DISCARD

Memory
for Odors

Memory
for Odors

Edited by
Frank R. Schab
Opinion Research Corporation
Robert G. Crowder
Yale University

LEA
LAWRENCE ERLBAUM ASSOCIATES, PUBLISHERS
1995   Mahwah, New Jersey   Hove, UK

Lawrence Erlbaum Associates, Inc., Publishers
10 Industrial Avenue
Mahwah, New Jersey 07430

Library of Congress Cataloging-in-Publication Data

Memory for odors / edited by Frank R. Schab, Robert G. Crowder.
    p. cm.
  Includes bibliographical references and index.
  ISBN 0-8058-0728-4
  1. Smell. 2. Memory. 3. Odors. I. Schab, Frank R.
II. Crowder, Robert G.
QP458.M45 1995
152.1′66 − dc20   95-15183
                                                         CIP

Books published by Lawrence Erlbaum Associates are printed
on acid-free paper, and their bindings are chosen for strength
and durability.

Printed in the United States of America
10 9 8 7 6 5 4 3 2 1

═Contents═

══ Preface ══

Beginning at least with the start of modern work on cognition, the question of how sensory experience relates to memory has been central, as shown in the imagery argument in the 1970s and in the pervasive issue of coding starting in the 1960s. Examining memory within a different and, for most of us, unfamiliar modality such as olfaction brings these questions to foreground status even more than they have been in the past, for all sensory modalities give rise to some type of experience and also to some type of memory. How are these related?

Here, we appreciate that *knowledge* and *memory* are both representations in the mind (brain) that were not previously available there. Indeed, the olfactory knowledge possessed by individuals such as chefs, wine-tasters, and Japanese Incense Masters is a wondrous kind of expertise to the rest of us. However, our concerns here, with some exceptions, are more with olfactory memory than with olfactory knowledge, the field of memory being concerned with cases where the temporal and spatial context in which an experience occurred are defining attributes of it.

We were led to this project initially by conversations with our colleague William Cain, whose agenda had for some time been to convince workers already committed to olfaction that genuinely cognitive factors indeed had an important influence on performance. We soon realized that we had been approaching the same domain with the diametrically opposite mandate—to convince cognitive psychologists that there was something genuinely olfactory to be considered in this literature on memory for odor, rather than just another level of processing. The research covered in these chapters should leave little doubt as to either of these complementary propositions.

This is the first book-length project gathering information on olfaction and memory that we know of. We have organized the field into subfields as we see it reflected now in the first wave of scientific activity on this subject. But we hope this will be a provocation: We hope that questions raised here will define directions for future research, directions we cannot now anticipate. Quite specifically, we shall be delighted if these future directions sharpen thinking about the general relationship between memory and sensation as well as about remembering odors.

Frank R. Schab
Robert G. Crowder

= 1 =

Introduction

Robert G. Crowder
Yale University

Frank R. Schab
Opinion Research Corporation

The power of odors to unlock human memory is celebrated in literature and anecdote but poorly documented by science. Odors, perhaps more than other stimuli, are widely believed to evoke vivid and complex past experiences easily: The most famous anecdotal report of an odor serving as a powerful memory cue is, of course, Marcel Proust's recollection of his aunt's home in the country following the smell of a *madelaine* soaked in tea. Yet in contrast to the frequency with which odors are thought to evoke memories of the past, scientific evidence is thus far scanty.

For years, voluminous data have been collected on odor sensitivity (e.g., Amoore, 1977, 1980; Fazzalari, 1978; Jones, 1957; Van Gemert & Nettenbreijes, 1977), whereas relatively few studies exist on memory for odors per se. Moreover, the memory data that do exist are so far only poorly integrated with the most modern attitudes on human memory (Schab, 1991; Schab & Cain, 1991). One major goal of this volume is to point the way toward a better state of affairs, one in which the study of odor memory is legitimatized as a proper specialization and is informed by the most promising ideas in the mainstream study of memory. We see especially three tendencies in modern memory theory that have not yet sufficiently penetrated the odor-memory work: memory coding, memory and knowledge, and implicit and explicit memory.

MEMORY CODING

The flourishing of the cognitive approach to learning and memory, unlike earlier approaches, stressed that stimuli are not themselves learned and retained but, rather, some format of coding is engaged by the stimulus and provides the retained information. Thus, researchers such as Conrad (1964) demonstrated that visually presented letters are retained in memory through the participation of a speech code. Many of the first demonstrations of visual imagery in memory showed shared capacity (interference) between the use of the visual system in an ongoing task and the simultaneous retention of information in visual form (Bower, 1972; Brooks, 1968).

These questions of coding have scarcely been raised, much less addressed, for odors in memory. To measure memory for odors we can give subjects a recognition test for a previously presented set of odor substances. A correct recognition response to an odor, such as straw-berry, must show that something has been acquired, retained, and retrieved. But what? The odor itself?

Other codes are possible. For example, the subject might have smelled the substance originally, identified it as such, and generated a visual image of a strawberry, which was retained until the time of testing. When the same odor was presented for recognition, it again was identified, and the generated image matched the remembered image of the presentation episode. The smell itself was in no sense recognized but the encoded event was—through the medium of visual imagery.

Another alternative possibility is perhaps even more plausible: The same target odor, strawberry, was presented originally, leading the subject to identify the smell verbally (e.g., "strawberry" or "That bubble gum in the red and blue wrapper"). At later recognition testing, strawberry was again presented, again verbalized in the same way as before, and a correct match was achieved, this time on the basis of a verbal label. (We examine this possibility in more detail in the later section on memory and knowledge.) What we need to answer, then, is: What is it about an odor that is learned at presentation and mediates performance on a later memory test?

A subordinate issue, forming part of coding analysis in general, is the concept of imagery. What sets an image apart from any memory must be that it preserves the coding format of the original experience, untrans-formed by any process of recoding. Thus, a visual image of a U.S. flag must carry some one-for-one isomorphism with the object originally seen, not a verbal description of it or a meaningful association to it (Shepard, 1978). *Visual imagery* is usually the term used when the memory was derived top-down, as from an instruction to "picture a U.S.

flag." The term *sensory memory*, or afterimage, is reserved for the case when this same visually coded information results from actually seeing the target object. The same opposition between top-down and bottom-up derivation of olfactory memory activity should logically be the case. But it must be remembered that the case needs to be made, experimentally, for this symmetry before we accept it.

Hebb (1968) believed that the same neural organizations (cell assemblies or phase sequences) were active in the two cases. Such neural activity derived from the sensory surface in the case of afterimages and from top-down instigation in the case of imagery. His favorite example was the *phantom-limb phenomenon* where itching, for example, may be experienced from a part of the body that was actually removed surgically. We may suppose that the same neural centers were stimulated by the limb itself, before amputation, and of course by some other agency after the limb in question was amputated. We focus on the question of odor imagery in more detail elsewhere in this volume (see Schab & Crowder, chapter 6, this volume).

MEMORY AND KNOWLEDGE

The distinction made by researchers such as Tulving (1972, 1983) between *episodic memory* and *generic knowledge* is overwhelmingly apt in guiding our thought about odor memory, but largely ignored. (Tulving preferred the term *semantic memory*, to distinguish from *episodic memory*, but we think *generic knowledge* better captures the opposition between the two.) A prototypical example of episodic memory would be recall or recognition of a particular word as a member of a previously presented list. Generic knowledge is tested by a question such as "What is the plural of the word mouse?" Both queries very obviously rely on memory, but the learning context (time and place of acquisition) is fundamental to the episodic-memory question and quite irrelevant to the generic-knowledge question. Hollingworth (1913) was the first to be explicit that in recall the context is given and the target is to be produced, whereas in recognition the target is given and the context is to be supplied (verification of context).

In odor memory experiments of either sort, recognition, rather than recall, is the retention measure of choice because odors obviously cannot be produced as the targets of memory retrieval. To identify or recognize a familiar odor by its name—as banana, shoe polish, vanilla, or whatever—theoretically rests on generic knowledge and not on the context of any specific learning episode. That is, recognizing these smells necessarily shows memory for odor, coded by olfactory (chemical) dimensions. But it does not demonstrate memory for olfactory *events*. For better or worse, the psychology of memory has been based on events, whether in the Ebbinghaus (1885/1964) or Bartlett (1932) traditions. Twenty years' worth of sporadic experimentation on short-term episodic recognition memory for odors (see Schab & Crowder, chapter 2, this volume) has produced quite modest knowledge beyond dismay that such memory is relatively at variance with conventional wisdom.

The two literatures on odor recognition and odor identification exist side-by-side, with no efforts to recognize the distinction, much less to make comparisons. For example, how are we to measure odor memory performance? One classic index used in the study of olfactory functioning is the ease with which subjects can name familiar odors, given a sniff, out of context (Doty, Shaman, Krefetz, & Dann, 1981; Douek, 1974). But just as odor identification decrements may reflect impaired sensory functioning or odor discrimination or impaired odor identification, or some combination of these, so may episodic odor memory performance reflect both episodic and generic odor memory. The knowledge-versus-memory issue is not all independent of the coding question we just discussed: If episodic recognition testing of odors were, at least partially, dependent on a verbal/semantic code, for normosmics (people with an unimpaired sense of smell), then a deficit in generic odor recognition would show up disguised as an episodic recognition-memory deficit. For example, subjects could cope with an episodic memory experiment by (a) first identifying the inspection odors with a verbal label or semantic association ("This is strawberry" or "This smells like that gum in the blue and red wrapper" or "This reminds me of summer visits to Grandpa's") and then (b) remembering these verbal/ semantic associations until the recognition testing, at which point they (c) identify the recognition candidates with the same verbal labels or semantic associations and (d) match these against the memorized ones. This would produce a theoretically spurious correlation between the forms of memory involved in knowledge and episodic testing, for a deficit in the episodic capacity (temporal-spatial marking of olfactory experiences) would not produce a correlated penalty in odor naming.

For such reasons, we should be especially interested in memory studies with odors that are difficult to name. Potentially, these allow some degree of dissociation of the memory for an odor experience with its identifiability. (However, even with strange odors never before smelled, subjects may still employ some form of verbal, or at least semantic, identification: "It smells kind of like . . ." or "It reminds me of. . . .") If naming suffers, for such difficult-to-name odors, as it surely does, without an appreciable decline in episodic recognition memory, then we may be encouraged to believe that olfactory experiences can be recognized, as such, with minimal participation of verbal mediation. The objection might be raised that difficult-to-label odors would suffer in memory experiments because of their obscurity, or unfamiliarity. However, we know from studies of verbal memory (Schulman, 1974) that rare stimuli are recognized *better* than familiar ones, although recalled worse. Recently, Schab, De Wijk, and Cain (1991) compared episodic recognition of common (e.g., strawberry, oregano, and cigarette butt) and uncommon (e.g., benzaldehyde, methylbutyrate, and linalyl acetate) odors and found uncommon odors were recognized significantly worse than common ones. This result, in part, may be due to difficulty of generating and attaching verbal/semantic information to the uncommon odors. However, this is one area where additional experiments are waiting to be done in order to integrate the study of odor memory and mainstream principles of (verbal) memory. One important question is: How much of episodic odor memory is memory for verbal/semantic associations generated to the odors at inspection and testing?

The same ambiguity about the form of coding we have discussed in episodic memory experiments (remembering the verbal description of odors rather than the odors themselves) does not plague odor identification, which tests memory for odors in the form of generic knowledge. Because the name is itself the target of retrieval in such tests it could not be an unwelcome mediator in that retrieval. Knowledge of what banana, for example, smells like must therefore depend on some stable representation of the precise chemical configuration.

IMPLICIT AND EXPLICIT MEMORY

One of the most exciting developments in the field of memory since the 1980s has been the emergence of tests of implicit memory. For example, priming effects in word-stem completion give evidence for an earlier presentation just as surely as do tests of recognition or recall. Priming is the better measure of retention, too, in that amnesics can be shown to have normal performance in priming (Graf, Squire, & Mandler, 1984), whereas they are virtually helpless in explicit recall and recognition. Such priming is also evident in tachistoscopic word recognition (Jacoby & Dallas, 1981) and picture naming (Snodgrass & Feenan, 1990). If any single new research trend has animated work in the area of memory during the 1980s, it was probably the introduction of implicit memory techniques. So far, we know of no published reports on odor memory using implicit testing. Here, more than elsewhere, this volume is intended as a call to action for investigators.

The notorious difficulty people sometimes have in retrieving the names of familiar odors, or recognizing such items from a short array of episodically presented odors, suggests to some that, unlike many of our experiences, odors fail to produce explicit, retrievable memory traces (Engen, 1982). But is retention of odors likewise poor? Tests of perceptual recognition, identification, or threshold measurement all potentially permit priming effects from some earlier experience with an odor as compared to appropriate nonprimed controls.

We have evidence from our laboratory concerning priming in odor naming, too (see Schab & Crowder, chapter 5, this volume), but that field has otherwise been, so far, innocent of implicit testing methods. Theoretical considerations do encourage the importance of implicit memory measures for odors: Scholars such as Tulving (1983) consider the techniques of implicit memory to be persuasive in both human and animal species, whereas the phenomenon of explicit memory, or recollection, is considered more uniquely human. What lower animal can, like us, reflect on an experience and be transported to that same or similar experience at some temporal remove? We shall not quibble about the power of some advanced mammals to do something of the sort, but surely the sorts of simple organisms from which we evolved were simultaneously capable of retention and yet incapable of explicit recollection. The chemical senses, including olfaction, were as prominent in these early species as they are secondary to us in comparison with the evolutionarily later vision and audition. It would follow that the place to look for olfactory retention should not be among the advanced evolutionary triumphs of memory but rather among the more primitive forms.

REFERENCES

Amoore, J. E. (1977). Specific anosmia and the concept of primary odors. *Chemical Senses and Flavor, 2,* 267–281.

Amoore, J. E. (1980). Properties of the olfactory system. In F. H. Suchomel & J. W. Weatherly, III (Eds.), *Odorization* (pp. 31–35). Chicago: Institute of Gas Technology.

Bartlett, F. C. (1932). *Remembering: A study in experimental and social psychology.* Cambridge, England: Cambridge University Press.

Bower, G. H. (1972). Mental imagery and associative learning. In L. W. Gregg (Ed.), *Cognition in learning and memory* (pp. 51–88). New York: Wiley.

Brooks, L. R. (1968). Spatial and verbal components of the act of recall. *Canadian Journal of Psychology, 22,* 349–368.

Conrad, R. (1964). Acoustic confusions in immediate memory. *British Journal of Psychology, 55,* 75–84.

Doty, R. L., Shaman, P., Krefetz, D. G., & Dann, M. (1981). Recent progress in the development of a clinically useful microencapsulated olfactory function test. In L. Surjan & G. Bodo (Eds.), *Proceedings of the XIIth ORL World Congress* (pp. 5–8). Budapest, Hungary: Hungarian Academy of Sciences.

Douek, E. (1974). *The sense of smell and its abnormalities.* London: Churchill Livingstone.

Ebbinghaus, H. (1964). *Memory: A contribution to experimental psychology.* New York: Dover. (Original work published 1885)

Engen, T. (1982). *The perception of odors.* New York: Academic Press.

Fazzalari, F. A. (1978). *Compilation of odor and taste threshold values data.* Philadelphia: American Society for Testing and Materials.

Graf, P., Squire, L. R., & Mandler, G. (1984). The information that amnesic patients do not forget. *Journal of Experimental Psychology: Learning, Memory, and Cognition, 10,* 164–178.

Hebb, D. O. (1968). Concerning imagery. *Psychological Review, 75,* 466–477.

Hollingworth, H. C. (1913). Characteristic differences between recall and recognition. *American Journal of Psychology, 24,* 532–544.

Jacoby, L. L., & Dallas, M. (1981). On the relationship between autobiographical memory and perceptual learning. *Journal of Experimental Psychology: General, 110,* 306–340.

Jones, F. N. (1957). An analysis of individual differences in olfactory thesholds. *American Journal of Psychology, 70,* 227–232.

Schab. F. R. (1991). Odor memory: Taking stock. *Psychological Bulletin, 109,* 242–251.

Schab, F. R., & Cain, W. S. (1991). Memory for odors. In D. G. Laing, R. L. Doty, & W. Breipohl (Eds.), *The human sense of smell* (pp. 217–240). New York: Springer.

Schab, F. R., de Wijk, R. A., & Cain, W. S. (1991, April). *Memory for odors over the course of one hundred seconds.* Paper presented at the 13th annual meeting of the Association for Chemoreception Sciences, Sarasota, FL.

Schulman, A. I. (1974). Memory for words recently classified. *Memory and Cognition, 2,* 47–52.

Schulman, A. I. (1976). Memory for rare words previously rated for familiarity. *Journal of Experimental Psychology: Human Learning and Memory, 2,* 301–307.

Shepard, R. N. (1978). The mental image. *American Psychologist, 33,* 125–137.

Snodgrass, J. G., & Feenan, K. (1990). Priming effects in picture fragmentation completion: Support for the perceptual closure hypothesis. *Journal of Experimental Psychology: General, 119,* 276–296.

Tulving, E. (1972). Episodic and semantic memory. In E. Tulving & W. Donaldson (Eds.), *Organization of memory* (pp. 381–403). New York: Academic Press.

Tulving, E. (1983). *Elements of episodic memory.* New York: Oxford University Press.

Van Gemert, L. J., & Nettenbreijer, A. H. (1977). *Compilation of odour threshold values in air and water.* Voorburg/Zeist, The Netherlands: National Institute for Water Supply and Central Institute for Nutrition and Food Research TNO.

Odor Recognition Memory

Frank R. Schab
Opinion Research Corporation

Robert G. Crowder
Yale University

Of all the forms of odor memory discussed in this volume, odor recognition is the most common and direct measure of odor memory. This is for good reason: Recall of odors themselves is obviously not an option in the way that recall of words is. Subjects can be asked to recall the *names* of odors to which they have been exposed (Lyman & McDaniel, 1990), but this form of testing may well affect the manner in which the targets are encoded (e.g., by encouraging subjects to encode in terms of odor names). So, investigators interested in memory for odor stimuli as such have gravitated toward recognition memory (although as we suggest here, there is still no guarantee that names are not prominent in the processing that occurs).

In the typical recognition paradigm, subjects encode a target odor (or a collection of target odors, a list) and, after a variable retention interval, decide either whether a probe is the same as the target odor, or whether the probe is an old stimulus (target odor) or a new one (foil). Memory performance is given by percent correct recognition judgments or some derivative measure based on accuracy.

Quite clearly, these experiments have very little to do with the everyday experience of recognizing an odor, as when Charlie Chaplin— walking along a sidewalk in the early moments of the film *Gaslight*— begins to make puzzled sniffing gestures and then bends to gravely inspect the sole of his shoe. (The odor turns out to have been escaping gas.) That recognition, too, is based on memory, necessarily, but such a form of memory we would refer to as *olfactory knowledge* and is not tied to any particular encoding experience. All studies reviewed here include a well-defined presentation event for the odors later to be recognized.

Although recognition is the most common technique used in the study of odor memory, only about 20 odor recognition studies have been reported so far. A search of keywords in the PsychLit scanning database turns up 1,144 titles under the keywords {WORD and REC-OGNITION and MEMORY} but only 25 under the keywords {ODOR and RECOGNITION and MEMORY}. Our mandate in this chapter is to review the available data on recognition memory for odors and to suggest promising avenues for future research. We argue that too few data exist to permit broad conclusions about odor memory.

For example, despite typical findings of relatively flat forgetting curves for odors, the lack of systematic investigations of stimulus and procedural variables (e.g., discriminability of target and distractor odors, retention interval activities) makes risky this conclusion that odors are relatively impervious to forgetting. Indeed, as we discuss later, recent work has shown significant forgetting for single odors over relatively brief retention intervals.

Furthermore, the notion that verbal-semantic factors play little or no role in odor recognition because of the difficulty associated with verbal identification of odors (see de Wijk, Schab, & Cain, chapter 3, this volume) is inappropriate because accurate odor identification is only one, though arguably the highest, level of verbal-semantic association to odors. For example, in the literature on face identification, results show that the retrieval of semantic information about the person is much easier than name retrieval and occurs even when name retrieval fails (Flude, Ellis, & Kay, 1989; Young, Ellis, & Flude, 1988). Similarly, an odor may evoke verbal-semantic associations (e.g., "running along the pier," "reminds me of something in Aunt Sue's summer cabin in Wisconsin") even when its name remains inaccessible or unknown. Such associations may assist or mediate odor recognition memory in the absence of precise identification with a single verbal label (see Crowder & Schab, chapter 1, this volume). Under intentional learning conditions, which characterize virtually all of the recognition studies reported to date, an unknown degree of *odor recognition* therefore could be recognition of the same verbal and/or semantic associations generated to the odor on acquisition, however wildly idiosyncratic they might have been, rather than recognition of the perceptual characteristics of the odor. Even when correct recognition occurs on trials where different verbal labels were generated to the same odor (e.g., Lehrner, 1990), we cannot be sure that recognition was based solely on a perceptual code; the different verbal labels or descriptions may belong to the same associative net as was evoked by the odor both times.

Critical to our understanding of odor recognition is the application of theoretical principles and experimental techniques that have evolved over the past two decades in verbal memory. Only through continued systematic investigations can we hope to provide answers to general questions about odor memory, and throughout this review we point to questions we deem important for careful study. This chapter is organized into three major sections: short-term odor recognition, long-term odor recognition, and conclusion and future directions. The distinction made here between short- and long-term retention is not so much an indication that we believe separate memory systems support short- and long-term retention of odors as it is a shorthand description of the different tasks subjects confront in experiments.

SHORT-TERM ODOR RECOGNITION

In a typical short-term odor memory experiment using recognition, subjects are presented with a single (or a few) target odor(s) on each trial. After a short period of distractor activity, lasting less than 1 minute, subjects decide whether a second odor is the same as the target odor(s).

Engen, Kuisma, and Eimas (1973) conducted such an experiment: Subjects in their study inspected either one or five odors and made a same–different judgment of a single test odor after retention intervals ranging from 3 to 30 sec filled with a second odor presentation, a backward counting task, or no task. The criterion was whether the single test odor matched either the single target presented on that trial or any of the five targets on five-odor trials. Results show that performance reliably improved between 3 and 12 sec and then declined again (Fig. 2.1; A' is an unbiased measure of accuracy or sensitivity). Apparently no differences were found between backward counting and presenting a distractor odor during the retention interval.

In a different type of study, Jones, Roberts, and Holman (1978, Experiment 2) asked subjects to remember one, three, or five stimuli and retention interval was defined by the number of intervening targets and distractors (1 to 15). Subjects presented the odors to themselves at their own pace, and the results of this study, also, indicate no evidence for forgetting as function of retention interval. Moreover, both of these studies show that memory was far from perfect, even for a single target odor at the briefest retention interval (e.g., 3 sec or one intervening

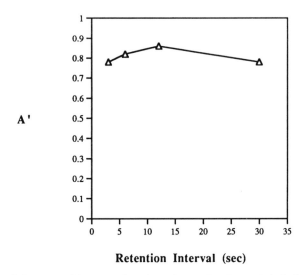

A'

Retention Interval (sec)

FIG. 2.1. Odor recognition as a function of retention interval (calculated from Engen, Kuisma, & Eimas, 1973, Figure 1, 5-alternative trials).

stimulus), suggesting a limitation at encoding, perhaps a discrimination problem. Once encoded, however, the odors were not forgotten.

But in a more recent study, Murphy, Cain, Gilmore, and Skinner (1991, Experiments 3 & 4) found virtually perfect performance in the recognition of a single odor after 30 sec.

Walk and Johns (1984) investigated odor recognition after a 26-sec period as a function of the type of distractor activity filling the second half of the retention period. The distractor activities included generating verbal associations to a similar odor, to the name of a similar odor, to the name of the target odor, or doing nothing. The results show that generating associations to another odor compromised memory for the target odor over the control condition, whereas associations generated to the name of the target odor improved target recognition. Walk and Johns concluded that the interference they observed was primarily perceptual in nature, but semantic interference could not be ruled out in their study (a) because it was not clear to what extent the perceptual characteristics of the distractor odor and the verbal-semantic associations generated in response to the distractor odor depressed target recognition, and (b) because performance in the condition where subjects generated associations to the name of a similar odor was not statistically different from the odor distractor condition.

Researchers of these odor recognition experiments borrowed the 30-sec retention interval from early studies of short-term verbal memory (Brown, 1958; Peterson & Peterson, 1959). But we may question whether a 30-sec interval is functionally comparable between the domains of verbal and olfactory memory. Sensory-perceptual processing of verbal-linguistic stimuli is faster by an order of magnitude than that of olfactory stimuli. Assuming the same forgetting mechanisms operate in verbal and olfactory domains, the longer encoding processes for odors might effectively shorten a nominal retention interval relative to verbal or visual stimuli. Accordingly, two recent studies (de Wijk, Schab, & Cain, 1994; Gilmore, 1991) using retention intervals of between 1 and 2 min report significant forgetting in target odor recognition. For this reason, we remain skeptical of the assertion that recognition memory functions are flat against retention interval, based on evidence such as we have just reviewed.

In the first of these studies, Gilmore (1991) presented subjects with five target odors and tested recognition with a single probe after 30 or 120 sec. The retention interval was filled with one of four distractor tasks. The control task made no demands of subjects. The remaining distractor conditions involved the presentation and processing of olfactory, visual, and verbal information. The results show significant forgetting of odors at the 120 sec retention interval, particularly for the verbal distractor task, but no decrement in recognition after 30 sec.

In a different study, de Wijk et al. (1994, Experiment 2) compared recognition of a single target odor over retention intervals of 8, 20, 40, and 100 sec filled with a semantic distractor task (deciding whether words referred to living or nonliving objects). Their results (Fig. 2.2) show that common odors are recognized better than uncommon odors. For both types of stimuli, little forgetting occurred for retention intervals of 40 sec or fewer, but, by 100 sec, a significant loss became evident. Furthermore, de Wijk et al. showed that the more knowledge of an odor

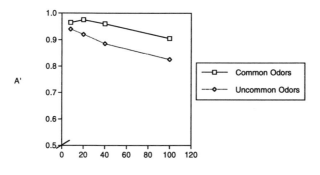

FIG. 2.2. Recognition of common and uncommon odors as a function of retention interval (from de Wijk et al. 1992).

subjects possessed, as measured by odor familiarity and identifiability, the more probable was correct odor recognition, a finding similar to those in studies of long-term odor memory (e.g., Rabin & Cain, 1984). This effect of odor knowledge may be restricted to encoding because the difference between identifiable or familiar odors, on the one hand, and unidentifiable or unfamiliar odors, on the other, occurred at the shortest retention interval (e.g., 8 sec) and remained constant as retention interval increased, suggesting no differential loss. Finally, the forgetting observed by de Wijk et al. did not appear to be due to proactive interference from previous trials: The number of errors did not increase with trials.

Together, these results suggest that recognition of one or a few odors over relatively brief intervals is not perfect as once was thought. Retention intervals used in other modalities do not necessarily apply automatically to olfaction.

A recent experiment by White (1992) finds a *recency effect* in short-term odor recognition of 5 odors, whereas an earlier study (Gabassi & Zanuttini, 1983) using 12 odors failed to find an effect for serial position. One interpretation of recency (Greene, 1986) is that it represents a paradigm case of the central circumstance of forgetting: We remember well those things that most recently happened, in a sequence of experiences, and remember more poorly those things that occurred earlier in the sequence. The failure of recency in the earlier study would thus correspond to findings of a flat forgetting function in the distractor technique, whereas White's (1992) recency effect would agree with later reports that forgetting functions are not flat, after all, for odor memory. All workers can agree that further investigation of order effects in odor memory is warranted.

LONG-TERM ODOR RECOGNITION

In contrast to the experiments of short-term memory reported earlier, long-term odor memory experiments typically require subjects to learn a list of target odors, not a single one or a handful (list) of them. After a relatively long retention interval, measured in tens of minutes, days, or even months, subjects decide whether each test odor had been presented in the earlier session. Usually half the test odors had been so presented and half are *new* in respect to the encoding episode.

Early long-term odor memory experiments yielded results and conclusions very similar to early short-term recognition studies — imperfect initial encoding, little subsequent forgetting, and no effects of odor familiarity or identifiability. In one study, subjects who learned common and uncommon odors recognized only 75% on an immediate recognition test. However, performance declined only to 65% after 1 month and remained above chance even after 1 year (Engen & Ross, 1973). Similarly, Lawless and Cain (1975) found recognition performance of 85% after 10 min which fell to 75% over the span of 28 days. The forgetting curves found in these two experiments are shown in Fig. 2.3. In neither study was knowledge of the odors, as measured by familiarity and identifiability, related to recognition performance. Other studies are in general agreement with these findings (e.g., Larjola & von Wright, 1976).

In a different experiment, Lawless and Engen (1977, Experiment 1) investigated interference in odor memory by comparing two different pairings of odors with pictures. In their AB-ABr design, 12 odors were paired with 12 pictures, first in one way (the AB list) and then in another arrangement 48 hours later (the ABr list). Two weeks later, subjects were

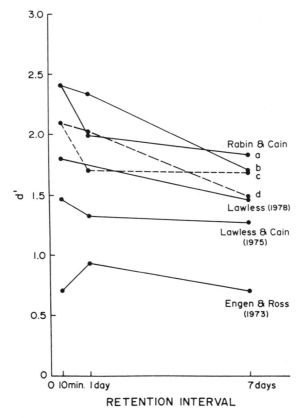

FIG. 2.3. Odor recognition as a function of retention interval (from Rabin & Cain, 1984).

tested on their memory for the pairings. Unlike similar studies with verbal stimuli, only proactive interference was found, and the second pairings had been largely forgotten by the time of testing. Lawless and Engen (1977) concluded that odor memory offers only a single associative link on a first-come, first-served basis and that this link is relatively impervious to interference from subsequent associations (retroactive interference).

Although these studies seem to imply that odor memory is inherently different from visual or verbal memory, Lawless (1978) recognized the importance of stimulus factors and compared recognition of odors with two types of visual stimuli, complex travel pictures and simple visual shapes. His results show that recognition for pictures was very near ceiling on immediate testing but declined rapidly. In contrast, memory for both odors and simple visual forms was poorer than that for pictures at an immediate test, but declined less severely over time; the retention curves were essentially parallel for odors and simple visual forms (Fig. 2.3).

In a careful series of paired-associate experiments, Davis (1975, 1977) pursued the comparison of olfactory stimuli with visual forms. He found that subjects more rapidly learned to associate verbal material with simple and relatively meaningless visual forms than with odors, although the visual stimuli were less familiar and discriminable than the odors. Nevertheless, the general assumption in these various studies has been that odors are encoded perceptually as relatively featureless stimuli and that semantic or verbal factors play little or no role in odor recognition.

This view has been revised by more recent work. An important factor in this revision was a study by Rabin and Cain (1984), which examined odor recognition as a function of within-subject measures of identifiability and familiarity, rather than the between-subject (normative) measures used in earlier studies. They showed that familiar and identifiable odors are remembered better than less familiar and less identifiable odors. This suggests that familiarity effects may be idiosyncratic with odors, rather than consensual as they are with verbal materials. But like the earlier studies, a relatively flat forgetting curve described performance over intervals as long as a week (Fig. 2.3). Although a progressive recognition loss is thus evident in most long-term odor recognition experiments, that loss rarely exceeds 10%, as suggested by earlier experiments.

Subsequent studies have established an effect of verbal or semantic coding, or prior knowledge, upon long-term odor memory. In two investigations, Lyman and McDaniel (1986, 1990) examined the effect of elaborative encoding on recognition memory. In their first study, subjects were exposed to a set of odors by (a) generating short verbal definitions for the odors, (b) relating a life episode for each odor, (c) forming a visual image of the odor sources, or (d) being left to their own devices. After a 7-day retention period, subjects who had provided short definitions and life episodes remembered significantly more odors than those who had generated visual images or learned the odors without an orienting task. In a follow-up study (Lyman & McDaniel, 1990, Experiment 1), subjects elaborated odors by processing a visual representation of the odor sources, the odor names, or both. Other groups learned the odors or their names without explicit elaboration. Subjects recalled the odor names and recognized the odors after a 1-week retention interval, and the recognition results show that the elaboration produced significantly better performance than no elaboration. Moreover, combined visual and verbal elaboration produced the best recognition performance.

Verbal-semantic processes also have been shown to cause significant *interference* with odor recognition. The difference is produced by effecting a suppression task during encoding rather than an elaboration task supporting that encoding. Perkins and Cook (1990), for example, directed subjects to learn odors while performing visual, verbal, or combined visual and verbal suppression tasks. Recognition was tested immediately and after 1 week. For the immediate test, only the conditions involving verbal suppression produced a decrement in odor recognition. After 1 week, recognition was significantly worse than for the immediate test, and performance grew worse with visual suppression, verbal suppression, and combined visual and verbal suppression. Perkins and Cook correctly noted that the obtained effects may have resulted from either verbal-semantic interference or general attention limitations, and additional work would be required to unconfound these sources of the recognition deficit.

Future work using the facilitation and interference paradigms should also consider the extent to which visual stimuli in such experiments are encoded verbally-semantically rather than visuospatially; the facilitative or inhibitory effects on odor recognition of nominally visual stimuli could be due, at least in part, to verbal-semantic processing.

CONCLUSION AND FUTURE DIRECTIONS

The nature of the code underlying odor recognition must become the cynosure of future research in odor memory. The extent to which verbal-semantic encoding enhances or replaces a perceptual code represents a crucial question. The literature to date suggests that odors are encoded with some difficulty, because even on immediate recognition tests performance is far from perfect, but performance declines only little (roughly 10%) thereafter. However, the few existing studies on odor recognition are insufficient to permit the conclusion that odor memory is special because of its relative imperviousness to the ravages of time.

One important question raised by Schab (1991) is the extent to which odors that are presented deliberately in an experiment on memory are encoded differently than odors encountered in everyday experience. If subjects in an experiment attempt verbal identification of the target odors and generate semantic associations to them, and then do the same at testing, but not with environmental odors they encounter in daily life, then we should not be surprised to see relatively little forgetting for experimental odors: The similarity of odor processing during learning and testing, and the dissimilarity of processing experimental odors and potentially interfering odors from the environment over the duration of the retention interval, may be responsible for the longevity of odor memory in experiments (cf. Morris, Bransford, & Franks, 1977). That is, if special processing modes are recruited in explicit memory experiments on odor, then the slight losses over a week, shown in Fig. 2.3, should not be surprising because everyday odor activities during that week probably included little of that special processing. This concern argues for odor recognition studies using incidental learning where subjects do not expect a subsequent memory test, as well as procedures that selectively inhibit or facilitate the processing of perceptual versus verbal-semantic information.

Recent findings showing increased odor recognition with increased familiarity are in conflict with verbal- and visual-recognition memory experiments which show that unfamiliar, or infrequent, stimuli are recognized better, albeit recalled worse, than familiar, or frequent ones (e.g., Shepard, 1967). On the surface, this difference would seem to suggest that odor recognition is qualitatively different from visual and verbal memory. However, the frequency effect on visual and verbal stimuli occurs for stimuli that are meaningful and easily encodable (e.g., words, travel pictures). In contrast, as the existing short-term and long-term recognition experiments reviewed here suggest, encoding is far from stable even after extremely brief retention intervals. Arguably, when initial encoding is nontrivial, as appears to be the case for odors, familiarity, as a measure of the number and quality of associations evoked by the odor, may outweigh the benefits of odor distinctiveness. A priori, it would seem that distinctiveness should have its greatest effect on memory when stimulus coding is automatically easy and the size of the category in memory to which the stimulus belongs is large (e.g., words, meaningful pictures). If this is true, the reversed frequency effect also should obtain for relatively meaningless visual stimuli.

In summary, we believe that there is no compelling evidence for a separate odor memory system characterized by different parameters than memory for other forms of information. Whether such evidence is forthcoming remains to be seen. In the meantime, it is more parsimonious to assume that odor recognition is not fundamentally different than memory for visual or auditory stimuli.

REFERENCES

Brown, J. (1958). Some tests of the decay theory of immediate memory. *Quarterly Journal of Experimental Psychology, 10,* 12–21.

Brown, R., & McNeill, D. (1966). The "tip of the tongue" phenomenon. *Journal of Verbal Learning and Verbal Behavior, 5,* 325–337.

Davis, R. G. (1975). Acquisition of verbal associations to olfactory stimuli of varying familiarity and to abstract visual stimuli. *Journal of Experimental Psychology: Human Learning and Memory, 104,* 134–142.

Davis, R. G. (1977). Acquisition and retention of verbal associations to olfactory and abstract visual stimuli of varying similarity. *Journal of Experimental Psychology: Human Learning and Memory, 3,* 37–51.

de Wijk, R. A., Schab, F. R., & Cain, W. S. (1994). *Short-term recognition memory for odors as a function of odor knowledge.* Manuscript in preparation.

Engen, T., Kuisma, J. E., & Eimas, P. D. (1973). Short-term memory of odors. *Journal of Experimental Psychology, 99,* 222–225.

Engen, T., & Ross, B. M. (1973). Long-term memory of odors with and without verbal descriptions. *Journal of Experimental Psychology, 100,* 221–227.

Flude, B. M., Ellis, A. W., & Kay, J. (1989). Face processing and name retrieval in an anomic aphasic: Names are stored separately from semantic information about people. *Brain and Cognition, 11,* 60–72.

Gabassi, P. G., & Zanuttini, L. (1983). Recognition of olfactory stimuli in short-term memory. *Giornale Italiano di Psicologia, 10,* 51–60.

Gilmore, M. M. (1991, April). *On the encoding of odors: Is there a visual and/or semantic component?* Paper presented at the 13th annual AChemS Conference, Sarasota, FL.

Greene, R. L. (1986). Sources of recency effects in free recall. *Psychological Bulletin, 99,* 221–228.

Jones, F. N., Roberts, K., & Holman, E. (1978). Similarity judgments and recognition memory for common spices. *Perception and Psychophysics, 24,* 2–6.

Larjola, K., & von Wright, J. (1976). Memory of odors: Developmental data. *Perceptual and Motor Skills, 42,* 1138.

Lawless, H. T. (1978). Recognition of common odors, pictures, and simple shapes. *Perception and Psychophysics, 24,* 493–495.

Lawless, H. T., & Cain, W. S. (1975). Recognition memory for odors. *Chemical Senses and Flavor, 1,* 331–337.

Lawless, H. T., & Engen, T. (1977). Associations to odors: Interference, memories, and verbal labeling. *Journal of Experimental Psychology, 3,* 52–59.

Lehrner, J. P. (1990). *Gender differences in long-term odor recognition memory: Verbal vs. sensory influences and the consistency of label use.* Unpublished manuscript.

Lyman, B. J., & McDaniel, M. A. (1986). Effects of encoding strategy on long-term memory for odours. *The Quarterly Journal of Experimental Psychology, 38,* 753–765.

Lyman, B. J., & McDaniel, M. A. (1990). Memory for odors and odor names: Modalities of elaboration and imagery. *Journal of Experimental Psychology: Learning, Memory and Cognition, 16,* 656–664.

Morris, C. D., Bransford, J. D., & Franks J. S. (1977). Levels of processing versus transfer appropriate processing. *Journal of Verbal Learning and Verbal Behavior, 16,* 519–533.

Murphy, C., Cain, W. S., Gilmore, M. M., & Skinner, R., B. (1991). Sensory and semantic factors in recognition memory for odors and graphic stimuli: Elderly versus young persons. *American Journal of Psychology, 104,* 161–192.

Perkins, J., & Cook, N. M. (1990). Recognition and recall of odours: The effects of suppressing visual and verbal encoding processes. *British Journal of Psychology, 81,* 221–226.

Peterson, L. R., & Peterson, M. J. (1959). Short-term retention of individual verbal items. *Journal of Experimental Psychology, 58,* 193–198.

Rabin, M. D., & Cain, W. S. (1984). Odor recognition: Familiarity, identifiability, and encoding consistency. *Journal of Experimental Psychology: Learning, Memory, and Cognition, 10,* 316–325.

Richardson, J. T. E., & Zucco, G. M. (1989). Cognition and olfaction: A review. *Psychological Bulletin, 105,* 352–360.

Schab, F. R. (1991). Odor memory: Taking stock. *Psychological Bulletin, 109,* 242–251.

Shepard, R. N. (1967). Recognition memory for words, sentences, and pictures. *Journal of Verbal Learning and Verbal Behavior, 6,* 156–163.

Walk, H. A., & Johns, E. E. (1984). Interference and facilitation in short-term memory for odors. *Perception and Psychophysics, 36,* 508–514.

White, T. (1992, April). *A comparison of item and order processing in olfactory and verbal short-term memory.* Paper presented at the fourth annual AChemS conference, Sarasota, FL.

Young, A. W., Ellis, A. W., & Flude, B. M. (1988). Accessing stored information about familiar people. *Psychological Research, 50,* 111–115.

= 3 =

Odor Identification

René A. de Wijk
Brown and Williamson Tobacco Corporation

Frank R. Schab
Opinion Research Corporation

William S. Cain
University of California at San Diego

When asked to estimate their ability to identify common objects (e.g., typical household products) by smell alone, people tend to be very confident about their ability (Cain, 1982). But those of us who have actually tried to name such odors in the absence of visual or other contextual cues have been surprised and vexed by the difficulty of the task; many odors seem very familiar but either fail to evoke a name or elicit only broad categories (e.g., fruit, edible). Although early experiments suggest that people can accurately identify only about 16 odors (Engen & Pfaffman, 1960) even after practice (Jones, 1968), more recent work (Desor & Beauchamp, 1974) indicates that the number is higher, especially for common odors and when feedback on the identification performance is provided. But, even then, performance is still less than perfect. Cain (1979) reported that correct identification of 80 odorants was less than 50% on the first trial, and improved to more than 90% over the course of five additional trials. Experts (e.g., perfumers), moreover, frequently attain impressive levels of identification performance, although this skill acquisition is measured in years rather than trials. Nevertheless, typical free identification of a set of familiar, everyday stimuli by the layperson rarely exceeds 50% correct. Roughly 10% of the incorrectly named stimuli are identified by reasonably close or related names (e.g., orange for lemon), whereas the remaining 40% of incorrectly named stimuli are called by clearly inappropriate names (e.g., turpentine for banana) or by no name at all.

Unlike the unrealistically high confidence many people aver regarding their ability to identify common odors, people typically have little confidence in their identifications when they give clearly inappropriate names. Frequently, they feel as though they know more about the odors and that they could produce more accurate labels at some later time (Cain, de Wijk, Lulejian, Schiet, & See, 1994). This must stem, in part, from the perception of familiarity that many common odors engender, regardless of the person's ability to identify those odors with precise verbal labels. Lawless and Engen (1977) coined the term *tip-of-the-nose* phenomenon to denote the experience of high familiarity of an odorant and the concomitant inability to identify it. But unlike the *tip-of-the-tongue* phenomenon (Brown & McNeill, 1966), which is generally induced by requiring the person to name an object on the basis of a description (e.g., the device used for navigation by early seafarers), in the tip-of-the-nose state, the person is unable to answer any questions about the name of the stimulus (e.g., how many syllables it has), but is usually capable of profiling the odor, suggesting that the two phenomena actually may be quite different.

Our relatively poor performance in free odor identification, which seems striking in comparison to our ability to identify the same objects presented visually, has been attributed by some to the absence of a special vocabulary for odors (Richardson & Zucco, 1989). But just as sounds (e.g., slamming door, screeching tire) come from specific items or actions, odors come from specific objects (e.g., strawberries, plastic), making special names redundant with actual object names; many objects are red and sweet, necessitating a special vocabulary in vision and taste, but generally only strawberries have a strawberry smell. Others have hypothesized that the connection between perceived odors and language is inherently weak (e.g., Engen, 1982, 1987), and support for this idea comes from the following two observations. First, once encoded, odors typically are remembered well over long periods of time.[1] And second, essentially no difficulty exists in retrieving object names when presentation is visual rather than olfactory. However, it is also possible that the weak relationship between odors and their names is the result of how we learn (or, better, fail to learn) about odors, rather than an inherent structural limitation between olfaction and semantic memory for object names. In our society, learning to name objects by

---

[1]More empirical work is needed, however, to determine to what extent the longevity of odor memory in experiments is due to differences in the way experimental and environmental odors are encoded (see Schab & Crowder, chapter 2, this volume).

smell is not formalized as is visual identification; school children are not taught that this smell is called "apple" and that smell, "leather." We usually learn gradually (and usually incidentally, following numerous pairings) that a given object, say ketchup, has a particular smell, rather than that a particular smell identifies the object. Exceptions to this norm also exist (e.g., frying bacon for many people in the United States).

In daily life, odors are perceived within a rich and meaningful context, and what we smell is what we expect on the basis of visual or contextual information. Ordinarily, odors only serve to support or confirm object identification. This explains why people may identify purple-colored apple juice as grape juice (e.g., Cain, 1980; DuBose, Cardello, & Maller, 1980). Unless the discrepancy between the object identified visually (or contextually) and suggested olfactorily is great (e.g., see strawberry and smell onion), the odor perception is integrated with the visual or contextual identification. Ecologically, as well as evolutionarily, veridical identification of odors with precise labels does not appear as important as categorical identification (e.g., fruit, spoiled, mate), or identification in terms of associated experiences (e.g., being ill, nearly drowning; Schab, 1991). An important question for future research is whether the rather weak association between odors and their names is due to an inherent structural limitation between olfaction and the lexicon, or to the way in which we learn odors.

Besides verbal-semantic limitations, however, mediocre performance in free odor identification tasks may also reflect sensory-perceptual limitations. On odor recognition tasks, where precise verbal identification of an odor is not necessary, a large percentage (circa 30%) of recognition failures occurs, even with retention intervals as short as a few seconds (de Wijk, Schab, & Cain, 1994; Engen, Kuisma, & Eimas, 1973; Engen & Ross, 1973; Lawless & Cain, 1975). These recognition failures, presumably, are the result of confusion among the odors of the experimental set, confusion between test odors and perceptually similar but nonpresented odors, or both. Performance on free odor identification tasks, similarly, may be limited by less than perfect odor discrimination. In the present chapter we argue that both discrimination and verbal-semantic factors determine free odor identification. We also note that most of the theoretical and empirical emphasis hitherto has focused almost exclusively on verbal factors. To buttress our case, we survey existing, and foreshadow new, information. In a final section we examine group differences in odor identification from the perspective that such differences provide valuable and complementary information on the nature and mechanism(s) of odor identification and are essential to any theoretical integration of empirical data on human odor identification.

ODOR DISCRIMINATION AND IDENTIFICATION

Cain (1979; Schab & Cain, 1991) suggested that poor odor discrimination plays a significant role in the relatively poor identification performance observed in most studies. Of course, in the extreme, all subsequent, higher order processing, including recognition memory and identification, can only be as accurate as the resolution of the sensory system. If the perceptual acuity of the olfactory sensory system is low compared to other sensory modalities, then odor identification performance must be correspondingly poor. Indeed, whereas visual discrimination between a lemon and an orange is trivial, success in discriminating between the smells of these two objects is far from guaranteed. (Of course, tactile discrimination may be even worse.) Even in side-by-side comparisons, where the impact of memory is minimized, subjects are found to make discrimination errors with common odors (Eskenazi, Cain, & Friend, 1986; Eskenazi, Cain, Novelly, & Friend, 1983; Rabin, 1988). In free identification tasks, moreover, subjects must not only discriminate each odor from all the others in the test battery, but also from those not presented at all; that is, from perceptually similar alternatives already in pre-existing memory.

   The claim that odor identification is, to a substantial degree, dependent upon odor discrimination is fueled by strong correlations between odor identification and side-by-side discrimination ($r = 0.5$ for normals, and $r = 0.8$ for persons with temporal lobe damage; Eskenazi et al., 1983) and between odor identification and absolute threshold ($r = 0.8$–0.9 for normals and persons with olfactory disorders; e.g., Cain & Rabin, 1989; Doty, Shaman, Applebaum, et al., 1984). In fact, the relatively strong relationship observed between odor identification and discrimination has motivated the use of identification tests as a primary tool in the clinical assessment of olfactory functioning (Cain, 1989; Doty, Shaman, & Dann, 1984). When the cognitive-semantic contribution to identification is reduced by using a multiple-choice identification procedure (Cain & Gent, 1986), in which the stage of name generation from semantic memory is bypassed, the task essentially becomes a discrimination task—one that is more easily administered than a threshold task. Of course, the level of performance on such multiple-choice tasks will depend on the similarity among the choices. Correspondingly, training with odor labels enhances discrimination among odors (Rabin, 1988).

   In a recent effort to investigate the relationship between identification and discrimination, de Wijk and Cain (1994b) found significant correlations between discrimination and identification of a given set of odors ($r = 0.60$, $p < 0.01$), between discrimination of one set of odors and identification of another ($r = 0.53$, $p < 0.01$), and between discrimination and consistency of identification, that is to say, the probability of applying the same label to a given odor over repeated presentations ($r = 0.61$, $p < 0.01$). Cain et al. (1994) found fluctuations, or inconsistencies, in odor identification performance for the same odors presented to the same subjects on different days. And de Wijk and Cain showed that these fluctuations in identification will occur even across trials within the same testing session. The magnitude of the correlation between discrimination and consistency of identification (as well as accuracy in single-presentation identification) suggests that many of the identification errors are in fact discrimination errors (e.g., perceiving peppermint as peppermint on one trial, and as wintergreen on another). The words subjects assign to odors (see Engen, 1987) also imply discriminative errors. The object lemon, for instance, may elicit the name lime, which suggests a specific discriminative confusion, but the object may also elicit the name fruit, which suggests a different type of discriminative error, one of vagueness. There is no reason to consider one error more inherently discriminative than the other.

VERBAL AND SEMANTIC FACTORS IN IDENTIFICATION

Discriminability may seem unlikely to account for the remarkably slow progress in learning to identify new odors, the rapid subsequent relearning observed with previously learned odors, and the sharp increase in identification performance after just one or two trials when name feedback is provided (e.g., Cain, 1979, 1980). At least some of the variance in such performance presumably involves a compromised link between the perceptual representation of an odor and its name in the mental lexicon (or other semantic information) (e.g., Engen, 1987). Ineffectual linkage could, as noted before, be the result either of an inherent structural limitation or of the way in which we learn odors. In any case, the compromised relationship between odors and their names appears to be unidirectional: Whereas presentation of an odor frequently will fail to activate the odor's name in semantic memory, activation of the odor's name by the experimenter, or the context, often leads to unambiguous perception of the odor in terms of the presented name, even when the actual odor presented is a degraded exemplar (artificial aroma) of a different, but perceptually similar, odor (Cain et al., 1994). In other words, the availability of an odor name, unless clearly inappropriate, can drive the perceptual experience.

One can speculate on the reasons for this effect. Without names, the odor is still perceivable, and, although precise identification may elude subjects, they can profile the quality of the odor in terms of various characteristics (e.g., fruity, fatty). Hence, subjects are capable of processing the odor partially. But this processing does not enhance odor identification (Cain et al., 1994), which suggests that odor identification does not emerge from an analysis of separate features of the odor. Most people are familiar with the effect that once a label is presented, the corresponding odor is perceived with a new clarity. Labels seem to reorganize the perception of the odor. This phenomenon has much in common with the visual perception of fragmented figures. One can spend a considerable amount of time looking at Fig. 3.1 without actually recognizing a meaningful figure. Once provided with the identification (dog), perception is reorganized and the figure is identified. A reorganized percept will result in superior encoding and, consequently, enhanced memory. Interestingly, this top-down influence of verbal-semantic information on odor experience apparently operates only when an odor is physically present; a convincing case for odor imagery (top-down production of odor experience in the physical absence of the odor) has not yet been made (see Crowder & Schab, chapter 6, this volume).

The importance of familiarity and, more specifically, identifiability for long-term memory has been demonstrated by Rabin and Cain (1984) and others (e.g., Lyman & McDaniel, 1986). Collectively, their work shows that familiar and correctly identified odors are better remembered than unfamiliar and incorrectly identified odors. And results of de Wijk, Schab, and Cain (1994) show that familiarity and identifiability of odors are important for short-term odor memory, too (Figs. 3.2a, 3.2b). An obvious conclusion is that people remember odor names whenever these are provided by the experimenter, the context, or the subjects themselves.

For obvious reasons most studies of identification have focused on verbal identification (i.e., the generation of odor names by the subject). But whether or not a person can generate an odor's name (candle wax), or even an idiosyncratic verbal response to the odor (Sunday school class), does not capture the complete spectrum of semantic odor identification. Thus, an odor may evoke semantic as well as perceptual associations (thoughts of certain people, visual images of certain places, etc.), but these may not lend themselves to overt verbalization. Although some readers may wish to argue that such ineffable associations are not identifications, there is a real sense in which they are the most significant identifications. The richness and distinctive-

FIG. 3.1. The first impression one typically gets from this fragmented figure is a meaningless pattern of black polygons against a white background. The figure becomes meaningful, or reorganized, when the viewer is told that the pattern depicts a dog sniffing the ground.

ness of such associations, moreover, should make the odors that produce them most memorable. This is an important reason that researchers must be careful not to interpret as evidence for the sensory-perceptual, as opposed to verbal-semantic, encoding of odors the observed fact that odors which are not identified veridically, or consistently, are often recognized at levels above chance (e.g., Lyman & McDaniel, 1986; Rabin & Cain, 1984). It is conceivable that the memory code for odors is primarily semantic in nature (cf. Crowder & Schab, chapter 1, this volume; Murphy, Cain, Gilmore, & Skinner, 1991). For future work in odor identification, the investigation of free identification performance, although difficult to score, continues to offer the best opportunity for understanding the processes involved.

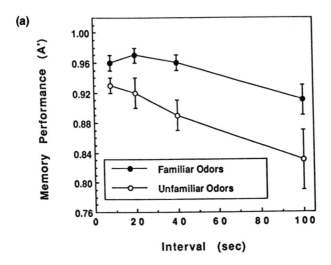

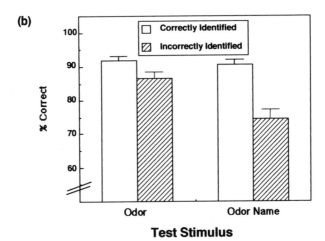

FIG. 3.2. (a) Results (±1 standard error of the mean, SEM) of a same-different recognition experiment (31 subjects) using 60 familiar odors (common household products) and 60 unfamiliar odors (chemicals) and retention intervals of 8, 20, 40, and 100 sec. The effects of familiarity and retention interval on recognition were significant ($p < 0.01$). Chance performance was 0.50. From de Wijk, Schab, and Cain (1994). (b) Results (± 1 SEM) of a recognition memory experiment (33 subjects) using 72 common household odors. Subjects learned target odors and were tested for short-term retention in a same-different procedure either with odors or corresponding odor names. Correctly identified target odors were better recognized than incorrectly identified target odors ($p < 0.01$), irrespective of the test stimulus (odor or odor name). From de Wijk, Schab, and Cain (1994).

GROUP DIFFERENCES IN ODOR IDENTIFICATION

Commensurate with its practical significance (e.g., detection of danger), most studies on odor identification have focused on comparing performance between different groups of people. The available results allow the following generalizations about odor identification: Young adults outperform old adults, young and middle-aged adults outperform children, women outperform men, and blind adults outperform sighted adults (e.g., de Wijk & Cain, 1994a; Murphy, 1986; Murphy & Cain, 1986; Schiffman, 1977).

Aging

Aging takes a toll on most sensory and various cognitive processes, and olfactory processes are no exception. Age-related deficits in olfaction have been found for threshold and suprathreshold sensitivity (Cain & Stevens, 1989; Enns & Hornung, 1988; Kimbrell & Furtchgott, 1963; Murphy, 1983; Schiffman, Moss, & Erickson, 1976; Stevens & Cain, 1985), recognition memory (Cain & Murphy, 1987; Murphy et al., 1991; Stevens, Cain, & Demarque, 1990), and odor identification (Doty, Shaman, & Dann, 1984; Schemper, Voss, & Cain, 1981; Wood & Harkins, 1987).

Although sensory losses doubtlessly exacerbate age-related problems in odor identification, evidence from several sources suggests that this deficit is due in large, or small, part to impairment in verbal-semantic processing. First, under some circumstances, odor identification continues to improve with age until middle adulthood (Doty, Shaman, Applebaum, et al., 1984; Eskenazi, Cain, & Friend, 1986), as the individual's growing experience with objects and their odors would suggest. But this experience-mediated improvement in odor identification ability is tempered by declining odor sensitivity (Venstrom & Amoore, 1968). Beyond middle adulthood, losses in both cognitive abilities (e.g., memory retrieval) and sensory acuity conspire to offset experiential gains. The age at which performance begins to decline probably depends on the difficulty of the identification task (e.g., size of the set to be identified). Murphy (1987) reported a decline in free identification for an 80-item set beginning in early adulthood. Second, the obtained age difference in identification is greatly attenuated when the cognitive demand is reduced through the use of a multiple-choice, rather than a free-identification, procedure (Stevens & Cain, 1987). However, multiple-choice items often refer to odors with very different qualities (e.g., the target odor "motor oil" might need to be recognized from a list of alternatives like: chocolate, apple, thyme, and motor oil).

It is very possible that a target odor that is perceived vaguely, is still identified correctly by eliminating obviously incorrect alternatives. Third, a significant age deficit is evident even when subjects are prescreened for their ability to discriminate odors (Schemper, Voss, & Cain, 1981).

Interestingly, older adults are less likely than young adults to benefit from training with their own, previously generated labels, or from longer exposure to the odors, but benefit as much as young adults from training with veridical labels (Schemper et al., 1981).

In a recent investigation involving a greater range of ages than any previous investigation, de Wijk and Cain (1994a) explored how 113 subjects, ranging from children to elderly adults, could identify the odors of everyday products (e.g., chocolate, tea, vinegar). Their battery of 17 different items included products sometimes involved in poisoning from accidental ingestion (e.g., scented and unscented hypochlorite bleach, mothballs). Net performance at identification followed an inverted U-shaped course over age, with the highest performance (53% hits) in young adults and approximately equally poor performance among the youngest group consisting of children to 14 years of age (32% hits), and the oldest group consisting of elderly people 69 to 88 years of age (33% hits). The reciprocal pattern was found for far misses: Children and old adults had the most far misses, young and middle-aged adults the lowest. Near misses remained relatively infrequent and stable across ages, with some decline in the elderly (Fig. 3.3). Age-related deterioration in quality discrimination for the adults, measured along with identification, paralleled the identification results.

Despite relatively large differences between age groups in absolute identification, item (odor) analyses showed that some odors (e.g.,

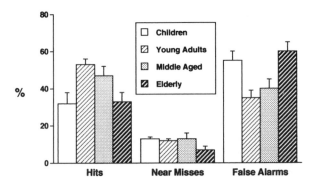

FIG. 3.3.   Percent veridical, near miss, and far miss identifications (± 1 SEM) for children, young adults, middle aged, and elderly persons. From de Wijk and Cain (1994a).

chocolate) were identified better than others (e.g., Lysol), and this pattern was similar across age groups: Average intercorrelations between groups equaled 0.78. For the children, the identifiability of odors correlated with the frequency of the corresponding odor names in standard text, suggesting that opportunities to learn the names of odors limit identification performance in that group.

When identification responses were sorted into categories of edible and inedible, correct performance improved by 88% over exact identification, with the performance of the children improving disproportionately to that of the other age groups. For products posing significant health risks if ingested (e.g., bleach), children were able to say correctly whether an odor represented something edible or nonedible on 79% of trials, as opposed to only 15% correct name identifications. In fact, identification for children, measured by the criterion of edibility, was similar to that for young adults. Elderly subjects identified edible products less often as edible, and inedible products more often as edible, than the other age groups (Fig. 3.4). Children, young adults, and the elderly sometimes assigned names of edible products to bleach, the most dangerous item in the set. Subjects more frequently identified the scented than the unscented bleach with names of edible objects, and fully 19% of the elderly identified scented bleach as edible, suggesting that scenting certain household products may prove dangerous to that group (Fig. 3.5).

This selective review demonstrates that odor identification is sensitive to an individual's age. During childhood and young adulthood, identi-

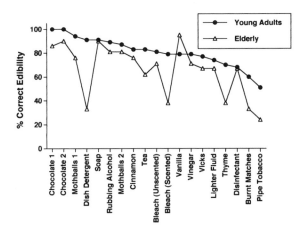

FIG. 3.4.   Percent correct assignment of edibility of young adults and elderly to the odors of 17 common products, two of which (chocolate, mothballs) appeared twice. Errors of edibility comprise of calling an inedible product edible and vice versa, and refusals to venture any guess. From de Wijk and Cain (1994a).

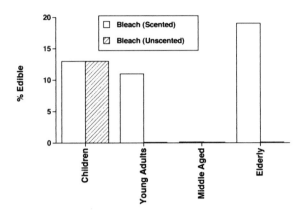

FIG. 3.5. Percent "edible" judgments of children, young adults, middle-aged adults, and elderly to the odors of scented and unscented bleach. From de Wijk and Cain (1994a).

fication performance improves, probably as experience with odors and their names increases. Eventually, however, both sensory and cognitive processes conspire to reduce identification performance.

Gender

Not only do both men and women predict that women are superior at odor identification, but women are actually better than men in correct identification and consistency of identification (Cain, 1982, 1984; Cain, Gent, Goodspeed, & Leonard, 1988; Doty, Shaman, Applebaum, et al., 1984; Doty, Shaman, & Dann, 1984). This superiority of women has been shown to exist across four different cultural groups (Doty, Applebaum, Zusho, & Settle, 1985). In one study (Cain, 1982), women produced more accurate odor labels (more hits and fewer far misses) right from the start, but both genders improved equally across additional test sessions when given corrective feedback (Fig. 3.6). The superiority of women in odor identification is a reliable empirical result. However, the source of this gender difference remains an open question. To date, proposed explanations for the effect include gender differences in verbal skills, socialization and odor experience, hormones, and olfactory sensitivity. This last possibility has received the most attention by researchers. Unfortunately, the results are far from clear: Some investigations imply that women are more sensitive to odors than men (e.g., Cain et al., 1988; Koelega & Köster, 1974), whereas others have failed to find a gender difference in sensitivity (e.g., Matzker, 1965; Venstrom & Amoore, 1968). For suprathreshold odor intensity, the verdict so far

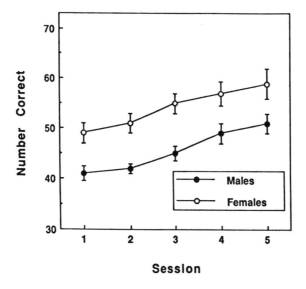

FIG. 3.6. Mean number of correct odor identifications (± 1 SEM) by males and females over the course of five sessions. From Cain (1982).

appears to be that no significant gender differences exist (Stevens, Bartoshuk, & Cain, 1984; Stevens & Cain, 1985).

CONCLUSION

Odor identification, as typically defined, requires the retrieval of a verbal label in response to the perception of an odor. But success at free odor identification generally is quite moderate, just as the relatively poor performance in paired-associate learning with odor stimuli predicts (Davis, 1975, 1977). Although many objects are difficult to identify on the basis of sight only (e.g., bleach) or sound only (e.g., wrench), it appears that common objects that are unique visually and olfactorily (e.g., cherry) are disproportionately difficult to identify by smell alone. We have suggested here that poor odor identification may be the result of limitations in sensory-perceptual discrimination among odors and weak odor-name associations due to an inherent structural limitation or the way in which we learn (or, more appropriately, fail to learn) about odors. What is needed now is programmatic empirical work on how these, and possibly other, factors conspire to produce the relatively poor performance frequently observed on free odor identification tasks.

But beyond the importance of odor identification in its own right, identification has been demonstrated in various studies to affect the way in which we perceive odors. We have argued that odor perception is the result of interactions between both top-down processes (verbal-semantic factors) and bottom-up processes (discrimination). The availability of an appropriate (even if only marginally appropriate) object name (identity) enhances processes like odor memory and odor discrimination, which have classically been considered subject only to sensory-perceptual factors. Hence, experimenters must always be mindful that subjects will likely attempt identification when confronted with an odor in an experiment. The effects of odor identification on other aspects of odor perception, like perception of odor mixtures, have not yet been investigated, but the fact that familiar odors are better recognized in mixtures than unfamiliar ones suggests that semantic processing is critical here, too (Rabin & Cain, 1989). Presumed identities (names), either self-generated or provided by others, seem to reorganize the odor percept into something meaningful, enhancing both encoding and retrieval of the odor. Difficulties in odor discrimination caused by aging, gender, and other factors are reduced or disappear if odor identities are provided during discrimination, even as increasing odor intensity results in improved identification performance.

We noted that identification of an odor by a single name is not the only way to make it meaningful. Odors are frequently identified with other semantic and perceptual associations that appear as no identification or inconsistent identification in the results of lab experiments. Therefore, a free identification procedure with experimenter-guided probing, though difficult to score, seems most promising for understanding odor identification and its relationship to other olfactory and cognitive processes. Moreover, future work should include both subject and item analyses, particularly when comparisons are made between odor identification and other aspects of olfactory functioning (e.g., discrimination), in order to separate true relationships between olfactory processes (or olfactory and cognitive processes) from interindividual differences in olfactory functioning.

ACKNOWLEDGMENTS

Preparation of this chapter was supported in part by grant DC 00284 from the National Institutes of Health.

REFERENCES

Brown, R., & McNeill, D. (1966). The "tip of the tongue" phenomenon. *Journal of Verbal Learning and Verbal Behavior, 5,* 325–337.

Cain, W. S. (1979). To know with the nose: Keys to odor identification. *Science, 203,* 467–470.

Cain, W. S. (1980). Chemosensation and cognition. In H. van der Starre (Ed.), *Olfaction and taste* (Vol. 7, pp. 347–357). London: Information Retrieval Ltd.

Cain, W. S. (1982). Odor identification by males and females: Predictions and performance. *Chemical Senses, 7,* 129–141.

Cain, W. S. (1984). What we remember about odors. *Perfumer and Flavorist, 9,* 17–21.

Cain, W. S. (1989). Testing olfaction in a clinical setting. *Ear, Nose, and Throat Journal, 68,* 316–328.

Cain, W. S., de Wijk, R. A., Lulejian, C., Schiet, F., & See, L.-C. (1994). *Odor identification: Stability, specificity, feeling of knowing, and discrimination.* Manuscript submitted for publication.

Cain, W. S., & Gent, J. F. (1986). Use of odor identification in clinical testing of olfaction. In H. L. Meiselman & R. S. Rivlin (Eds.), *Clinical measurement of taste and smell* (pp. 170–186). New York: Macmillan.

Cain, W. S., Gent, J. F., Goodspeed, R. B., & Leonard, G. (1988). Evaluation of olfactory dysfunction in the Connecticut Chemosensory Clinical Research Center. *Laryngoscope, 98,* 83–88.

Cain, W. S., & Murphy, C. L. (1987). Influence of aging on recognition memory for odors and graphic stimuli. *Annals of the New York Academy of Sciences, 510,* 212–215.

Cain, W. S., & Rabin, M. D. (1989). Comparability of two tests of olfactory functioning. *Chemical Senses, 14,* 479–485.

Cain, W. S., & Stevens, J. C. (1989). Uniformity of olfactory loss in aging. *Annals of the New York Academy of Sciences, 561,* 29–38.

Davis, R. G. (1975). Acquisition of verbal associations to olfactory stimuli of varying familiarity and to abstract visual stimuli. *Journal of Experimental Psychology: Human Learning and Memory, 104,* 134–142.

Davis, R. G. (1977). Acquisition and retention of verbal associations to olfactory and abstract visual stimuli of varying similarity. *Journal of Experimental Psychology: Human Learning and Memory, 3,* 37–51.

de Wijk, R. A., & Cain, W. S. (1994a). Odor identification by name and by edibility: Life-span development and safety. *Human Factors, 36,* 182–187.

de Wijk, R. A., & Cain, W. S. (1994b). Odor quality: Discrimination versus free and cued identification. *Perception and Psychophysics, 56,* 12–18.

de Wijk, R. A., Schab, F. R., & Cain, W. S. (1994). *Short-term recognition memory for odors as a function of odor knowledge.* Manuscript submitted for publication.

Desor, J. A., & Beauchamp, G. K. (1974). The human capacity to transmit olfactory information. *Perception and Psychophysics, 16,* 551–556.

Doty, R. L., Applebaum, S., Zusho, H., & Settle, R. G. (1985). Sex differences in odor identification ability: A cross-cultural analysis. *Neuropsychologia, 23,* 667–672.

Doty, R. L., Shaman, P., Applebaum, S. L., Giberson, R., Sikorski, L., & Rosenberg, L. (1984). Smell identification ability: Changes with age. *Science, 226,* 1441–1443.

Doty, R. L., Shaman, P., & Dann, M. (1984). Development of the University of Pennsylvania Smell Identification Test: A standardized microencapsulated test of olfactory functioning. *Physiology and Behavior, 32,* 489–502.

DuBose, C. N., Cardello, A. V., & Maller, O. (1980). Effects of colorants and flavorants on identification, perceived flavor intensity, and hedonic quality of fruit-flavor beverages. *Journal of Food Science, 45,* 1393–1400.

Engen, T. (1982). *The perception of odors.* New York: Academic Press.

Engen, T. (1987). Remembering odors and their names. *American Scientist, 75,* 497–503.

Engen, T., Kuisma, J. E., & Eimas, P. D. (1973). Short-term memory of odors. *Journal of Experimental Psychology, 99,* 222–225.

Engen, T., & Pfaffman, C. (1960). Absolute judgments of odor quality. *Journal of Experimental Psychology, 59,* 214–219.

Engen, T., & Ross, B. M. (1973). Long-term memory of odors with and without verbal descriptions. *Journal of Experimental Psychology, 100,* 221–227.

Enns, M. P., & Hornung, D. E. (1988). Comparisons of the estimates of smell, taste and overall intensity in young and elderly people. *Chemical Senses, 13,* 131–139.

Eskenazi, B., Cain, W. S., & Friend, K. (1986). Exploration of olfactory aptitude. *Bulletin of the Psychonomic Society, 24,* 203–206.

Eskenazi, B., Cain, W. S., Novelly, R. A., & Friend, K. B. (1983). Olfactory functioning in temporal lobectomy patients. *Neuropsychologia, 21,* 365–374.

Jones, F. N. (1968). The informational content of olfactory quality. In N. N. Tanyloç (Ed.), *Theories of odors and odor measurement.* Istanbul, Turkey: College Research Center.

Kimbrell, G. M., & Furtchgott, E. (1963). The effect of aging on olfactory threshold. *Journal of Gerontology, 18,* 364–365.

Koelega, H. S., & Köster, E. P. (1974). Some experiments on sex differences in odor perception. *Annals of the New York Academy of Sciences, 237,* 234–246.

Lawless, H. T., & Cain, W. S. (1975). Recognition memory for odors. *Chemical Senses and Flavor, 1,* 331–337.

Lawless, H. T., & Engen, T. (1977). Associations to odors: Interference, memories, and verbal labeling. *Journal of Experimental Psychology, 3,* 52–59.

Lyman, B. J., & McDaniel, M. A. (1986). Effects of encoding strategy on long-term memory for odours. *The Quarterly Journal of Experimental Psychology, 38,* 753–765.

Matzker, J. (1965). Riechen und Lebensalter-Riechen und Rauchen. *Archiv für Ohren-, Nasen-, und Kehlkopfheilkunde, 185,* 755–760.

Murphy, C. (1983). Age-related effects on the threshold, psychophysical function, and pleasantness of menthol. *Journal of Gerontology, 38,* 217–222.

Murphy, C. (1986). Taste and smell in the elderly. In H. L. Meiselman & R. S. Rivlin (Eds.), *Clinical measurement of taste and smell* (pp. 343–371). New York: Macmillan.

Murphy, C. (1987). Olfactory psychophysics. In T. E. Finger & W. L. Silver (Eds.), *Neurobiology of taste and smell* (pp. 251–273). New York: Wiley.

Murphy, C., & Cain, W. S. (1986). Odor identification: The blind are better. *Physiology and Behavior, 37,* 177–180.

Murphy, C., Cain, W. S., Gilmore, M. M., & Skinner, R. B. (1991). Sensory and semantic factors in recognition memory for odors and graphic stimuli: Elderly versus young persons. *American Journal of Psychology, 104,* 161–192.

Rabin, M. D. (1988). Experience facilitates olfactory quality discrimination. *Perception and Psychophysics, 44,* 532–540.

Rabin, M. D., & Cain, W. S. (1984). Odor recognition: Familiarity, identifiability, and encoding consistency. *Journal of Experimental Psychology: Learning, Memory, and Cognition, 10,* 316–325.

Rabin, M. D., & Cain, W. S. (1989). Attention and learning in the perception of odor mixtures. In D. G. Laing, W. S. Cain, R. L. McBride, & B. W. Ache (Eds.), *Perception of complex smells and tastes* (pp. 173–188). Sidney, Australia: Academic Press.

Richardson, J. T. E., & Zucco, G. M. (1989). Cognition and olfaction: A review. *Psychological Bulletin, 105,* 352–360.

Schab, F. R. (1991). Odor memory: Taking stock. *Psychological Bulletin, 109,* 242–251.

Schab, F. R., & Cain, W. S. (1991). Memory for odors. In D. G. Laing, R. L. Doty, & W. Breipohl (Eds.), *The human sense of smell* (pp. 217–240). New York: Springer.

Schemper, T., Voss, S., & Cain, W. S. (1981). Odor identification in young and elderly persons: Sensory and cognitive limitations. *Journal of Gerontology, 36,* 446–452.

Schiffman, S. S. (1977). Food recognition by the elderly. *Journal of Gerontology, 32,* 586–592.

Schiffman, S. S., Moss, J., & Erickson, R. P. (1976). Thresholds of food odors in the elderly. *Experimental Aging Research, 2,* 389–398.

Stevens, J. C., Bartoshuk, L. M., & Cain, W. S. (1984). Chemical senses and aging: Taste versus smell. *Chemical Senses, 9,* 167–179.

Stevens, J. C., & Cain, W. S. (1985). Age–related deficiency in the perceived strength of six odorants. *Chemical Senses, 10,* 517–529.

Stevens, J. C., & Cain, W. S. (1987). Old-age deficits in the sense of smell gauged by thresholds, magnitude matching, and odor identification. *Psychology and Aging, 2,* 36–42.

Stevens, J. C., Cain, W. S., & Demarque, A. (1990). Memory and identification of simulated odors in elderly and young persons. *Bulletin of the Psychonomic Society, 28,* 293–296.

Venstrom, D., & Amoore, J. E. (1968). Olfactory threshold in relation to age, sex, or smoking. *Journal of Food Science, 33,* 264–265.

Wood, J. B., & Harkins, S. W. (1987). Effects of age, stimulus selection, and retrieval environment on odor identification. *Journal of Gerontology, 42,* 584–588.

The Neuropsychology of Odor Memory

Robert G. Mair
Loredana M. Harrison
David L. Flint
University of New Hampshire

There are two broad claims that can be made to justify a chapter on the neuropsychology of odor memory. The first is that the study of mental functions and their dissolution in brain disease provides a useful tool for analyzing cognitive processes that are not normally dissociable in the intact brain. In other sensory modalities, it has proved possible to separate functions related to primary sensory capacity from processes related to recognition, identification, and memory. For olfaction, our concern is whether there is a functional distinction between discrimination and recognition, or whether impairments can be demonstrated for odor identification or memory in persons able to detect and recognize differences between odorants.

The second claim of neuropsychology is that, by careful analysis of clinical syndromes in terms of known neuroanatomy, it is possible to determine the neural systems that are necessary for particular cognitive processes. Beyond providing an interesting roadmap, such analyses allow us to understand the basic complexity of each system. For example, visual systems are now known to diverge in functionally distinct pathways from primary sensory cortex through projections in the circumstriate belt to higher order association cortices in parietal and inferotemporal cortices. For olfaction, our concern is with the identification of the pathways that underlie cognitive aspects of perception and their relationship to processes from other sensory modalities as well as systems involved in memory and language.

THE NEUROPSYCHOLOGY OF SENSORY PROCESSES

In 1881, Hermann Munk demonstrated that destruction of dorsal regions of occipital cortex impairs the ability of dogs to recognize visual stimuli without apparently affecting their capacity for sight. Munk (1881/1950) reported that his dogs were able to avoid obstacles while moving about a room but failed to respond to stimuli (a whip, familiar people or dogs) that once elicited emotional responses or to the appearance of food placed in their path even when they were hungry. Munk argued that the dogs had lost their visual memory images and thus the capacity for recognition, while retaining the capacity to see optical sensations, a condition he termed *seelenblind* or mindblind. Freud has been credited with coining the term *agnosia* to refer to disorders affecting recognition as opposed to perceiving or naming stimuli (cf. Benton, 1985). Subsequent investigators have described a number of agnosias affecting visual, auditory, and tactile modalities.

In this discussion vision is used to exemplify distinctions between information-processing structures within the brain. This is done primarily because a lot is known about the anatomy, physiology, and functional organization of central visual processes. Since Kuffler's (1953) studies of receptive field properties of cat retinal ganglion cells, a variety of anatomical, physiological, and behavioral methods have been used to analyze the organization of visual pathways from retina to striate cortex and through the extrastriate cortex to temporal and parietal cortices (cf. Andersen, 1987; Gross, 1973; Lennie, Trevarthen, VanEssen, & Wassle, 1990; Livingstone & Hubel, 1988; Maunsell & Newsome, 1987; Mishkin, 1972). The literature in this field is extensive and well beyond the scope of this chapter. Nevertheless, several simple ideas have emerged from the convergence of experimental results that provide a general framework from which olfaction can be considered.

First, lesions that produce areas of visual loss or scotomas are restricted to pathways from retina to primary visual cortex. This was established by the elegant analyses of visual cortical lesions in the first half of the 20th century (cf. Foerster, 1929; Kluver, 1942; Lashley, 1948) and is routinely verified in clinical practice with cases that present with neurologically based loss of vision (cf. Tomsak, 1990). Lesions of higher order visual areas within extrastriate cortex have been associated with more specific perceptual deficits. Those affecting projections to parietal cortices have been reported to disrupt the perception of motion or position without affecting object recognition (Damasio & Benton, 1979; Zihl et al., 1983). In contrast, those involving projections to temporal cortex, particularly visual area 4, can impair the perception of color (achromatopsia) or of faces (prosopagnosia or face agnosia) (Damasio, Tranel, & Demasio, 1990; Pearlman, Birch, & Meadows, 1979).

The patient described by Pearlman et al. (1979) is particularly instructive. This was a 44-year-old man who had earlier passed a color vision exam to become a custom inspector, and was also an amateur painter. Following bilateral infarcts involving parts of striate and extrastriate cortex, he was left with prosopagnosia, topographic disorientation, and achromatopsia that persisted chronically to the time of the report (8 years after onset). Although his acuity was normal and he retained his ability to read and to recognize objects (but not faces), the patient complained that he was unable to see colors, stating that it was like "seeing a black-and-white movie" (p. 254). The patient relied on his wife to select his clothing and to choose colors for painting. He was, however, able to name the colors that common objects should be (and was thus not anomic for colors) and reported seeing desaturated colors (calling a deeply saturated red "very pale pink") (p. 256).

In humans, lesions of the inferior parietal lobule produce a complex syndrome of impairment that affects processes related to visual attention as well as visuospatial orientation and perception (cf. Andersen, 1987; Mesulam, 1981). On the other hand, lesions affecting occipitotemporal projections have been associated with impairments in visual object recognition. Neurologists have traditionally distinguished between associative and apperceptive visual agnosia (cf. Damasio & Tranel, 1990; Milner & Teuber, 1968). *Apperceptive agnosia* refers to deficient recognition of objects due to a failure to perceive them clearly. A patient with apperceptive visual agnosia would not only fail to recognize an object, but would also be deficient in copying drawings and matching like objects. Although the structural basis of this impairment is not fully established, it has been argued that it results from subtotal lesions of striate and extrastriate cortex (cf. Alexander & Albert, 1983; Bauer & Rubens, 1985). *Associative agnosia* refers to the inability to recognize objects in the face of a preserved capacity to perceive them (as shown by normal drawing and matching to sample performance). Although neuropathologic data are scant, it has been argued that associative agnosia results from lesions affecting connections between temporo-occipital visual areas and limbic and speech related areas (cf. Alexander & Albert, 1983; Bauer & Rubens, 1985). This localization of function is consistent with a body of evidence that, in monkeys, inferotemporal cortex is critical for visual recognition and memory (Iwai & Mishkin, 1969; Kluver, 1942; Mishkin, 1982).

From the view of olfaction, this brief review of visual processing has several lessons. Complete sensory loss (or a primary sensory deficit) over any area of the visual field occurs with lesions affecting primary sensory pathways. After the level of striate cortex, lesions affect limited kinds of information (color, faces, motion) or specific psychological functions (object recognition, visual learning, visuospatial perception). Presumably this reflects the divergence of visual pathways into functionally distinct and parallel information-processing systems. Damage to any one system past striate cortex would not prevent the processing of other types of information by parallel systems and thus would not result in an absolute scotoma. To the extent that odor perceptions represent different kinds of information and involve distinct (and morphologically separable) functions, it may be possible to isolate component processes of olfaction through careful analysis of clinical syndromes in humans or experimental lesions in animals.

There are two other broad dissociations of function that can be made within the visual system. These involve the naming or verbal identification of visual information and memory for visual information. Modality-specific naming disorders have been demonstrated in cases of alexia without agraphia in which words can be written but not read, and color anomia in which colors can be discriminated in a matching or ordering task but cannot be named. These conditions are associated with lesions of the left posterior occipital lobe that render subjects blind in the right hemifield, and present visual information from crossing the splenum of the corpus callosum and reaching left hemisphere language areas (Friedman & Albert, 1985; Geschwind & Fusillo, 1966). Geschwind (1967) argued that such modality-specific naming deficits in the absence of sensory disorders result from the isolation of sensory regions from speech areas within the brain. The observation of naming deficits in patients with intact perceptual capabilities provides evidence that processes related to naming and recognition depend on functionally distinct and morphologically separable mechanisms within the brain.

The relationship between memory and perception is somewhat more problematic. The occurrence of a perceptual disability makes it difficult to determine whether deterioration in performance after a delay is the direct result of a memory impairment or is a secondary consequence of a failure to adequately encode stimulus information. Perceptual disorders are known to occur in a number of amnesic syndromes. For instance, Korsakoff's syndrome is associated with perceptual deficits in multiple sensory modalities as well as severe global impairments in short-term memory (Mair et al., 1986). Similarly, perceptual deficits are known to coincide with the specific amnesias associated with unilateral temporal lobectomies (cf. Milner, 1968a, 1968b; Milner & Teuber, 1968).

Generally, it is the disproportionate impairment in performance after a delay that leads to an emphasis on memory rather than perception as the source of the deficit. For instance, Milner (1968b) reported that patients with right, nondominant temporal lobectomies are impaired in face-recognition memory to a greater extent when there was a 90-sec rather than a 0-sec memory delay. These same subjects were unimpaired on measures of verbal memory.

Figures 4.1 and 4.2 show examples from our laboratory of the short-term memory impairments of Korsakoff patients for visual and verbal stimuli. Figure 4.1 shows results from a hue recognition memory study (Flint & Mair, 1991) in which Korsakoff and control subjects were shown a hue sample and were then asked to select that hue from among four distractors. Distractors were selected to represent hard, medium, and easy discrimination problems based on the similarity of distractors to the target on the Farnsworth–Munsell scale (Farnsworth, 1957). All subjects showed consistent differences in performance based on the difficulty of the discrimination problem. The Korsakoff subjects showed evidence of a perceptual deficit by performing significantly worse than controls when there was no memory delay. This is consistent with previous evidence from other studies that Korsakoff patients who show no signs of specific color blindness are impaired in their ability to sort colors based on similarity (Mair et al., 1986). The Korsakoff patients also showed signs of memory impairment in the extent to which their performance decayed over the 28-sec retention interval for

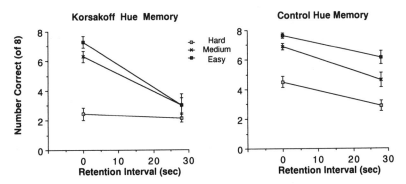

FIG. 4.1   Mean performance of Korsakoff ($N = 7$) and matched abstinent alcoholic control ($N = 8$) subjects on a color hue recognition memory task. Error bars represent standard error of the mean. Data are from Flint and Main (in preparation). Subjects were instructed to select a target hue from among four distractors at retention intervals of 0 and 28 sec. Task difficult was varied by manipulating the similarity of distractors from the target. Korsakoff subjects showed signs of a significant discrimination deficit at the 0-sec delay as well as a disproportionate decay in performance when the memory delay was increased to 28-sec. See text for details.

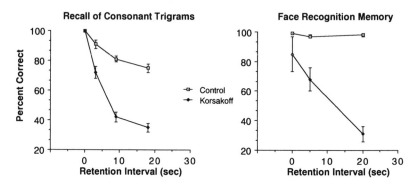

FIG.4.2. Mean performance of Korsakoff ($N = 10$) and matched nonalcoholic control subjects ($N = 8$) on two measures of short-term memory decay. Error bars represent standard error of the mean. Data are from Mair et al. (1980). The recall of consonant trigrams shows signs of a rapid decay in performance of Korsakoff subjects without impairment at the 0-sec interval. On the face recognition memory task, Korsakoff subjects were impaired at the 0 sec interval and showed signs of a disproportionate decay in performance at longer retention intervals. See text for details.

the medium and easy problems. This was verified by the observation of a significant interaction between group (Korsakoff vs. control) and delay (0 vs. 28 secs) for this measure. Data from the hard discrimination task were not included in this analysis because of the apparent floor effect in the Korsakoff performance.

A similar result can be shown for recognition memory for pictures of unfamiliar human faces. Figure 4.2 shows data replotted from Mair, Capra, McEntee, and Engen (1980). Face recognition was measured by having subjects locate a photograph of an unfamiliar face from a 5 × 5 matrix of similar photographs. There were three delay conditions: simultaneous matching of the target to the matrix, matching immediately after removal of target, and matching after removal of target and completion of a 15-sec distractor task. The Korsakoff subjects exhibited a significant impairment when the memory demands were minimized in the simultaneous matching condition (= 0-sec retention in Fig. 4.2). They showed evidence of a memory impairment in their disproportionate deficits in immediate matching, when the target had to be held in memory during the scanning of the matrix (= 5-sec delay in Fig. 4.2), and in delayed matching when the target had to be held in memory during the distractor task as well as the scanning operation (= 20-sec delay in Fig. 4.2). These trends were verified statistically by a significant interaction between group condition (Korsakoff vs. control) and matching condition (simultaneous vs. immediate vs. delayed).

Korsakoff patients showed a cleaner example of short-term memory impairment on the consonant trigrams task (Fig. 4.2, replotted from

Mair et al., 1980; see also Butters & Cermak, 1980). In this task, subjects are asked to recall a meaningless combination of three consonants after distractor-filled delays of 0, 3, 9, or 18 secs. In Fig. 4.2 results are combined for three different modes of presentation: auditory (reading aloud at the rate of 1 consonant/sec, visual successive (presenting consonants written on a card at the rate of 1/sec, and visual simultaneous (presenting the three consonants together on one card for 3 sec). In each of the modes of presentation, all subjects performed without error at the 0 sec delay, although the Korsakoff patients showed a significantly greater decay in performance with increases in the retention interval.

Apart from Korsakoff's disease, rapid decay of memory for visual, auditory, and tactile stimuli have been reported in amnesias associated with bilateral medial temporal lobe pathology affecting hippocampus and with medial diencephalic lesions produced by tumors, infarcts, and trauma (Benson & McDaniel, 1990; Milner & Teuber, 1968; Squire, 1987). Analyses of animals with experimental brain lesions have verified the importance of these areas in memory processes (Amaral, 1987; Goldman-Rakic, 1987; Mishkin, 1982; Squire, 1987). The observation of memory impairments that are disproportionate to any perceptual deficits suggests that for these sensory modalities there are morphologically distinct systems critical for memory that are separate from pathways that are critical for perception.

OLFACTION BEYOND PYRIFORM CORTEX

Functional Considerations

In most treatments, odor perception and memory are analyzed on the basis of conscious cognitive judgments of odorous stimuli. In considering the neural substrates that underlie such explicit and specific forms of olfactory perception and memory, it is important to recognize first that olfactory information may be processed through other channels for functions that do not rely on explicit judgments of odors. One such function involves the role of olfaction in the perception of flavor. Flavors are derived from the senses of smell, taste, and touch but are not easily separated into their sensory components (cf. McBurney, 1986). Flavor may be somewhat analogous in this sense to the perception of spatial location. Information about spatial location is derived from multiple sensory inputs (vision, audition, touch, and smell) and is thought, by some, to be represented separately from modality-specific information within the hippocampus (cf. O'Keefe & Nadel, 1978; Otto & Eichenbaum, 1991).

To the layperson, the perception of flavor is most commonly associated with the sense of taste rather than smell. It is not uncommon for persons suffering anosmia of acute onset to present with the primary complaint that foods have lost their flavor, and the belief that their deficit is gustatory rather than olfactory (Finelli & Mair, 1990). Flavor can also be separated from other forms of odor perception by the influence of internal state conditions (fasting, satiation) on hedonic tone. While the pleasantness of flavors or food-related odors depends on such factors, the hedonic value of nonfood-related odors are not altered by manipulations of internal state conditions (Cabanac, 1971; Duclaux, Feisthauer, & Cabanac, 1973; Mower, Mair, & Engen, 1977). The neural basis of flavor perception is not established, however, there is strong circumstantial evidence that olfactory projections to hypothalamus may play an important role in mediating food-related olfactory responses (LeMagnen, 1971; Price, 1985).

The sense of smell is also reputed to function automatically as an arousal system (cf. Engen, Gilmore, & Mair, 1991). Odors can intrude on consciousness and signal the presence of a warning stimulus (the smell of gas or smoke, an unexpected putrid odor). This monitoring can be unattended, as can be shown in common experience by the ability to detect warning signals even when attention is engaged in other ongoing tasks. Presumably, the ability to respond automatically to such changes in the olfactory background represents a process comparable to *preattentive* processes in other sensory systems (cf. Julesz, 1987) and involves automatic (or unattended) forms of recognition and memory. Other evidence of implicit odor memory has come from studies of priming (see Schab & Crowder, chapter 2, this volume). These phenomena have received scant attention in the literature. They are mentioned here to acknowledge the possibility that there may be information channels specialized for such implicit responding that are distinct from those involved in making explicit cognitive judgments of olfactory stimuli.

Thalamocortical Mechanisms

Olfactory information travels along the first nerve to the olfactory bulb and then by the lateral olfactory tract to ipsilateral paleocortical structures known collectively as primary olfactory cortex (Fig. 4.3). The discovery that direct olfactory bulb projections did not extend beyond this into the hippocampus and related limbic structures (then known

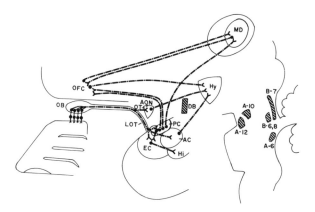

FIG. 4.3. Schematic representation of olfactory pathways in humans. Olfactory centers represented include: OB- olfactory bulb, LOT- lateral olfactory tract, OT- olfactory tubercle, AON- anterior olfactory nucleus, PC- pyriform cortex, EC- entorhinal cortex, AC- amygdaloid complex, Hy- hypothalamus, Hi- hippocampal system, MD- mediodorsal nucleus of the thalamus, OFC- orbitofrontal cortex. Some of the neurochemical systems innervating olfactory bulb and primary olfactory cortex are indicated by black striped areas. These include: cholinergic processes that arise from the diagonal (DB), dopaminergic processes primarily from the ventral tegmental area (A-10), noradrenergic processes primarily from the locus coeruleus (A-6) and brainstem serotonergic nuclei (B-6, 7, & 8). A-12 represents dopaminergic systems innervating the pituitary.

collectively as the *rhinencephalon* or smell brain) led to the view in the 1950s that olfactory discrimination depends on a relatively modest patch of primitive cortex (Brodal, 1947; Pribram & Kruger, 1954). This view was consistent with contemporary behavioral studies that emphasized the importance of the olfactory bulb and its immediate projections. In a widely cited series of experiments, Swann (1934, 1935) trained 130 rats to discriminate shavings scented with either anise or creosote in a T-maze. They found that this behavior was disrupted by lesions of the olfactory bulb or immediate retrobulbar regions but not of other sites. Subsequent investigators verified this finding and demonstrated that simple olfactory discrimination was not impaired by lesions of any other structures associated with the rhinencephalon (Allen, 1940, 1941; Brown & Ghiselli, 1938; Lashley & Sperry, 1943).

A major breakthrough occurred in the early 1960s with the discovery of projections from pyriform cortex to the mediodorsal thalamic nucleus (MDn; Powell, Cowan, & Raisman, 1963, 1965). Prior to this, analyses of central olfactory projections emphasized connections with hypothal- amus that were presumed to be related to neuroendocrine or feeding behaviors (Lundberg, 1960; Nauta, 1961; Scott & Pfaffmann, 1967). Powell et al. (1963) recognized the important implication of this discovery: There might be a neocortical olfactory area within the frontal cortical projections of MDn that was presumably related to cognitive aspects of olfactory perception.

Subsequent investigators have demonstrated projections from pyriform cortex to MDn in a number of mammalian species (cf. Jones, 1985), and they have shown that there is a heavier direct projection from pyriform lobe to orbital and ventral agranular frontal cortex in rodents (cf. Price, 1985). In retrospect, comparable projections from pyriform cortex to the *ventrolateral area of the prefrontal cortex* (after Allen, 1943) in dogs and to the *agranular insular cortex* of rabbits were described in earlier work (cf. Allison, 1953) based on degeneration and electrophysiological mapping techniques. Figure 4.3 shows a schematic representation of central olfactory pathways involving hypothalamus, thalamus, and orbitofrontal cortex. It should be noted that the direct projection from pyriform cortex to orbitofrontal cortex has not been verified in primates although Potter and Nauta (1979) demonstrated a heavy projection to olfactory areas in orbitofrontal cortex from prorhinal cortex, a portion of the entorhinal area reported to receive inputs from both pyriform cortex and olfactory bulb.

The functional significance of olfactory thalamocortical projections is not established. There are several lines of evidence that these pathways play an important role in processes related to the discrimination, recognition, or memory for odors. Electrophysiological studies have verified that the MDn contains cells responsive to odors in monkeys (Motokizawa, 1974; Yarita, Ilno, Tanabe, Kogure, & Takagi, 1980) and rats (Price & Slotnick, 1983). Further, there is at least one report that olfactory neurons respond to fewer odorants (i.e., more selectively) as one moves from olfactory bulb to primary olfactory cortex to lateral preorbital frontal cortex (Tanabe, Ilno, & Takagi, 1975). Such an increase in response selectivity in higher order olfactory neurons is consistent with the idea that projections from thalamus to orbitofrontal cortex are involved in discriminating differences between odorants.

Lesion studies have only partially confirmed this view. Thalamic lesions involving MDn have been reported to disrupt measures of olfactory discrimination learning, but not olfactory detection, in rats (Eichenbaum, Fagan, & Cohen, 1980; Mair, Knoth, Rabchenuk, & Langlais, 1991; Slotnick & Kaneko, 1981; Staubli, Schottler, & Nejat-Bina, 1987) and hamsters (Sapolsky & Eichenbaum, 1980). Other reports have indicated that lesions of presumed olfactory areas in frontal cortex can impair performance of complex or difficult odor mediated responses without disrupting the basic capacity to detect and respond selectively to odors in dogs (Allen, 1940, 1941), monkeys (Tanabe, Yarita, Ilno, Ooshima, & Takagi, 1975), and rats (Eichenbaum et al., 1980; Eichenbaum, Morton, Potter, & Corkin, 1983). The specific importance of MDn-orbitofrontal projections is supported by evidence that lesions of amygdalo-hypothalamic pathways in rats do not produce comparable discrimination deficits (Eichenbaum et al., 1986; Slotnick, 1985; Slotnick & Kaneko, 1981) but do disrupt performance on odor and taste-potentiated aversions (Bermudez-Rattoni, Rusiniak, & Garcia, 1983), odor preference learning (Beaulieu, Morris, & Petrides, 1988), and odor-mediated aspects of reproductive behaviors (Devor, 1973; Macrides, Firl, Schneider, Bartke, & Stein, 1976).

Taken together, these lesion studies support the concept that olfactory information diverges into at least two pathways: one to hypothalamus that mediates olfactory aspects of feeding or neuroendocrine functions, the other involving thalamocortical projections that is critical for discrimination learning and related processes of recognition and memory. Although there is broad agreement that thalamo-cortical mechanisms play some role in odor-discrimination learning, there is uncertainty over the precise nature of this role. Eichenbaum et al. (1980) showed that MDn lesions in rats disrupt performance of a difficult discrimination between novel or similar odorants, while sparing the capacity to detect weak concentrations of odorants or to perform a relatively easy, pretrained discrimination between dissimilar odorants. The increased deficit observed for the similar odorants is consistent with a direct role in discriminating differences in odor quality; however, the reduction in the deficit produced by pretraining indicates that the impairment is not a simple sensory discrimination deficit. Slotnick and Kaneko (1981) confirmed that lesions of MDn do not disrupt detection of weak concentrations of odorants. However, they found that these lesioned rats were impaired in the reveral, but not the initial acquisition, of an odor discrimination. Since the odor discrimination was the same in initial acquisition and reversal trials, the impairment observed by Slotnick and Kaneko must be considered as evidence that MDn lesions impair cognitive rather than sensory aspects of odor discrimination learning.

Staubli et al. (1987) reached a similar conclusion in their study of olfactory learning set formation. Following surgery, they trained rats to perform a series of olfactory discrimination problems involving different pairs of odorants. Although animals with MDn lesions were impaired in the initial problems in the series, they exhibited positive transfer across problems and eventually improved to a level comparable to controls. The capacity of MDn lesioned animals to learn later problems (with novel odor pairs) as readily as controls is inconsistent with a simple inability to discriminate differences between odors. Staubli et al. (1987) argued that the deficit was related to an ability to learn the procedural, rather than the sensory aspects of the task. More recently, Mair, Knoth, et al. (1991) compared serial reversal learning based on auditory, olfactory, and spatial cues for rats having thalamic lesions affecting MDn thalamocortical projections produced by pyrithiamine-induced thiamine deficiency (PTD). For all modalities, lesioned animals were able to learn tasks to criterion although they made significantly more errors in doing so. Recovered PTD animals also showed comparable transfer in spatial serial reversal learning, the only modality in which transfer effects could be fully analyzed. These findings are consistent with other evidence that the thalamic lesions involving MDn, produced by either PTD treatment (Knoth & Mair, 1991; Mair, Knoth, et al., 1991; Mair, Otto, Knoth, Robchenuk, & Langlais, 1991) or radiofrequency lesions (Mair et al., 1990), disrupts the capacity for working memory across sensory modalities while sparing the capacity for reference memory. A spared capacity for odor reference memory is consistent with the ability of MDn-lesioned animals to perform discriminations to criterion (Mair, Knoth, et al., 1991; Slotnick & Kaneko, 1981; Staubli et al., 1987), to perform normally in detection tasks (Eichenbaum et al., 1980; Slotnick & Kaneko, 1981), and to perform normally in discrimination problems learned prior to surgery (Eichenbaum et al., 1980) or after extensive postsurgical training on comparable discrimination problems (Staubli et al., 1987).

The Hippocampus

In the early 20th century, the hippocampus was regarded as an important element in the rhinencephalon or smell brain. The discovery (discussed earlier) that olfactory bulb afferents were limited to primary olfactory cortex led to a rejection of this view and the more modern belief that hippocampus is primarily involved in nonolfactory functions (Brodal, 1947). More recent evidence has shown that olfactory inputs reach hippocampus through connections with entorhinal cortex and that the hippocampus has outputs that influence primary olfactory cortex (Price, 1985; Swanson & Köhler, 1986; Switzer, de Olmos, & Heimer, 1985). Thus, although olfactory connections with hippocampus are not as robust as once believed, they do exist.

Electrophysiological studies have related the activity of hippocampal neurons to olfactory functions (Macrides, 1976; Otto & Eichenbaum, 1991), although the literature clearly indicates that the hippocampus is primarily involved in processes related to memory or spatial perception and not olfaction per se. Lesions of the hippocampal system disrupt performance on simultaneous two-choice olfactory discriminations (Eichenbaum, Fagan, Mathews, & Cohen, 1988; Staubli et al., 1987); however, they do not impair performance on single choice go/ no go discriminations (Eichenbaum et al., 1988; Otto, Schottler, Staubli, &

Lynch, 1987). Based on these and other findings, Otto and Eichenbaum (1991) argued that the hippocampus is necessary to encode relations between odorants (or other stimuli) but not for discriminating differences between them.

Modulatory Systems

The olfactory bulb receives numerous afferents from the central nervous system as well as from the first nerve. Although many of these afferents arise from central olfactory areas and can thus be thought of as feedback systems, several arise from forebrain cholinergic as well as brainstem adrenergic and serotonergic nuclei that are thought to be important modulators of general brain activity (Foote & Morrison, 1987; Halász & Shepherd, 1983; Macrides & Davis, 1983). These nuclei are indicated by areas of black stripes in Fig. 4.3. These systems are of interest to the present chapter because of evidence that pathologic changes in these systems may mediate cognitive impairments produced by neurologic and psychiatric diseases (cf. Stahl, Iversen, & Goodman, 1987). Although each of these modulatory systems has been related hypothetically to aspects of olfaction, experimental studies have so far failed to establish a clear functional role for any of them (for a more complete review, see Mair & Harrison, 1991).

THE NATURE OF CENTRAL OLFACTORY IMPAIRMENT

Clinical Syndromes

Olfactory perception has been reported to be impaired by a remarkable diversity of diseases affecting the central nervous system (cf. Finelli & Mair, 1990). Several of these disorders are associated with systemic pathology that provide little insight into the neural basis of the olfactory deficits. Impairments of smell function of uncertain origin have been reported in patients with Alzheimer's disease (Esiri & Wilcock, 1984; Koss, Weiffenbach, Haxby, & Friedland, 1988; Serby, Corwin, Movatt, Conrad, & Retrosen, 1985), Parkinson's disease (Ansari & Johnson, 1975; Doty, Deems, & Stellar, 1988; Doty, Riklan, Deems, Reynolds, & Stellar, 1989; Ward, Hess, & Calne, 1983), Huntington's chorea (Moberg et al., 1987), and schizophrenia (Hurwitz, Kopala, Clark, & Jones, 1988) as well as in healthy elderly persons (Doty & Snow, 1988; Schiffman, 1986). The diversity of neural systems affected by these conditions raises the cautionary point that tasks used to measure olfactory perception may be sensitive to impairments of psychological or physiological processes that are not specifically olfactory. In this context, it is interesting to note reports that left parietal lobe lesions produce a syndrome of right (contralesion) unilateral neglect that extends to olfaction (Bellas, Novelly, Eskenazi, & Wasserstein, 1988). Olfactory afferents are not known to reach the parietal lobe on either side of the brain. Further, unlike other sensory systems, the central olfactory projections are ipsilateral to the sensory field. Thus, the observation of contralateral olfactory neglect following right parietal lesions provides a clear demonstration of a perceptual impairment (failure to respond to odors presented to the contralesion nostril) that results from a lesion outside pathways thought to respond to that stimulus.

Olfactory impairments have been described within three clinical populations having pathology localized along central olfactory pathways: patients with Korsakoff's disease (Gregson, Free, & Abbott, 1981; Jones, Moskowitz, & Butters, 1975; Jones, Moskowitz, Butters, & Glosser, 1975; Jones, Butters, Moskowitz, & Montgomery, 1978; Mair et al., 1980, 1986; Potter & Butters, 1980), patients with frontal cortical lesions that impinge on orbitofrontal cortex (Jones-Gotman & Zatorre, 1988; Potter & Butters, 1980), and patients with temporal lobe disease or extirpation (Eichenbaum, Morton, Potter, & Corkin, 1983; Eskenazi, Cain, Novelly, & Friend, 1983; Eskenazi, Cain, Novelly, & Mattson, 1986; Jones-Gotman & Zatorre, 1988; Mair & Engen, 1976; Rausch & Serafetindes, 1975).

Olfactory impairments have been reported for measures of olfactory discrimination, recognition, and identification following unilateral temporal lobectomies involving anterior portions of temporal cortex and including uncus, amygdala, and variable amounts of hippocampus (Eskenazi et al., 1983, 1986; Jones-Gotman & Zatorre, 1988). The performance of these same patients on odor detection tasks were either equivalent to controls (Jones-Gotman & Zatorre, 1988) or *clinically normal* and not correlated with higher order olfactory deficits (Eskenazi et al., 1983, 1986). Jones-Gotman and Zatorre (1988) found no difference in odor identification performance for 41 temporal lobectomy patients with small hippocampal lesions and 30 with large hippocampal lesions. A comparable pattern of impairment has been reported for the noted case H. M. who was rendered amnesic following a bilateral temporal lobectomy that included uncus, amygdala, and the anterior two thirds of hippocampus (Eichenbaum et al., 1983). H. M. is reported to perform normally on measures of absolute olfactory sensitivity although he performs poorly on measures of odor discrimination, identification, and recognition.

There are several olfactory pathways that might be disrupted by temporal lobectomies. In humans, the pyriform cortex is divided into frontal, insular, and temporal parts (Takimoto, Sakamoto, & Mitsui,

1962). The anterior temporal lobe contains a large portion of pyriform cortex as well as primary olfactory projection areas in the amygdaloid complex and entorhinal cortex (Takimoto et al., 1962; Truex & Carpenter, 1969). Thus, the temporal lobectomies might disrupt olfactory projections to thalamocortical targets, with sparing of pathways mediated by the olfactory tubercle and frontal and insular zones of pyriform cortex; hypothalamus, sparing pathways through the anterior olfactory nucleus; and hippocampus, which apart from direct damage may be denervated of olfactory processes relayed through lateral olfactory tract projections to entohinal cortex.

Patients with unilateral frontal cortical removals have been reported to be impaired in odor discrimination (Potter & Butters, 1980) and odor identification (Jones-Gotman & Zatorre, 1988) although they performed as well as controls in odor detection tasks. In both studies, impairments were limited to patients with cortical removals that included presumed olfactory areas in orbitofrontal cortex. Jones-Gotman and Zatorre (1988) reported that frontal cortical removals sparing orbitofrontal cortex were not associated with a significant impairment of odor identification (Fig. 4.5). However, because surgeries sparing this region tended to be smaller, it was not possible to distinguish between the possibilities that this deficit reflects overall lesion size or the specific involvement of orbitofrontal cortex.

There are a number of reports indicating that olfactory functions are impaired in Korsakoff's disease. Earlier reports show deficits in psychophysical scaling of odor intensity (Jones, Moskowitz, Butters, et al., 1975; Jones et al., 1978) and chance level performance in identification and recognition memory tasks (Jones, Moskowitz, & Butters, 1975). Based on these data, Jones and her colleagues inferred that Korsakoff patients were hyposmic. This hypothesis was tested and rejected by Mair et al. (1980) who demonstrated a normal capacity to detect a weak concentration of n-Butanol (2.05 mM in an equilibrium sniffer) by a group of Korsakoff paitents. These same subjects were also tested for short-term odor recognition memory (Fig. 4.4). There were two stimulus conditions: one with pairs of similar odorants (the hard task) and one with dissimilar odorants (the easy task) as targets and distractors. Like hue and face recognition memory (Figs. 4.1, 4.2), the Korsakoff subjects performed significantly worse at minimal delays. The decay of odor memory could be analyzed for the easy problems since the performance of the Korsakoff subjects was well above chance. Unlike hue or face recognition memory, Korsakoff patients did not exhibit an abnormally rapid rate of decay in odor memory. This comparison is simplified by the equivalent performance of Korsakoff patients on easy trials and controls on hard trials.

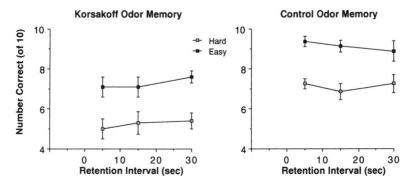

FIG. 4.4. Mean performance for Korsakoff ($N = 10$) and matched nonalcoholic controls ($N = 8$) for odor recognition memory. Error bars represent standard error of the mean. Data are reanalyzed from results reported originally by Mair et al. (1980). Results are shown for pairs of odors selected (on the basis of scaling data) to be relatively similar (hard to discriminate) or dissimilar (easy to discriminate). See text for details.

Potter and Butters (1980) modified the methods of Mair et al. (1980) and obtained generally similar results with a group of Korsakoff subjects studied earlier by Jones and colleagues (described earlier). Using a similar detection procedure (with butanol concentrations of 0.13 mM and 125 mM rather than a single concentration of 2.05 mM), they found that their Korsakoff patients could reliably detect weak concentrations of odorants although their detection performance was significantly worse than controls. Using much stronger (undiluted) odorants well above detection limits, they found that Korsakoff patients were impaired in their ability to discriminate differences between pairs of odorants including some drawn from the similar and dissimilar sets used earlier by Mair et al. (1980). Taken together, these studies provide evidence that Korsakoff's disease disrupts the ability to discriminate between odorants and that this deficit is not due to either an inability to detect the odorants or a rapid decay of odor memory.

Beyond observations of deficits in groups of subjects, there are several reports that indicate that olfactory deficits are a consistent feature of Korsakoff's disease. Gregson et al. (1981) demonstrated impairments in odor naming, labeling, and memory tasks among 12 Korsakoff patients and showed by stepwise discriminant analysis that the combination of these three measures provided a strong separation with matched alcoholic and nonalcoholic control subjects. Mair et al. (1986) measured odor identification in 26 Korsakoff subjects with the University of Pennsylvania Smell Identification Test (UPSIT), a standardized measure odor identification (Doty et al., 1984). The Korsakoff subjects averaged 41% correct (Fig. 4.5) and only two (8%) scored above 65% correct, a

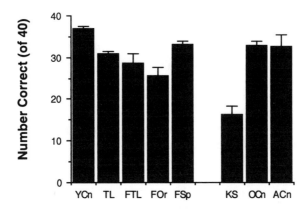

FIG. 4.5. Mean performance on the University of Pennsylvania Smell Identification Test (UPSIT) from two studies. Data are replotted from Jones-Gotman and Zatorre (1988) for subjects with unilateral extirpations of temporal lobe (TL) (N = 71), fronto-temporal lobes (FTL) (N = 10), frontal lobes including orbital cortex (FOr) (N = 16), frontal lobes sparing orbital cortex (FSp) (N = 13), and age appropriate (younger) controls (YCn) (N = 20). Data are combined for right and left sided removals for all groups except FTL (which include right-sided removals only). Data are reanalyzed from Mair et al. (1986) for patients with alcoholic Korsakoff's syndrome (KS) (N = 26), age-appropriate (older) controls (OCn) (N = 21), and age-appropriate abstinent alcoholic controls (ACn) (N = 8).

level achieved by virtually every subject in a large normative sample (N = 1,256). Although Korsakoff's disease has been associated with neurochemical pathology (cf. McEntee & Mair, 1990), there are several reasons to suspect that the impairments of this disease result from lesions of MDn. Amnesic cases of the Wernicke–Korsakoff syndrome exhibit consistent lesions of the medial magnocellular zone of MDn (Victor, Adams, & Collins, 1989), an area that corresponds to the location of olfactory thalamocortical projections (see earlier discussion of thalamocortical mechanisms). Further, in experimental animals, lesions affecting MDn or its cortical projections can product impairments in measures of memory (Goldman-Rakic, 1987; Mair, Lacourse, Koger, & Fox, 1990) and olfactory discrimination learning while sparing performance on tasks measuring odor detection (see earlier discussion of thalamocortical mechanisms).

Anosmia

The loss or decreased ability to detect odors (anosmia or hyposmia) can result from nasal obstructions that prevent volatile substances from reaching the receptor epithelium or from lesions disrupting the first nerve, the olfactory bulb, or its projections through the lateral olfactory tract (Finelli & Mair, 1990). In a study of brain computed tomography (CT) scans of 354 patients with hyposmia and/or hypogeusia, head trauma comprised the largest fraction (n = 97). Of head trauma cases with positive CT findings (N = 42), 37 had subfrontal pathology in the area of the first nerve or olfactory bulb, 3 had subtemporal lesions in the anteromedial region associated with primary olfactory cortex, and 2 showed signs of generalized atrophy (Schellinger, Henkin, & Smirniotopoulos, 1983). The olfactory tract can also be compressed by pressure exerted from tumors, especially meningiomas of the olfactory groove. In one study of 29 cases of olfactory groove meningiomas in whom smell could be tested, 26 exhibited bilateral and 3 exhibited unilateral anosmia (Bakay, 1984). This clinical evidence is consistent with a large body of experimental evidence that anosmia is produced only by lesions that include the olfactory nerve, olfactory bulb or the connections of the bulb to primary olfactory cortex (see earlier discussion of thalamocortical mechanisms).

Although lesions of the olfactory nerve, bulb, or tract can produce anosmia, there is good evidence that lesions affecting more central olfactory pathways can impair higher order aspects of olfactory perception (discrimination, recognition, identification) while sparing the capacity to detect weak odorants in both humans (see earlier discussion of clinical syndromes) and experimental animals (see earlier discussion of thalamocortical mechanisms). Taken together, the data suggest that the loss of primary sensory capacity for olfaction results only from lesions that prevent olfactory input from reaching primary olfactory cortex. Apparently lesions, such as temporal lobectomies that eliminate parts of primary olfactory cortex and affect higher order aspects of olfaction, do not prevent reliable detection of weak odorants. This is comparable to the situation in vision (see earlier discussion of the neuropsychology of sensory processes) in which lesions producing scotomas occur at relatively peripheral levels (pathways from retina through the geniculate to striate cortex). These data are consistent with two broad possibilities. First, it is possible that information required to make an odor detection judgment can reach consciousness through channels separate from those that are disrupted by lesions impairing recognition, or discrimination. Second, it is possible that the capacity for detection can survive partial destruction of a pathway sufficient to disrupt higher order olfactory processes.

Discrimination

Discrimination, or the capacity to respond based on differences between odorants, is required for tasks measuring odor recognition, identification, and memory. It is difficult to measure odor discrimination directly. Unlike vision or touch, odors must be sampled one at a time, and, thus, discrimination must be based on comparisons of successive samples. Simultaneous testing is limited by the difficulty human observers have in distinguishing stimuli presented simultaneously to the two nostrils. Further, the duration of the nasal respiratory cycle and the time course of olfactory adaptation place minimal limits on the delay (retention interval) of successive stimuli. In animal studies, sensory discrimination is generally measured by training rats to perform a successive (go/no go) discrimination with a single odor port in which odors vary between trials, or a choice discrimination between two ports in which different odors are available in each port on a given trial. After extensive training (or pretraining in lesion studies) with consistent stimuli, the demands on procedural learning are minimized and performance is taken as a measure of discriminability (cf. Mackintosh, 1983). As noted earlier (see thalamocortical mechanisms), animals with lesions of central olfactory pathways have been shown to be impaired in olfactory discrimination learning. In most cases, however, they have been shown to improve with practice and to perform at criterion (or as well as controls) when given sufficient training. These deficits have thus been interpreted as impairments of higher order processes rather than as deficits in simple sensory discrimination.

In humans, olfactory discrimination has been studied using several procedures. Unfortunately, all of these procedures require comparison of successively sampled stimuli and, thus, none demonstrate discrimination deficits that cannot be attributed to memory impairment. Eskenazi et al. (1983) used an oddity procedure to demonstrate discrimination deficits in patients with unilateral temporal lobectomies. Subjects were given three vials of odorant, two of which contained the same stimulus, and were asked which two smelled the same. To compensate for the influence of memory, subjects were allowed to sample the odors in the vials as often as desired. The temporal lobectomy patients performed significantly worse than controls (70.9% vs. 87.3% correct). Mair et al. (1980) used a recognition memory procedure to compare the capacity of Korsakoff and control subjects to discriminate differences between sets of similar and dissimilar odoarants. Recognition judgments were made at retention intervals of 5, 15, and 30 secs. Korsakoff subjects were impaired with both sets of stimuli (Fig. 4.4). Since their performance was above chance for dissimilar odorants and did not decay as a function of retention interval, it was argued that their deficit was one of discrimination, not memory.

Potter and Butters (1980) used a variation of this procedure to provide evidence of discrimination deficits in Korsakoff's disease patients as well as in patients with prefrontal disease. They used four pairs of odorants selected to represent differing degrees of similarity (or discriminability). Discrimination was tested by having subjects make multiple recognition judgments of each pair of odorants at a fixed recognition interval (15 sec). Each odorant pair was tested in a block of 32 trials, 16 with the target presented twice and 16 with the target followed by the distractor. This successive comparison procedure has elements of a yes–no recognition memory task (with only one retention interval) and of a go/no go procedure in which discrimination is measured for one pair of stimuli over a block of trials. By this measure, discrimination was impaired by Korsakoff's disease and by frontal lobectomy. This same procedure was used later to demonstrate a discrimination deficit in the case of H. M. (Eichenbaum et al., 1983). Although the impairments observed with this procedure are consistent with deficient discrimination, the data do not rule out the alternative possibility that the deficit is the result of a rapid decay in odor memory in the 15-sec interstimulus interval. Further, although this measure of discrimination was based on 32 trials with the same stimuli, the analysis of the data did not indicate whether the performance improved with practice. This issue seems important to the question of discrimination impairment given the observations that the apparent discrimination deficits of lesioned animals disappear with practice (discussed earlier).

Taken together, the data are consistent with the possibility that lesions of olfactory projections from primary olfactory cortex (affected by temporal lobectomy), through MDn (affected by Korsakoff's disease), to orbitofrontal cortex (affected by prefrontal disease) impair the ability to discriminate differences between odorants. The possibilities remain, however, that these deficits reflect either the memory demands of comparing two successive stimuli or the disruption of higher cognitive processes that could be overcome by practice.

Recognition and Identification

Recognition and identification require the capacity to discriminate an odorant as distinct from other odorants, and to be cognizant of its meaning or to associate it with either its source or an appropriate label. To demonstrate a specific impairment in such higher level processes, it is necessary to show a loss of the appreciation of meaning or identity that does not include elementary processes such as discrimination or detection. There have been relatively few attempts to assess odor recognition. Several studies have used matching procedures in which subjects sample a commonly experienced (*ecologically valid*) odorant and match it to a container or object with which it is normally associated

(Eichenbaum et al., 1983; Eskenazi et al., 1983; Mair & Engen, 1976). In one notable study, Eskenazi et al. (1983) provided convergent evidence of a recognition impairment in unilateral temporal lobectomy patients by demonstrating impairments for: (a) matching odorants to tactile stimuli, (b) matching odorants to visual stimuli, (c) matching odorants to verbal labels, and (d) making functional judgments of hard-to-identify odorants. In this study, however, the lobectomy patients also demonstrated impairments in discrimination that were correlated significantly with matching performance. Thus, like apperceptive visual agnosia (see earlier discussion of the neuropsychology of sensory processes), impairments in recognition seem secondary to a more elementary impairment of sensory perception.

Evidence has been presented that the ability to identify odorants by matching them with verbal labels is impaired by temporal lobectomy (Eichenbaum et al., 1983; Eskenazi et al., 1983, 1986; Jones-Gotman & Zatorre, 1988), Korsakoff's syndrome (Mair et al., 1986), and frontal lobectomy (Jones-Gotman & Zatorre, 1988) (Fig. 4.5). However, these same groups of subjects have also been shown to be impaired in their capacity to make same–different judgments of odorants (discussed earlier) and, thus, their failure to identify odorants can reasonably be ascribed to a more basic impairment of discriminative processes. Evidence has been reported that patients with aphasia are deficient in odor naming even though they retain a capacity for discrimination demonstrated by matching nonverbal pictures to odors (Goodglass, Barton, & Kaplan, 1968). According to Goodglass et al., aphasia impairs naming uniformly across sensory modalities in a manner that "supports the notion of a process which intervenes between the perception of any stimulus and the arousal of its name" (p. 494). Thus, it appears that odor naming shares pathways in common with naming in other sensory modalities. It is also apparent that odor naming can be disrupted by lesions of such naming centers without a concomitant impairment in olfactory discrimination.

The impairments noted on identification tasks provide evidence against the argument that rapid decay of odor memory accounts for the deficits observed following diseases affecting olfactory thalamocortical projections (i.e., temporal lobectomy, Korsakoff's disease, or frontal lobectomy). Tasks used to measure discrimination involve comparisons between odorants presented at different points in time and, thus, are susceptible to disruption by impairments of working (or episodic) memory (discussed earlier). In contrast, identification tasks involve the matching of a current sensation to a previously acquired label and, thus, depend on reference (or semantic) memory but not working (or episodic) memory (cf. Squire, 1987). There is a body of evidence relating diseases affecting olfactory thalamocortical projections (i.e., temporal lobectomy, Korsakoff's disease, and prefrontal lobectomy) to impairments of aspects of working memory (cf. Amaral, 1987; Goldman-Rakic, 1987; Mishkin, 1982; Squire, 1987). The observation of olfactory impairments in identification tasks argues against the implication of working memory deficits as the cause of these olfactory impairments.

Memory

In other sensory modalities, impairments in memory can be dissociated from impairments of perception by demonstrating a disproportionate decay in recognition or recall after a delay (see earlier discussion of the neuropsychology of sensory processes). For olfaction, however, such a dissociation has not been reported. Although patients with Korsakoff's disease show signs of rapid memory decay for tactile, visual, and auditory modalities (Butters, Lewis, Cermak, & Goodglass, 1973; Riege, 1977; Strauss & Butler, 1978; see Figs. 4.1, 4.2), they exhibit signs of discrimination impairment without rapid memory decay for odors (Fig. 4.4). It is also striking that conditions notably associated with memory impairments are also associated with impairments of olfactory perception that do not seem to be a direct result of amnesia. These conditions include: bilateral temporal lobectomy (discussed earlier), Korsakoff's disease (discussed earlier), Alzheimer's disease (Esiri & Wilcock, 1984; Koss et al., 1988; Serby et al., 1985), and aging (Doty & Snow, 1988; Schiffman, 1986). The apparent association of memory deficits with olfactory perceptual impairment suggests that these processes may share a critical dependence on the same neurological centers or pathways. Such a commonality of neurological substrates could also account for the apparent lack of reports (to our knowledge) of any patients exhibiting a rapid decay in odor memory with an intact capacity for odor perception. Although lesions of memory centers (presumably involving medial temporal lobe or midline diencephalon) can produce rapid forgetting of visual, auditory or tactile stimuli without disrupting perception, lesions of these same centers disrupt the capacity for more elementary aspects of odor perception. Unlike other sensory modalities, there is no evidence that there are morphologically distinct centers mediating the perception of, and memory for, odors.

Laterality

One of the more interesting aspects of central olfactory impairment is the observation of equivalent deficits following unilateral lesions of either hemisphere. There is abundant evidence in other modalities of perceptual deficits produced by unilateral lesions. However, for vision, audition, and touch, lesions of the dominant and nondominant hemispheres tend to disrupt different aspects of sensory perception (Milner, 1974; Nass & Gazzaniga, 1987; Teuber, 1975). In olfaction, however, this has not proven to be the case. For both frontal and temporal lobes, extirpation of tissue in the left and right hemispheres has been reported to produce comparable impairments for a variety of olfactory tasks (reviewed earlier). It is particularly striking that cerebral dominance has no apparent effect on the matching of odors to verbal labels (Eskenazi et al., 1983, 1986; Jones-Gotman & Zatorre, 1988). These data suggest that in humans there is redundancy in olfactory processes mediated by the two hemispheres. The possibility remains, however, that dominant and nondominant lesions affect different aspects of olfactory perception, but testing procedures have not been sensitive to these differences.

Gordon and Sperry (1969) showed that patients with surgically disconnected hemispheres can name odors presented to the left, but not right, nostril. Additionally, when odors were sampled by the right nostril, subjects could identify odorants with their left (but not right) hands by either pointing to an appropriate visual target or identifying an appropriate tactile stimulus. This indicates that the right hemisphere retained a capacity for olfactory discrimination. Odorants sampled by the left nostril could also be identified manually by the right (but not the left) hand, indicating that the left hemisphere retained a capacity for olfactory discrimination. The reader should be reminded that the right hemisphere controls the left hand, but receives olfactory input from the right nostril. The specific correspondence between nostril and contralateral hand is consistent with the idea that each hemisphere has a separate capacity for olfactory discrimination and that this information does not cross between hemispheres when the cerebral commissures are severed. The inability of split brain patients to name odorants presented to the right nostril suggests that odor naming is a left hemisphere function. This is consistent with the observation (discussed earlier) that unilateral dominant hemisphere lesions disrupt the naming of odors as well as visual, auditory, and tactile stimuli (Goodglass et al., 1968).

The observations of Gordon and Sperry (1969) indicate that in humans each hemisphere has a separate capacity to discriminate between odorants. Comparisons between patients with left and right lobectomies indicate that dominant and nondominant lesions disrupt performance on the same measures of olfactory perception (Eskenazi et al., 1983, 1986; Jones-Gotman & Zatorre, 1988). If there is complete redundancy in the functions served by each hemisphere, then why do unilateral lesions disrupt odor perception? One possible explanation is that the coordinated functioning of both hemispheres is necessary for optimal olfactory performance. If this is the case, then unilateral lesions disrupting olfactory function in one hemisphere should produce impaired odor perception, but not to the extent of bilateral lesions involving olfactory pathways in both hemispheres. Although data do not exist to explicitly test this proposition, there is evidence consistent with it. Korsakoff's disease produces bilateral lesions of MDn and thus can be presumed to affect thalamocortical projections in both hemispheres. Figure 4.5 compares Korsakoff patients wih subjects having unilateral lobectomies of frontal and temporal cortices for performance on the University of Pennsylvania Smell Identification Test (UPSIT). Since lobectomy patients tend to be younger, control data are presented for younger controls (YCn) that are age appropriate for patients with unilateral lobectomies (Jones-Gotman & Zatorre, 1988). Data for Korsakoff patients are presented with age-appropriate older normal controls (OCn) and abstinent alcoholic controls (ACn) (Mair et al., 1986). Compared to age-appropriate controls, UPSIT performance was reduced by 16% for temporal lobectomies (TL), 22% for frontotemporal lobectomies including orbitofrontal areas (FTL), 31% for frontal lobectomies including orbitofrontal cortex (FOr), and 10% for frontal lobectomies sparing orbitofrontaol cortex (FSp). In contrast, the performance of Korsakoff patients was 50% lower than age-appropriate controls. Without question, there are numerous confounding variables that prevent one from drawing strong inferences from these data. Nevertheless, the larger deficit apparent for Korsakoff patients is consistent with the prediction that olfactory deficits should be greater for bilateral disease.

ACKNOWLEDGMENT

This work was supported by grant NS26855 from NINDS to the first author.

REFERENCES

Alexander, M. P., & Albert, M. L. (1983). The anatomical basis of visual agnosia. In A. Kertesz (Ed.), *Localization in neuropsychology* (pp. 393–415). New York: Academic Press.

Allen, W. F. (1940). Effect of ablating the frontal lobes, hippocampi, and occipito-parieto-temporal (excepting pyriform areas) lobes on positive and negative olfactory conditioned reflexes. *American Journal of Physiology, 128,* 754–771.

Allen, W. F. (1941). Effect of ablating the pyriform-amygdaloid areas and hippocampi on positive and negative olfactory conditioned reflexes and on conditioned olfactory differentiation. *American Journal of Physiology, 132,* 81–92.

Allen, W. F (1943). Distribution of cortical potentials resulting from insufflation of vapors into the nostrils and from stimulating the olfactory bulbs and the pyriform lobe. *American Journal of Physiology, 139,* 553–555.

Allison, A. C. (1953). The morphology of the olfactory system in the vertebrates. *Biology Review, 28,* 195–244.

Amaral, D. G. (1987). Memory: Anatomical organization of candidate brain regions. In V. B. Mountcastle, F. Plum, & S. R. Geiger (Eds.), *Handbook of physiology: The nervous system* (pp. 211–294). Bethesda, MD: American Physiological Society.

Anderson, R. A. (1987). Inferior parietal lobule function in spatial perception and visuomotor integration. In V. B. Mountcastle, F. Plum, & S. R. Geiger (Eds.), *Handbook of physiology: The nervous system* (pp. 483–518). Bethesda, MD: American Physiological Society.

Ansari, K. A., & Johnson, A. (1975). Olfactory function in patients with Parkinson's Disease. *Journal of Chronic Diseases, 28,* 493–497.

Bakay, L. (1984). Olfactory meningioma: The missed diagnosis. *Journal of the American Medical Association, 251,* 53–55.

Bauer, R. M., & Rubens, A. B. (1985). Agnosia. In K. M. Heilman & E. Valenstein (Eds.), *Clinical neuropsychology* (pp. 187–242). New York: Oxford.

Beaulieu, N., Morris, R., & Petrides, M. (!988). Lesions of the basolateral amygdala and of the pyriform cortex impair acquisition of a conditioned odor preference. *Society for Neuroscience Abstracts, 14,* 1226.

Bellas, D. N., Novelly, R. A., Eskenazi, B., & Wasserstein, J. (1988). The nature of unilateral neglect in the olfactory sensory system. *Neuropsychologia, 26,* 45–52.

Benson, D. F., & McDaniel, K. D. (1990). Memory disorders. In W. G. Bradley, R. B. Daroff, G. M. Fenichel, & C. D. Marsden (Eds.), *Neurology in clinical practice: Principles of diagnosis and management* (pp. 1389–1406). Boston, MA: Butterworth-Heinemann.

Benton, A. L. (!985). Visuoperceptual, visuospatial, and visuoconstructive disorders. In K. M. Heilman & E. Valenstein (Eds.), *Clinical neuropsychology* (pp. 151–186). New York: Oxford.

Bermudez-Rattoni, R., Rusiniak, K. W., & Garcia, J. (1983). Flavor-illness aversions: Potentiation of odor by taste is disrupted by application of novocaine to the amygdala. *Behavioral Neural Biology, 37,* 61–75.

Brodal, A. (1947). The hippocampus and the sense of smell. A review. *Brain, 70,* 179–222.

Brown, C. W., & Ghiselli, E. E. (1938). Subcortical mechanisms in learning. IV. Olfactory discrimination. *Journal of Comparative Physiology and Psychology, 26,* 109–120.

Butters, N., & Cermak, L. S. (1980). *Alcoholic Korsakoff's Syndrome: An information-processing approach to amnesia.* New York: Academic Press.

Butters, N., Lewis, R., Cermak, L. S., & Goodglass, H. (1973). Material specific memory deficits in alcoholic Korsakoff patients. *Neuropsychologia, 11,* 291–299.

Cabanac, M. (1971). Physiological role of pleasure. *Science, 173,* 1103–1107.

Damasio, A. R., & Benton, A. L. (1979). Impairment of hand movements under visual guidance. *Neurology, 29,* 170–174.

Damasio, A. R., & Tranel, D. (1990). Disorders of recognition. In W. G. Bradley, R. B. Daroff, G. M. Fenichel, & C. D. Marsden (Eds.), *Neurology in clinical practice: Principles of diagnosis and management* (pp. 123–128). Boston, MA: Butterworth-Heinemann.

Damasio, A. R., Tranel, D., & Damasio, H. (1990). Face agnosia and the neural substrates of memory. *Annual Review of Neuroscience, 13,* 89–109.

Devor, M. (1973). Components of mating behavior dissociated by lateral olfactory tract transection in hamsters. *Brain Research, 64,* 437–441.

Doty, R. L., Deems, D. A., & Stellar, S. (1988). Olfactory dysfunction in Parkinson's: A general deficit unrelated to neurologic signs, disease stage, or disease duration. *Neurology, 38,* 1237–1244.

Doty, R. L., Riklan, M., Deems, D. A., Reynolds, C., & Stellar, S. (1989). The olfactory and cognitive deficits of Parkinson's disease: Evidence for independence. *Annals Neurology,* 25, 166–171.

Doty, R. L., Shaman, P., & Dann, M. (1984). Development of the University of Pennsylvania Smell Identification Test: A standardized microencapsulated test of olfactory function. *Physiology and Behavior, 32,* 489–502.

Doty, R. L., & Snow, J. B., Jr. (1988). Age-related alterations in olfactory structure and function. In F. L. Margolis & T. Getchell (Eds.), *Molecular neurobiology of the olfactory system* (pp. 355–374). New York: Plenum.

Duclaux, R., Feisthauer, J., & Cabanac, M. (1973). Effets du repas sur l'agrement d'odeurs alimentaires et nonalimentaires chez l'homme. *Physiological Behavior, 10,* 1029–1033.

Eichenbaum, H., Fagan, A., & Cohen, N. J. (1986). Normal olfactory discrimination learning set and facilitation of reversal learning after medial-temporal damage in rats: Implications for an account of preserved learning abilities in amnesia. *Journal of Neuroscience, 6,* 1876–1884.

Eichenbaum, H., Fagan, A., Mathews, P., & Cohen, N. J. (1988). Hippocampal system dysfunction and odor discrimination learning in rats: Impairment or facilitation depending on representational demands. *Behavioral Neuroscience, 102,* 331–339.

Eichenbaum, H., Morton, T. H., Potter, H., & Corkin, S. (1983). Selective olfactory deficits in case H. M. *Brain, 106,* 459–472.

Eichenbaum, H., Shedlack, K. J., & Eckmann, K. W. (1980). Thalmocortical mechanisms in odor-guided behavior. I. Effects of lesions of the mediodorsal thalamic nucleus and frontal cortex on olfactory discrimination in the rat. *Brain Behavior Evolution, 17,* 255–275.

Engen, T., Gilmore, M., & Mair, R. G. (1991). Odor. Memory. In T. Getchell, R. Doty, L. Bartoshuk, & J. Snow (Eds.), *Taste and smell in health and disease* (pp. 315–328). New York: Raven Press.

Esiri, M. M., & Wilcock, G. K. (1984). The olfactory bulbs in Alzheimer's Disease. *Journal of Neurology, Neurosurgery, and Psychiatry, 47,* 56–60.

Eskenazi, B., Cain, W. S., Novelly, R. A., & Friend, K. B. (1983). Olfactory functioning in temporal lobectomy patients. *Neuropsychologia, 3,* 365–374.

Eskenazi, B., Cain, W. S., Novelly, R. A., & Mattson, R. (1986). Odor perception in temporal obe epilepsy patients with and without temporal lobectomy. *Neuropsychologia, 24,* 553–562.

Farnsworth, D. (1957). *The Farnsworth–Munsell 100 Hue Test Manual.* Baltimore: Macbeth.

Finelli, P. F., & Mair, R. G. (1990). Disturbances of taste and smell. In W. G. Bradley, R. B. Daroff, G. M. Fenichel, & C. D. Marsden (Eds.), *Neurology in clinical practice: Principles of diagnosis and management* (pp. 209–216). Boston, MA: Butterworth-Heinemann.

Flint, D. L., & Mair, R. G. (1991). *Recognition memory is enhanced in Korsakoff's Disease by increasing the frequency of exposure, but not discriminability of visual stimuli.* Unpublished manuscript.

Foerster, O. (1929). Beitrage zur pathophysiologie der sehbahn undder sehsphare. Section 3. Zur frage der somatotopischen gliederung der area striata. *Jahrbuch fur Psychologie und Neurologie, 39,* 477–482.

Foote, S. L., & Morrison, J. H. (1987). Extrathalamic modulation of cortical function. *Annual Review of Neuroscience, 10,* 67–95.

Friedman, R. B., & Albert, M. L. (1985). Alexia. In K. M. Heilman & E. Valenstein (Eds.), *Clinical neuropsychology* (pp. 49–74). New York: Oxford.

Geschwind, N. (1967). The varieties of naming disorders. *Cortex, 3,* 97–112.

Geschwind, N., & Fusillo, M. (1966). Color-naming defects in association with alexia. *Archives of Neurology, 15,* 137–146.

Goldman-Rakic, P. S. (1987). Circuitry of primate prefrontal cortex and regulation of behavior by representational memory. In V. B. Mountcastle, F. Plum, & S. R. Geiger

(Eds.), *Handbook of Physiology: The nervous system* (pp. 373–418). Bethesda, MD: American Physiological Society.

Goodglass, H., Barton, M. I., & Kaplan, E. F. (1968). Sensory modality and object naming in aphasia. *Journal of Speech and Hearing Research, 11,* 488–496.

Gordon, H. W., & Sperry, R. W. (1969). Lateralization of olfactory perception in the surgically separated hemispheres of man. *Neuropsychologia, 7,* 111–120.

Gregson, R. A. M., Free, M. I., & Abbott, M. W. (1981). Olfaction in Korsakoff's, alcoholics and normals. *British Journal of Clinical Psychology, 20,* 3–10.

Gross, C. G. (1973). Visual functions of inferotemporal cortex. In R. Jung (Ed.), *Handbook of sensory physiology, Vol. VII, Part 3,* (pp. 452–482). Berlin: Springer-Verlag.

Halász, N., & Shepherd, G. M. (1983). Neurochemistry of the vertebrate olfactory bulb. *Neuroscience, 13,* 579–619.

Hurwitz, T., Kopala, L., Clark, L., & Jones, B. (1988). Olfactory deficits in Schizophrenia. *Biological Psychiatry, 88,* 123–128.

Iwai, E., & Mishkin, M. (1969). Further evidence on the locus of the visual area in the temporal lobe of the monkey. *Experimental Neurology, 25,* 585–594.

Jones, E. G. (1985). *The thalamus* (pp. 649–664). New York: Plenum Press.

Jones, B. P., Butters, N., Moskowitz, H., & Montgomery, K. (1978). Olfactory and gustatory capacities of alcoholic Korsakoff patients. *Neuropsychologia, 16,* 332–337.

Jones, B. P., Moskowitz, H., & Butters, N. (1975). Olfactory discrimination in alcoholic Korsakoff patients. *Neuropsychologia, 13,* 173–179.

Jones, B. P., Moskowitz, H., Butters, N., & Glosser, G. (1975). Psychophysical scaling of olfactory, visual, and auditory stimuli by alcoholic Korsakoff patients. *Neuropsychologia, 13,* 387–393.

Jones-Gotman, M., & Zatorre, R. J. (1988). Olfactory identification deficits in patients with focal cerebral excision. *Neuropsychologia, 26,* 387–400.

Julesz, B. (1987). Preattentive human vision: Link between neurophysiology and psychophysics. In V. B. Mountcastle, F. Plum, & S. R. Geiger (Eds.), *Handbook of physiology: The nervous system* (pp. 585–604). Bethesda, MD: American Physiological Society.

Kluver, H. (1942). Functional significance of the geniculo-striate system. *Biological Symposia, 8,* 253–299.

Knoth, R. L., & Mair, R. G. (1991). Response latency and accuracy on a pretrained nonmatch to sample task in rats recovered from pyrithiamine induced thiamine deficiency. *Behavioral Neuroscience, 105,* 375–385.

Koss, E., Weiffenbach, J. M., Haxby, J. V., & Friedland, R. P. (1988). Olfactory detection and recognition performance and disassociation in early Alzheimer's Disease. *Neurology, 38,* 1288–1232.

Kuffler, S. W. (1953). Discharge patterns and functional organization of mammalian retina. *Journal of Neurophysiology, 16,* 37–68.

Lashley, K. S. (1948). The mechanism of vision: XVIII. Effects of destroying the visual "associative areas" of the monkey. *Genetic Psychology Monographs, 37,* 107–166.

Lashley, K. S., & Sperry, R. W. (1943). Olfactory discrimination after destruction of the anterior thalamic nuclei. *American Journal of Physiology, 139,* 446–450.

LeMagnen, J. (1971). Olfaction and nutrition. In L. M. Beidler (Ed.), *Handbook of sensory physiology: Vol. IV, Part 1* (pp. 465–482).

Lennie, P., Trevarthen, C., Van Essen, D., & Wassle, H. (1990). Parallel processing of visual information. In L. Spillmann & J. S. Werner (Eds.), *Visual perception: The neurophysiological foundations* (pp. 103–128). San Diego: Academic Press.

Livingstone, M., & Hubel, D. (1988). Segregation of form, color, movement, and depth: Anatomy, physiology, and perception. *Science, 240,* 740–749.

Lundberg, P. O. (1960). Cortico-hypothalamic connections in the rabbit. *Acta Physiologica Scandinovia, (Suppl. 171), 49,* 1–80.

Mackintosh, N. J. (1983). *Conditioning and associative learning*. Oxford: Clarendon Press.

Macrides, F. (1976). Dynamic aspects of central olfactory processing. In D. Müller-Schwarze & M. M. Mozell (Eds.), *Chemical signals in vertebrates* (pp. 499–514). New York: Plenum Press.

Macrides, F., & Davis, B. J. (1983). The olfactory bulb. In P. C. Emson (Ed.), *Chemical neuroanatomy* (p. 391). New York: Raven Press.

Macrides, F., Firl, A. C., Schneider, S. P., Bartke, A., & Stein, D. G. (1976). Effects of one stage or serial transections of the lateral olfactory tracts on behavior and plasma testosterone levels in male hamsters. *Brain Research, 109,* 97–109.

Mair, R. G., Capra, C., McEntee, W. J., & Engen, T. (1980). Odor discrimination and memory in Korsakoff's psychosis. *Journal Experimental Psychology: Human Perception Performance, 6,* 445–458.

Mair, R. G., Doty, R. L., Kelly, K. M., Wilson, C. S., Langlais, P. J., McEntee, W. J., & Vollmecke, T. A. (1986). Multimodal sensory discrimination deficits in Korsakoff's psychosis. *Neuropsychologia, 24,* 831–839.

Mair, R. G., & Engen, T. (1976). Some effects of aphasic lesions on odor perception. *Sensory Processes, 1,* 33–39.

Mair, R. G., & Harrison, L. M. (1991). Influence of drugs on smell function and memory. In D. G. Laing, R. L. Doty, & W. Breipol (Eds.), *The human sense of smell* (pp. 335–359). Berlin: Springer-Verlag.

Mair, R. G., Knoth, R. L., Rabchenuk, S. A., & Langlais, P. J. (1991). Impairment of olfactory, auditory, and spatial serial reversal learning in rats recovered from pyrithiamine induced thiamine deficiency. *Behavioral Neuroscience, 105,* 360–374.

Mair, R. G., Lacourse, D. M., Koger, S., & Fox, G. D. (1990). In the rat, RF lesions of thalamus and fornix produce different patterns of impairment on a delayed non-matching to sample task. *Society for Neuroscience Abstracts, 16,* 608.

Mair, R. G., Otto, T., Knoth, R. L., Rabchenuk, S. A., & Langlais, P. J. (1991). An analysis of aversively conditioned learning and memory in rats recovered from pyrithiamine induced thiamine deficiency. *Behavioral Neuroscience, 105,* 351–359.

Maunsell, J. H. R., & Newsome, W. T. (1987). Visual processing in monkey extrastriate cortex. *Annual Review of Neuroscience, 10,* 363–401.

McBurney, D. H. (1986). Taste, smell and flavor terminology. Taking the confusion out of fusion. In H. L. Meiselman & R. S. Rivlin (Eds.), *Clinical measurement of taste and smell* (pp. 117–125). New York: MacMillan.

McEntee, W. J., & Mair, R. G. (1990). The Korsakoff Syndrome: A neurochemical perspective. *Trends in Neuroscience, 13,* 340–344.

Mesulam, M. M. (1981). A cortical network for directed attention and unilateral neglect. *Annals of Neurology, 10,* 309–325.

Milner, B. (1968a). Disorders of memory after brain lesions in man. Preface: Material-specific and generalized memory loss. *Neuropsychologia, 6,* 175–179.

Milner, B. (1968b). Visual recognition and recall after right temporal lobe excision in man. *Neuropsychologia, 6,* 191–209.

Milner, B. (!974). Hemispheric specialization: Scope and limits. In F. O. Schmitt & F. G. Worden (Eds.), *The neurosciences: Third study program* (pp. 75–89). Cambridge, MA: MIT Press.

Milner, B., & Teuber, H. L. (1968). Alteration of perception and memory in man: Reflections in methods. In L. Weiskrantz (Ed.), *Analysis of behavioral changes.* New York: Harper and Row.

Mishkin, M. (1972). Cortical visual areas and their interactions. In A. G. Karczmar & J. C. Eccles (Eds.), *The brain and human behavior* (pp. 188–238). New York: Springer.

Mishkin, M. (1982). A memory system in the monkey. *Philosophical Transactions Royal Society London. [Biol.], 298,* 85–95.

Moberg, P. J., Pearlson, G. D., Speedie, L. J., Lipsey, J. R., Strauss, M. E., & Folstein, S. E. (1987). Olfactory recognition: Differential impairments in early and late Huntington's and Alzheimer's diseases. *Journal of Clinical Experimental Neuropsychology, 9*, 650–664.

Motokizawa, F. (1974). Olfactory input to the thalamus: Electrophysiological evidence. *Brain Research, 67*, 334–337.

Mower, G. D., Mair, R. G., & Engen, T. (1977). Influence of internal factors on the perceived intensity and pleasantness of gustatory and olfactory stimuli. In M. R. Kare & O. Maller (Eds.), *The chemical senses and nutrition* (pp. 103–118). New York: Academic Press.

Munk, H. (1950). On the functions of the cortrx. In G. Von Bonin (Ed.), *Some papers on the cerebral cortex* (pp. 97–117). Springfield, IL: Charles E. Thomas. (Original work published 1881)

Nass, R. D., & Gazzaniga, M. S. (1987). Cerebral lateralization and specialization in human central nervous system. In V. B. Mountcastle, F. Plum, & S. R. Geiger (Eds.), *Handbook of physiology: The nervous system* (pp. 701–762). Bethesda, MD: America Physiological Society.

Nauta, W. (1961). Fiber degeneration following lesions of the amygdaloid complex in the monkey. *Journal of Anatomy, 95*, 515–532.

O'Keefe, J., & Nadel, L. (1978). *The Hippocampus as a Cognitive Map*. Oxford: Oxford University Press.

Otto, T., & Eichenbaum, H. (1991). Olfactory learning and memory in the rat: A "model system" for studies of the neurobiology of memory. In M. Serby & K. L. Chobor (Eds.), *Science of Olfaction* (pp. 213–244). New York: Springer-Verlag.

Otto, T., Schottler, F., Staubli, U., & Lynch, G. (1987). Hippocampal denervation facilitates olfactory learning-set formation and does not impair memory in a successive-cue go/no go task. *Society Neuroscience Abstracts, 13*, 1066.

Pearlman, A. L., Birch, J., & Meadows, J. C. (1979). Cerebral color blindness: An acquired defect in hue discrimination. *Annals of Neurology, 5*, 253–261.

Potter, H., & Butters, N. (1980). An assessment of olfactory deficits in patients with damage to prefrontal cortex. *Neuropsychologia, 18*, 621–628.

Potter, H., & Nauta, W. J. H. (1979). A note on the problem of olfactory associations of the orbitofrontal cortex in the monkey. *Neuroscience, 4*, 361–367.

Powell, T. P. S., Cowan, W. M., & Raisman, G. (1963). Olfactory relationships of the diencephalon. *Nature, 199*, 710–712.

Powell, T. P. S., Cowan, W. M., & Raisman, G. (1965). The central olfactory connections. *Journal of Anatomy, 99*, 791–813.

Pribram, K. H., & Kruger, L. (1954). Functions of the "olfactory brain". *Annals of N.Y. Academy of Science, 32*, 109–139.

Price, J. L. (1985). Beyond the primary olfactory cortex: Olfactory-related areas in the neocortex, thalamus, and hypothalamus. *Chemical Senses, 10*, 239–258.

Price, J. L., & Slotnick, B. M. (1983). Dual olfactory representation in the rat thalamus: An anatomical and electrophysiological study. *Journal of Comparative Neurology, 215*, 63–77.

Rausch, R., & Serafetindes, E. A. (1975). Specific alterations of olfactory function in humans with temporal lobe lesions. *Nature, 255*, 557–558.

Reige, W. (1977). Inconstant nonverbal recognition memory in Korsakoff patients and controls. *Neuropsychologia, 15*, 269–276.

Sapolsky, R. M., & Eichenbaum, H. (1980). Thalamo-cortical mechanisms in odor-guided behavior: Vol. II. Effects of lesions of the medioidorsal thalamic nucleus and frontal cortex on odor preferences and sexual behavior in the hamster. *Brain Behavior and Evolution, 17*, 276–290.

Schellinger, D., Henkin, R. T., & Smirniotopoulos, J. G. (1983). CT of the brain in taste and smell dysfunction. *American Jouranl of Neuroradiology, 4,* 752–754.

Schiffman, S. S. (1986). Taste and smell in disease. *New England Journal of Medicine, 308,* 1275–1279.

Scott, J., & Pfaffmann, C. (1967). Olfactory input to the hypothalamus: Electrophysiological evidence. *Science, 158,* 1592–1594.

Serby, M., Corwin, J., Movatt, A., Conrad, P., & Retrosen, J. (1985). Olfaction in dementia. *Journal of Neurology, Neurosurgery, and Psychiatry, 48,* 848–849.

Slotnick, B. M. (1985). Olfactory discrimination in rats with anterior amygdala lesions. *Behavioral Neuroscience, 99,* 956–963.

Slotnick, B. M., & Kaneko, N. (1981). Role of mediodorsal thalamic nucleus in olfactory discrimination learning in rats. *Science, 214,* 91–92.

Squire, L. (1987). *Memory and brain.* New York: Oxford.

Stahl, S. M., Iversen, S. D., & Goodman, E. C. (1987). *Cognitive neurochemistry.* Oxford: Oxford University Press.

Staubli, U., Schottler, F., & Nejat-Bina, D. (1987). Role of dorsomedial thalamic nucleus and piriform cortex in processing olfactory information. *Behavioral Brain Research, 25,* 117–129.

Strauss, E., & Butler, R. B. (1978). The effect of varying types of interference on haptic memory in the Korsakoff patient. *Neuropsychologia, 16,* 81–90.

Swann, H. G. (1934). The function of the brain in olfaction: Vol. I. The results of destruction of olfactory and other nervous structures upon the discrimination of odors. *Journal of Comparative Neurology, 59,* 175–201.

Swann, H. G. (1935). The function of the brain in olfaction: Vol. II. *American Journal of Physiology, 111,* 257–262.

Swanson, L. W., & Köhler, C. (1986). Anatomical evidence for direct projections from the entorhinal area to the entire cortical mantle in the rat. *Journal of Neuroscience, 6,* 3010–3023.

Switzer, R. C., de Olmos, J., & Heimer, L. (1985). Olfactory system. In G. Paxinos (Ed.), *The rat nervous system: Vol. 1. Forebrain and midbrain.* Orlando, FL: Academic Press.

Takimoto, T., Sakamoto, E., & Mitsui, Y. (1962). A cytoarchitectural study of the anterior perforated substance and its neighboring structures in man. *Tokoshima Journal of Experimental Medicine, 9,* 8–23.

Tanabe, T., Ilno, M., & Takagi, S. F. (1975). Discrimination of odors in olfactory bulb, piriform-amygdaloid areas, and orbitofrontal cortex of the monkey. *Journal of Neurophysiology, 38,* 1284–1296.

Tanabe, T., Yarita, H., Ilno, M., Ooshima, Y., & Takagi, S. F. (1975). An olfactory projection area in the orbitofrontal cortex of the monkey. *Journal of Neurophysiology, 38,* 1284–1296.

Teuber, H. L. (1975). Effects of focal brain injury on human behavior. In D. B. Tower (Ed.), *Vol. 2: The Clinical Neurosciences* (pp. 457–480). New York: Raven Press.

Tomsak, R. L. (1990). Visual loss. In W. G. Bradley, R. B. Daroff, G. M. Fenichel, C. D. Marsden (Eds.), *Neurology in clinical practice: Principles of diagnosis and management* (pp. 143–148). Boston, MA: Butterworth-Heinemann.

Truex, R. C., & Carpenter, M. B. (1969). *Human Neuroanatomy, Sixth Edition.* Baltimore: Williams and Wilkins.

Victor, M., Adams, R. D., & Collins, G. H. (1989). *The Wernicke-Korsakoff Syndrome, Second Edition.* Philadelphia: F. A. Davis.

Ward, C. D., Hess, W. A., & Calne, D. B. (1983). Olfactory impairment in Parkinson's Disease. *Neurology, 33,* 943–946.

Yarita, H., Ilno, M., Tanabe, T., Kogure, S., & Takagi, S. F. (1980). A transthalamic olfactory pathway to orbitofrontal cortex in the monkey. *Journal of Neurophysiology, 43,* 69–85.

Zihl, J., & Von Cramon, D. (1979). The contribution of the "second" visual system to directed visual attention in man. *Brain, 102,* 835–856.

Zihil, J., von Cramon, D., & Mai, N. (1983). Selective disturbance of movement vision after bilateral brain damage. *Brain, 106,* 313–340.

= 5 =

Implicit Measures of Odor Memory

Frank R. Schab
Opinion Research Corporation

Robert G. Crowder
Yale University

The vast preponderance of our scientific knowledge about human memory comes from experiments on explicit, or direct, memory tests, in which the rememberer consciously recollects events experienced at some earlier time. Explicit tests include the standard procedures of recall, recognition, and reconstruction that underlie such everyday experiences as remembering the name that goes with a particular face, retrieving the gist of last night's news broadcast, and recognizing the voice on the telephone as belonging to a particular old college friend.

Over the past decade, however, attitudes on memory have evolved significantly, largely based on procedures that test previous learning implicitly, or indirectly. On implicit tests, the subject is by definition not trying to recollect previous experiences. Memory is demonstrated by a facilitatory effect of a previous stimulus exposure on subsequent processing of that same stimulus (or a related one) in the absence of any conscious recollection of the previous experience (e.g., Graf & Schacter, 1985; Richardson-Klavehn & Bjork, 1988; Roediger, 1990). Tests of implicit memory include such repetition-based improvement in perceptual identification, word-stem completion (the stem ALC____ as a cue for the target ALCOHOL), and word-fragment completion (the fragment _LC_H__ as a cue for the same target). In perceptual identification, to take another example, subjects first are exposed to a series of stimuli (e.g., pictures of objects), and later are shown degraded examples of the original stimuli as well as novel stimuli (Snodgrass & Feenan, 1990). Shorter latency and/or greater accuracy at labelling degraded versions of the previously presented stimuli, as compared to baseline (novel stimuli), reflects memory (priming) for the earlier exposure just as surely as a traditional recognition or recall test.

Lest we exaggerate the novelty of testing memory by implicit, rather than explicit, measures, we should remind ourselves that the very first systematic experimental studies of memory (Ebbinghaus, 1885/1964) anticipated implicit tests. The savings method of Ebbinghaus was devised deliberately to elude the process of explicit recollection and rely, instead, on the facilitation in learning time for a particular list that resulted from previous study of that same list. Thus, it is historically more accurate to observe that implicit memory was reintroduced after being ignored and abandoned for nearly a hundred years after its introduction, rather than being recently discovered

Evidence for a theoretical distinction between processes underlying explicit and implicit memory comes from three sorts of dissociation between performance on implicit and explicit tasks. (Dissociations are cases when, in response to some variable, the two kinds of memory tests do not respond in the same way.) Dissociations between implicit and explicit memory are frequently observed as a function of experimental or task variables (Graf & Mandler, 1984; Graf, Mandler, & Haden, 1982; Jacoby & Dallas, 1981; Jacoby & Witherspoon, 1982; Roediger & Blaxton, 1987a; Schacter, 1987; Schacter & Graf, 1986). For example, Jacoby and Dallas (1981) showed that whereas performance on explicit tests is quite sensitive to depth of processing, performance on implicit tests is much less influenced by that variable. The reverse is true for surface characteristics of the information (e.g., stimulus modality, sex of speaker), which affect implicit but not explicit test performance (see Roediger & Blaxton, 1987b; Weldon, 1991).

A second type of dissociation is based on such nonclinical subject variables as age. Experiments show that performance on implicit memory tests is far less affected than on explicit tests by normal aging (Light, Singh, & Capps, 1986; Parkin & Streete, 1988) or drug state (Hashtroudi, Parker, DeLisi, Wyatt, & Mutter, 1984). The third dissociation also rests on subject differences, but this time on comparisons of normal and clinical populations: Patients suffering from anterograde amnesia generally exhibit very poor recall and recognition of information presented after the onset of amnesia, but perform at levels similar to normals—often completely unimpaired—when tested with implicit procedures (Cohen & Squire, 1980; Graf, Shimamura, & Squire, 1985; Warrington & Weiskrantz, 1974).

These dissociations have led some to suggest that different memory systems are involved when subjects perform implicit and explicit tests (e.g., Sherry & Schacter, 1987; Squire, 1987; Tulving & Schacter, 1990). But viable alternative explanations exist for the obtained dissociations, including, for example, the degree to which the type of processing at encoding and retrieval match (Roediger & Blaxton, 1987b; Roediger, Srinivas, & Weldon, 1989; Weldon, 1991). Furthermore, uncertainty surrounding the meaning of conscious recollection, and the distinctiveness of the implicit–explicit dichotomy vis-à-vis other popular memory dichotomies (e.g., semantic–episodic, declarative–procedural) cloud the issue further (Hirst, 1989). Also, most acts of remembering, especially recognition, arguably involve both conscious recollection and subconscious processes (Mandler, 1980), and so we may not assume any experimental tasks give us a *pure form* of processes underlying either implicit or explicit remembering.

These theoretical puzzles notwithstanding, all workers would agree that the implicit–explicit distinction has provided a host of new laboratory techniques and has stimulated new ideas in the study of verbal and pictorial memory. We believe that the application of implicit testing procedures to odor memory could have a similar effect in that domain. Until now, however, the literature on odor memory has been completely innocent of implicit measures. The mission of this chapter is to bring implicit measures to the field and help lay the foundation for future work on implicit odor memory. In particular, we do not pretend that the experiments reported here settle, for once and for all, the issue of whether implicit tests show odor memory. As far as we know, these experiments are the totality of the experimental literature on the subject, and we hope others will pursue the matter.

We report here four repetition priming experiments with odors as stimuli. The first of these investigated the effect of prior odor experience on subsequent odor *identification* performance. The second and third experiments examined priming as measured by odor *detection* thresholds and odor *identification* thresholds, respectively. An odor detection threshold represents the minimum concentration of a particular odor a subject can reliably distinguish from a no-odor control. An odor identification threshold, on the other hand, is the minimum concentration of an odor at which the subject can identify the odor by name. In general, for the same odor and same subject, the odor detection threshold will be lower than the odor identification threshold. The fourth experiment, finally, used suprathreshold odors and a *latency* measure of facilitation.

EXPERIMENT 1

In our first attempt to show priming for odors, we compared the effects of presenting (a) an odor along with its name, to presenting (b) the odor name only, on subsequent suprathreshold odor identification. As discussed in chapters 1 and 3, the extent to which odors are encoded semantically is unknown, largely because people probably cannot easily smell a familiar substance and not think of its name or a close associate. Therefore, in our estimation, a name-only control is essential when investigating *perceptual* processing of odors.

We presented 12 subjects (10 male and 2 female Yale undergraduates who had volunteered in return for course credit) with 20 jars in Session 1. Half of these contained an odor and half contained no odor. Subjects were told in advance that some of the jars would contain "very faint" odors (actually no odor at all). As each jar was presented, subjects were told the name of the odor they were actually, or supposedly, smelling and rated each for pleasantness and familiarity. If subjects could not smell the odor (i.e., the name-only condition), they based their rating on the odor's name.

In Session 2, 5 minutes later, subjects were presented with 30 odors in similar jars and asked to identify each odor by name. All 30 were well above threshold, so the limit was on identification and not perception. Ten of the odors had been presented earlier (odor + name condition), whereas 10 others had been presented in name only (name-only condition). The remaining 10 odors had not been presented in any form during Session 1 (control condition). The order of odor presentation in Session 2 was randomized across subjects. Each odor occurred an equal number of times in each of the three conditions across subjects. We provided at least 20 sec between successive odor presentations to reduce adaptation effects.

The odors belonged to objects commonly found in the average household (e.g., bleach, onion, peanut butter) and are listed in Appendix A. Performance measures on the identification task were accuracy and latency to identify the odors. Latencies were measured by the experimenter with a stopwatch and so were only a rough measure of identification latency. Figure 5.1 shows the proportion of correct identification as a function of the three priming conditions. We used a strict criterion in determining correct identification: For the odor of Juicy Fruit gum, for example, only the label "Juicy Fruit gum" was acceptable, and "gum" was scored as an incorrect response. But qualitatively identical results obtained with a more liberal scoring criterion (e.g., "gum" for "Juicy Fruit gum").

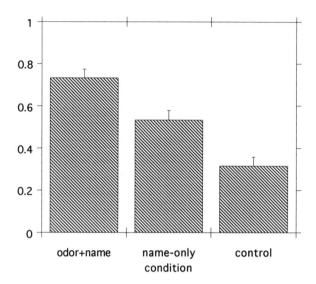

FIG. 5.1. Mean proportion correct odor identification (+1 SE) in Experiment 1 as a function of priming condition.

As Fig 5.1 suggests, odor identification was enhanced relative to the control condition when just the target odor's label had been presented in Session 1, without the actual odor. Beyond this name priming, however, presentation of the odor itself, in addition to its name, in Session 1 led to the best odor identification performance in Session 2, suggesting a priming effect for the olfactory cues in odors. An analysis of variance confirmed these descriptions, revealing a significant condition effect, $F(2,22) = 15.68$, p $= .0001$, with Newman–Keuls comparisons demonstrating that each of the three conditions was significantly different from the other two. The reaction time results (Fig. 5.2) parallel the accuracy results and show that subjects were slowest in identifying new odors and fastest in identifying odors in the odor + name condition, with identification in the name-only condition falling in between, $F(2,22) = 22.09$, $p = .0001$. Newman–Keuls tests show that all three conditions differed significantly from one another.

Clearly, presentation of an odor with its corresponding name enhanced subsequent identification beyond that engendered by presentation of the odor's name. The odor thus served to prime identification performance beyond the effects of the odor's name alone. This result indicates either that (a) the activation of an odor's perceptual representation, in conjunction with the activation of its verbal label, enhances subsequent odor identification by temporarily strengthening the associ-

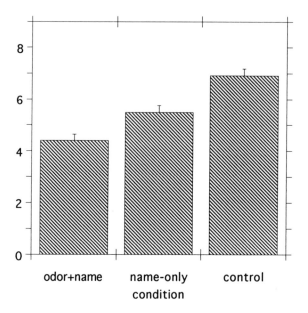

FIG. 5.2.   Mean response time (+1 SE) to identify odors in Experiment 1 as a function of priming condition.

ation between the odor's perceptual representation and its verbal code or (b) the presentation of an odor with its corresponding verbal label strengthens the accessibility of that verbal label until the subsequent odor identification task more than does presentation of the label only.

Which of these two effects is responsible for the greater identification facilitation following odor + name experience than name-only experience might be addressed by an experiment: In such an experiment, name processing would be *elaborated* in the name-only condition, for example by asking subjects to describe the typical uses for the object. The finding that memory for the odor's name is superior in the name-only condition, but that odor identification is superior for the odor + name condition, would support the hypothesis that a previous odor experience temporarily strengthens the association between that odor and its name.

Interestingly, despite the observed benefit of presenting the odor and its corresponding name during Session 1, as compared with the other conditions, odor identification in Session 2 for the odor + name condition was still far from perfect at 73%. Compared with stimuli from other modalities, say pictures of common objects, and a mere 5-min retention interval, an error rate of 27% would seem excessive. This error rate, which is comparable to that found on odor recognition tasks (see Schab & Crowder, chapter 2, this volume), may reflect a generally weak association between odors and their verbal labels in the lexicon (Engen, 1987; Schab, 1991) and/or poor odor discrimination (Cain, 1979; Schab & Cain, 1991). Further work on the relationship between odors and their names clearly is important for understanding the representation of odors in memory.

The main result of Experiment 1 is of course, the successful demonstration of implicit memory for odors through a test of priming. Our evidence for an olfactory basis of this priming is our having equalized the factor of naming through providing labels in both the odor + name and name-only conditions. Although both of these two conditions show better identification performance on the Session 2 test than the control condition, the former is reliably better than the latter. To our knowledge, this is the first published extension of the priming result to odors, although perhaps priming has been unmeasured and unnoticed in previous experiments with protocols arranged for other purposes.

EXPERIMENT 2

Our second experiment examines the effects of previous exposure of (a) odor names only and (b) odor names with their corresponding odors on the subsequent *detection* of odors at low concentrations. We commented earlier on how the results of Experiment 1 could be interpreted as depending either on the association between an odor and its label or on elaborative processing somehow engendered by the contiguity of a label and its proper odor. These complexities do not attach to the task of deciding simply whether an odor is present, at very weak intensity, or not at all. However, there, too, an earlier exposure to an odorant might be expected to facilitate performance through priming.

In Session 1, 18 subjects (9 male and 9 female Yale undergraduates, under than 30 years of age) were presented with a series of six, 60-ml squeezable plastic bottles with small holes at the top. Each bottle contained an odorous solution or de-ionized water. Subjects were given an odor name with each bottle, and three of the six bottles contained an undiluted odor corresponding to the name (odor + name condition). The three remaining bottles contained only water (name-only condition). Subjects were instructed to sniff while squeezing the bottles and rate the odor for familiarity and pleasantness on 7-point scales. They were warned that some odors might be "quite weak" and to base their ratings on the odor's name if they could not smell the odor.

In Session 2, 5 min later, subjects were given a detection-threshold test on nine odors (three presented earlier along with their names, three presented earlier in name only, and three new control odors). Ten concentrations of each odor were prepared in one third steps, and threshold testing followed the ascending staircase method. On each trial, subjects were given two bottles, one containing an odor and the other containing water only. Several water bottles were used to deny subjects any nonolfactory cues to the blanks. Threshold was defined as the odor concentration at which the subject correctly identified which bottle contained the odor on four consecutive trials. Each odor was assigned to the three conditions (odor+name, name only, control) equally often and the order of threshold testing was randomized across subjects. Appendix B lists the odors used in this experiment.

The main results of Experiment 2 are shown in Fig. 5.3. In contrast to Experiment 1 where previous exposure to a name, both with and without the corresponding odor, improved subsequent odor identification, exposure to an odor+name combination or name only did not affect subsequent threshold sensitivity to that odor: Threshold concentrations were not statistically different across the three conditions, $F(2,32) < 1.0$. In addition, although an ANOVA failed to find a statistically significant effect for gender, $F(1,16) = 2.14$, $p = .16$, women were consistently more sensitive (i.e., had lower odor thresholds) than men, $\chi^2 = 4.52$, p < .05. Our sample size may have been too small for a meaningful comparison across sex, but we also note that sex differences in absolute odor sensitivity—differences favoring women—are

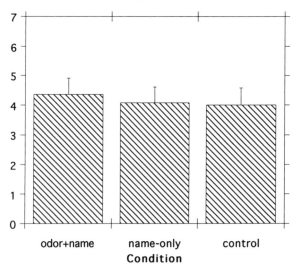

FIG. 5.3. Mean threshold concentration (+1 SE) for each priming condition in Experiment 2.

apparently found as often as not, so our unreliable effect here is perhaps variation rather than error.

Our failure to find facilitation in threshold detection with odors and odor names as primes in Experiment 2 may possibly have been due to an insensitive procedure. However, we calculated the power of our procedure to detect a threshold difference of two dilution steps. With our total of 18 subjects, the power of the present procedure is a respectable .83. We thus rejected with some degree of confidence the possibility that our failure to find odor priming in Experiment 2 was due to an insensitive procedure. Of course, another interpretation would be simply that priming does not occur with odors. Because we had evidence from Experiment 1 to the contrary, we turned our attention to a different explanation.

Experiment 2 required subjects to detect the presence of an odor under conditions in which there was never any doubt about the identity of the target odor. It is possible, however, that repetition priming for odors occurs, as Experiment 1 suggested, but only when the *quality* of the odor is at stake. A comparable effect in color vision would be to find that priming by an earlier exposure of blue would prime a decision as to what color a faint test patch was, but would not prime the intensity at which blue was reliably discriminated from grey.[1] Hence, the inability of Experiment 2 to detect odor priming may have occurred because we required subjects to *detect*, rather than *identify*, the odors. In Experiment 3, therefore, subjects tried to identify the odors.

EXPERIMENT 3

The three parts of Experiment 3 were originally considered three separate experiments, but are reported here as a single investigation for ease of exposition. The basic procedure was similar to that of Experiment 2, with the notable exception that identification thresholds were tested rather than detection thresholds. In Session 1, odors and blanks (water with no odors) were presented along with a label, and subjects were told that some of the odors would be extremely faint (name-only condition) whereas others would be quite strong (odor + name condition). In Session 2, conducted approximately 5 min later, identification thresholds were measured for odors corresponding to odor + name, name-only, and control (new odors) conditions. Odors served in the

---

[1]We certainly do not claim that this is the case for color vision; the example merely illustrates the pattern of results from the first two experiments here.

three priming conditions an equal number of times, and priming condition was a within-subjects variable.

Part 1

In Part 1, identification thresholds were measured for nine odors, three of which were assigned to each of the priming conditions. The odors were the same as those employed in Experiment 2 (Appendix B), and 10 dilutions (one third steps) were prepared for each odor. Fifteen subjects (all younger than 30 years) were recruited from the Yale summer community and participated in return for pay. As in Experiment 2, stimuli were presented in 60-ml plastic bottles, which subjects squeezed to deliver the headspace of each bottle to their noses. In Session 1 subjects were given six bottles, allegedly with an odor in each, although only three bottles actually contained an odor (odor + name condition); the remaining three contained only water (name-only condition). Subjects were exposed to these six stimuli in random order. While presenting a bottle, the experimenter informed the subject of the name of the stimulus. After sniffing a stimulus, the subject rated it for pleasantness and familiarity on 7-point scales.

All nine odors were then presented at each concentration level in random order. Before presenting a bottle, the experimenter gave the subjects a number between 1 and 20 which the subjects used to find a card in a rolodex situated immediately in front of them. On each card in the rolodex were printed four odor labels, one of which was the correct label for the upcoming odor. The subjects then received the stimulus and indicated which of the four labels they thought was the correct one. Approximately 20 sec separated successive stimulus presentation to minimize adaptation effects. The experimenter recorded for each of the 90 stimulus presentations (9 odors at 10 concentrations each) whether the subject correctly identified the odor.

The mean correct identifications per experimental condition for Part 1 are shown in the left panel of Fig. 5.4. Clearly there is no evidence for odor priming. This interpretation is supported by an analysis of variance which failed to find any significant effect for priming condition, $F(2,28) < 1$.

Contrary to our expectation, Part 1 of Experiment 3 failed to show odor priming when identification was required rather than detection, as had been the case in Experiment 2. This failure to find odor priming is not easily ascribed to an insensitive experiment because the mean number of odors correctly identified was a predictable and sensitive function of odor concentration (regression function of the latter on the former was $.47x + 1.86$, with $r^2 = .95$).

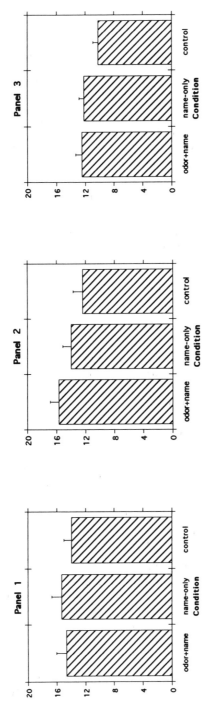

FIG. 5.4. Mean number of correct odor identifications (+1 SE) in Experiment 3 as a function of priming condition. Maximum number of correct identifications possible per condition in Part 1 is 30 (3 odors/condition x 10 concentration levels/odor). Maximum number of correct identifications possible per condition in Parts 2 and 3 is 20.

Part 1 (of Experiment 3) and Experiment 2 agree in discouraging the existence of repetition priming (implicit memory) for odor experiences. But tantalized by the positive outcome of Experiment 1 and attracted by the proposition that repetition priming might be a basic property of the nervous system and all its modular parts, we did not let it go at that. One rationalization for why no priming was obtained for odors in Part 1 is that the procedures used in the two sessions, rating pleasantness and familiarity in Session 1 versus identifying weak odors in Session 2, differ so much as to obscure priming effects. Although presumably the same neural units would underlie perception of the very same odor stimulus in weak and stronger versions, other aspects of these two activities, in Sessions 1 and 2, might engage quite different mental representations. The apparent dependency of priming effects on the similarity between learning and testing procedures (e.g., Roediger & Blaxton, 1987b) motivates this concern. Part 2 directly addresses this methodological explanation of the obtained null result.

Part 2

Part 2 essentially is identical to Part 1 with two exceptions. First, the number of odors was reduced from nine to six to facilitate subject testing (almond, Brut, and vanilla were dropped). Two odors were assigned to each of the three standard priming conditions, and these odor pairings were rotated through conditions across subjects using the same experimental design as in Part 1. Second, rather than having subjects rate suprathreshold concentrations in Session 1, subjects were given an identification threshold test in both experimental sessions. The increasing method of limits was used to prime four stimuli, two for which the odor was actually present and increasing in strength across trials, and two for which only water was present. For the two name-only stimuli, subjects were told at the end of the series of water bottles what the odor supposedly was, and it was remarked that the odor was "incredibly faint." In other words, subjects received the names to four odors in Session 1, two which they smelled and identified and two which they did not smell. Twelve new subjects (6 men and 6 women) from the same source were recruited for Part 2.

The procedure employed on testing paralleled the one used in Part 1, and the mean number of correct identifications in Session 2 are shown in Fig. 5.4, Panel 2, as a function of priming condition. The means suggest that identification accuracy was greater in the odor+name condition than in the name-only and control conditions. An ANOVA on the identification scores shows a marginally significant effect for condition, $F(2,11) = 3.19$, $p = .06$, and planned comparisons show a marginally significant difference between the odor+name and control conditions, $F(1,33) = 3.62$, $p = .066$. However, no other comparison approaches significance. And although the pattern of thresholds across conditions is what we predicted originally (greatest facilitation for the odor+name than the name-only condition), the data fail to show a statistically reliable difference between the odor+name and the name-only condition, making it impossible to distinguish between odor and name priming as the source of the marginal facilitation observed. Presentation of the odor, in addition to the odor's name, did not further enhance subsequent identification thresholds as compared with the name-only condition. Mean number of odors correctly identified by subjects again was, as in Part 1, a sensitive function of odor concentration (.24x + 2.91, $r^2 = .88$).

Part 3

The pattern of results obtained in Part 2, however, was encouraging to us (compare Fig. 5.1 with the center panel of Fig. 5.4), so we decided to conduct an exact replication of Part 2 in another attempt to show odor priming. Twenty-one Yale undergraduates (10 men, 11 women), volunteering in return for course credit, participated in Part 3. Mean identification thresholds for the three priming conditions are shown in Fig. 5.4, Panel 3. As in Part 2, it appeared that earlier presentation of the odor names was associated with lower identification thresholds than for controls, but that the additional experience with the odors along with the names did not further facilitate identification over the previous exposure to the odor names. Subsequent analyses shows a significant main effect for condition, $F(2,20) = 3.37$, $p = .04$. Planned comparisons indicate that the odor+name and control conditions differed significantly from one another, $F(1,60) = 4.57$, $p = .037$, and that the name-only and control conditions were marginally significantly different from one another, $F(1,60) = 3.50$, $p = .067$. However, the comparison of most interest, between the odor+name and name-only conditions, was far from significant, $F(1,60) < 1.0$. Mean number of odors correctly identified, again, was a sensitive function of odor concentration (.31x + 1.80, $r^2 = .95$).

Thus, Part 3 finds evidence for name priming, but no evidence of authentic odor priming. The occurrence of name priming is consistent across our experiments here and agrees with numerous studies demonstrating repetition priming with words. Except for our first experiment, we have been unsuccessful in demonstrating priming based on olfactory experience with the kinds of experiences and the kinds of tests used in these experiments.

EXPERIMENT 4

Having seemingly exhausted the threshold method, we returned to a suprathreshold latency measure in our final effort to find support for odor priming. The data from Experiment 1 (Fig. 2) encourage such an expectation.

In Experiment 4, each of 36 common odors (Appendix C) was assigned to one of three experimental conditions: odor + name, imagery + name, and control. Our interest in imagery (see Crowder & Schab, chapter 6, this volume) led us to include the second condition; for now, it may be considered comparable to the name-only conditions tested elsewhere in the research covered in this chapter. Each odor was rotated through these conditions such that it occurred an equal number of times in each condition across subjects. Eighteen subjects (11 women, 7 men), recruited from introductory psychology courses at Yale, participated in the experiment in return for course credit.

In Session 1, subjects rated the intensity of 24 stimuli: 12 odors presented with their names (odor + name) and 12 odor names presented with the instructions to image the smell of the odor and rate intensity based on the image (imagery + name). The presentation order of these 24 stimuli was random. Twelve additional stimuli, the controls, were not presented in any form during Session 1.

In Session 2, 5 min later, subjects rated the pleasantness of all 36 odors, also in random order. These 36 odors were presented by the experimenter in plastic bottles to the left hands of subjects at intervals of 15 sec between odors. A Mac Plus computer controlled stimulus randomization and all timing functions (accurate to within 1/60th of a sec). Subjects kept their right hands on the key pad of the computer and pressed *enter* as they sniffed each odor. The time between this key press and the entry of a digit between 1 and 9 for the rating, served as the measure of latency. In Session 3, subjects rated all odorants for intensity. Because of time constraints, the order of stimuli was the same as in Session 2, and odors were presented at the rate of 1 every 7 seconds.

We reasoned that odor priming would be observed as shorter latencies in Session 2 for the odor + name stimuli than the control stimuli. In addition, if the odor imagery instructions, given for the 12 stimuli in the imagery + name condition in Session 1, afforded some access to the perceptual representation of the odors, then the imagery + name condition should also show shorter rating latencies than the control condition (see Crowder & Schab, chapter 6, this volume).

Mean latencies for all three conditions are shown in Fig. 5.5. Apparently, latency did not differ across the three conditions. The only

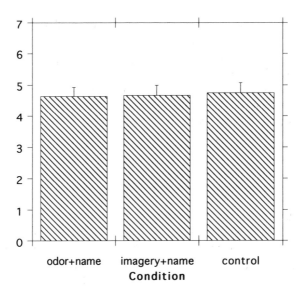

FIG. 5.5. Mean latency to make pleasantness ratings (± 1 SEM) in Experiment 4 as a function of condition.

significant effect on latency was a main effect for sex, which shows that women made their ratings faster than men, $F(1,16) = 7.35$, $p = .02$. Analyses on odors rather than subjects also failed to find any effects for condition.

With mean rating as the dependent variable, rather than latency to make those ratings, condition was the only significant factor, $F(2,32) = 4.27$, $p = .02$, and a Newman–Keuls test shows that both odor + name and control odors were rated as more pleasant than imagery + name odors. Why this result obtained is unclear, and it does not help explain the absence of an effect for condition on latency. Pleasantness ratings correlated modestly and positively with latency in all three conditions (all rs about .20).

Intensity ratings, given in Session 1 to odor + name and imagery + name stimuli, failed to correlate with latency of pleasantness ratings for identical odors in Session 2. However, intensity ratings given in Session 3 correlated modestly and negatively with latency (all rs about −.25).

Finally, an analysis on latency in Session 3 (intensity ratings), shows the same pattern of results found for Session 2: A significant main effect for sex, $F(1,16) = 8.69$, $p = .01$, and no other effects. The only comparison that shows a marginal effect for condition was the latency difference between intensity ratings given in Sessions 1 and 3 for conditions odor + name and imagery + name. The interaction between condition and session was marginally significant, $F(1,17) = 4.22$, $p = .06$, and shows that the latency difference (Session 1 minus Session 3) was greater for odor + name stimuli than for imagery + name stimuli. This marginal effect is suspect, however, because it ignores part of the data (control odors). Also, Session 3 was conducted immediately after Session 2, with the same order of odors as Session 2, and with a faster presentation rate. The power of Experiment 4 to detect an effect size of 1 sec was calculated as .83.

CONCLUSION

As a quest for demonstrating priming in odor memory, our empirical efforts paint a surprisingly bleak picture. After multiple experiments we must conclude, in balance, that implicit memory for odor experiences is not yet on a solid factual basis. Our first experiment did indeed show that presentation of a suprathreshold odor can enhance subsequent ability to identify that odor above and beyond previous presentation of the odor's name. This was the only experiment to find strong priming effects for odors.

Experiments 2 and 3 examined, respectively, the effects of previous exposure to an odor and/or to its name on odor detection and odor identification thresholds. Odor detection thresholds were unaffected by priming condition. Odor identification thresholds seemed sensitive to previous exposure to an odor's *name* (name priming) but were not differentially affected by the additional presentation of the corresponding odor. Of course, such priming effects on odor identification following an earlier presentation of the odor's name are neither unexpected no. particularly interesting with regard to our present purpose. Much discussion could be generated over whether this name priming is conceptually mediated or based on perceptual aspects of the odor name itself (Hirshman, Snodgrass, Mindes, & Feeman, 1990; Tulving, Hayman, & Macdonald, 1991). However, either alternative is clearly not a case of priming specific to the processing of olfactory stimuli, and so we leave this issue with no further comment. Experiment 4, finally, sought to measure priming by comparing the latency to rate odors presented earlier with that for novel odors. No such temporal advantage was found, in contradiction to Experiment 1, with the exception of one marginal and slightly dubious analysis (difference scores between two sessions).

We might be criticized for never having included a *pure* odor priming condition among our experiments. In the present research, whenever an odor was presented in Session 1, it was presented in company with its name. The presentation of an odor-name combination, to a proponent of this objection, may have predisposed subjects to focus on the name of the odor rather than the odor quality itself, when an odor was presented, thereby reducing the likelihood of odor-specific facilitation. This position predicts no priming effects on tasks where the odor name is irrelevant, such as detecting faint odors (Experiment 2) and rating odors (Experiment 4), and only name priming on tasks where the name is critical, such as suprathreshold identification and identification threshold determination. We have three responses to this criticism: First, in Experiment 1, subjects received the same priming procedures as in Experiment 2 and Part 1 of Experiment 3, and significantly greater facilitation was observed in the odor + name than the name-only condition. Second, no name priming was found in Part 1 of Experiment 3. And moreover, in Parts 2 and 3 of that experiment, identification accuracy in the odor + name and name-only conditions was far from the theoretical performance ceiling and showed as much variability as the control condition. Remembering four or six names clearly is not beyond the ability of our adult subjects, and the strategy of choosing the familiar name on identification testing, we predict, would have produced more than the marginal name priming effects found here. And third, we assume that subjects, when confronted with an odor in the context of an experiment, usually will attempt to identify it verbally, particularly when they know (or suspect) that they will be required to process the odor again later (see Crowder & Schab, chapter 1, this volume). By this reckoning, when presented with an odor-only prime, some subjects on some trials will attempt and succeed at verbal identification, thereby eliminating the distinction between odor and name priming made by the experimenter. In our experiments we chose to control this factor by always providing the odor's name, believing that careful control over variables is preferable to ambiguous results. Thus, the absence of a pure-odor priming exposure should not be held up as an objection to our experimental results.

Although each of the present experiments in isolation might be criticized on one point or another, taken together they make a convincing case: Under experimental conditions where priming generally is found for visual or lexical stimuli, little or none is found for odors. Obviously, the experiments reported here are not exhaustive, and null results should not and can not be taken as evidence for the nonexistence of odor priming under all circumstances. Converging evidence from other laboratories is not only desirable but essential at this point. Many useful studies of odor memory with implicit measures remain to be conducted. Of particular value now are additional experiments on repetition priming; comparisons of priming for olfactory, visual, and lexical stimuli in the same experiment; and investigations on semantic priming. We hope that the present results and discussion serve as a kind of catalyst for more intensive research on odor memory in general and odor priming in particular.

As stated earlier, it would be preposterous to conclude that implicit memory simply does not occur for odors and that this absence should be accepted as fact. On the other hand, the most optimistic conclusion to the contrary would be that implicit memory for odors has been elusive and inconsistent among our experiments. This inconsistency presents us with the dilemma of explaining priming effects for some experimental situations and not others. But given that our experiments in this chapter constitute the entire literature, we consider the research in this chapter more as showing how the issue can be studied than as answering the guiding questions raised here.

APPENDIX A: STIMULI USED IN EXPERIMENT 1

almond extract	nutmeg
apple sauce	onion powder
bleach	oregano
Brut cologne	peanut butter
cheese	pencil shavings
cinnamon	pickle
coffee	rubbing alcohol
crayon	rubber bands
garlic powder	sherry
school glue	Ivory soap
grape drink	soy sauce
Juicy Fruit Gum	spearmint
licorice	vanilla extract
lighter fluid	Vicks vap-o-rub
maple syrup	vinegar

APPENDIX B: STIMULI USED IN EXPERIMENTS 2 AND 3

Stimulus	Base Concentration
almond extract	.046%
Brut cologne	.046%
lemon extract	.056%
orange extract	.090%
peppermint extract	.046%

rum extract	.046%
strawberry extract	.046%
vanilla extract	.271%
vinegar	.369%

APPENDIX C: STIMULI USED IN EXPERIMENT 4

apple	licorice
banana	maple syrup
beer	mothball
black pepper	onion
bleach	orange
blueberry	oregano
butterscotch	peanut butter
cheese	pencil shavings
cigar	peppermint
cinnamon	popcorn
crayon	potato chips
curry powder	rubber
gasoline	rubbing alcohol
grape juice	strawberry
honey	tuna
ketchup	vanilla
leather	vinegar
lemon	whisky

REFERENCES

Cain, W. S. (1979). To know with the nose: Keys to odor identification. *Science, 203,* 467–470.

Cohen, N. J., & Squire, L. R. (1980). Preserved learning and retention of pattern-analyzing skill in amnesia: Dissociation of "knowing how" and "knowing that." *Science, 210,* 207–209.

Ebbinghaus, H. E. (1964). *Memory: A Contribution to Experimental Psychology.* New York: Dover. (Original work published 1885; translated 1913)

Engen, T. (1987). Remembering odors and their names. *American Scientist, 75,* 497–503.

Graf, P., Mandler, G., & Haden, P. (1982). Simulating amnesic symptoms in normal subjects. *Science, 218,* 1243–1244.

Graf, P., & Mandler, G. (1984). Activation makes words more accessible, but not necessarily more retrievable. *Journal of Verbal Learning and Verbal Behavior, 23,* 553–568.

Graf, P., & Schacter, D. L. (1985). Implicit and explicit memory for new associations in normal and amnesic subjects. *Journal of Experimental Psychology: Learning, Memory, and Cognition, 11,* 501–518.

Graf, P., Shimamura, A. P., & Squire, L. R. (1985). Priming across modalities and priming across category levels: Extending the domain of preserved function in amnesia. *Journal of Experimental Psychology: Learning, Memory, and Cognition, 11,* 385–395.

Hashtroudi, E. S., Parker, L. E., DeLisi, R. J., Wyatt, S. A., & Mutter, J. (1984). Intact retention in acute alcohol amnesia. *Journal of Experimental Psychology: Learning, Memory, and Cognition, 10,* 156–163.

Hirshman, E., Snodgrass, J. G., Mindes, J., & Feeman, K. (1990). Conceptual priming in fragment completion. *Journal of Experimental Psychology: Learning, Memory and Cognition, 16,* 634–647.

Hirst, W. (1989). On consciousness, recall, recognition, and the architecture of memory. In S. Lewandowsky, J. C. Dunn, & K. Kirsner (Eds.), *Implicit memory* (pp. 33–46). Hillsdale, NJ: Lawrence Erlbaum Associates.

Jacoby, L. L., & Dallas, M. (1981). On the relationship between autobiographical memory and perceptual learning. *Journal of Experimental Psychology: General, 110,* 306–340.

Jacoby, L. L., & Witherspoon, D. (1982). Remembering without awareness. *Canadian Journal of Psychology, 36,* 300–324.

Koelega, H. S., & Köster, E. P. (1974). Some experiments on sex differences in odor perception. *Annals of the New York Academy of Sciences, 237,* 234–246.

Lawless, H. T. (1978). Recognition of common odors, pictures, and simple shapes. *Perception and Psychophysics, 24,* 493–495.

Light, L. L., Singh, A., & Capps, J. L. (1986). Dissociation of memory and awareness in young and older adults. *Journal of Clinical Experimental Neuropsychology, 8,* 62–74.

Mandler, G. S. (1980). Recognizing: The judgment of previous occurrence. *Psychological Review, 87,* 252–271.

Parkin, A. J., & Streete, S. (1988). Implicit and explicit memory in young children and adults. *British Journal of Psychology, 79,* 361–369.

Richardson-Klavehn, A., & Bjork, R. A. (1988). Measures of memory. *Annual Review of Psychology, 39,* 475–543.

Roediger, H. L., III. (1990). Implicit memory: Retention without remembering. *American Psychologist, 45,* 1043–1056.

Roediger, H. L., III, & Blaxton, T. A. (1987a). Effects of varying modality, surface features, and retention interval on priming in word-fragment completion. *Memory & Cognition, 15,* 379–388.

Roediger, H. L., III, & Blaxton, T. A. (1987b). Retrieval modes produce dissociations in memory for surface information. In D. Gorfein & R. R. Hoffman (Eds.), *Memory and cognitive processes: The Ebbinghaus centennial conference* (pp. 349–377). Hillsdale, NJ: Lawrence Erlbaum Associates.

Roediger, H. L., III, Srinivas, K., & Weldon, M. S. (1989). Dissociations between implicit measures of retention. In S. Lewandowsky, J. C. Dunn, & Kirsner, K. (Eds.), *Implicit memory* (pp. 67–84). Hillsdale, NJ: Lawrence Erlbaum Associates.

Schab, F. R. (1991). Odor memory: Taking stock. *Psychological Bulletin, 109,* 242–251.

Schab, F. R., & Cain W. S. (1991). Memory for Odors. In D. G. Laing, R. L. Doty, & W. Breipohl (Eds.), *The human sense of smell* (pp. 217–240). New York: Springer.

Schacter, D. L. (1987). Implicit memory: History and current status. *Journal of Experimental Psychology: Learning, Memory, and Cognition, 13,* 501–518.

Schacter, D. L., & Graf, P. (1986). Effects of elaborative processing on implicit and explicit memory for new associations. *Journal of Experimental Psychology: Learning, Memory, and Cognition, 12,* 432–444.

Sherry, D. F., & Schacter, D. L. (1987). The evolution of multiple memory systems. *Psychological Review, 94,* 439–454.

Snodgrass, J. G., & Feenan, K. (1990). Priming effects in picture fragmentation completion: Support for the perceptual closure hypothesis. *Journal of Experimental Psychology: General, 119,* 276–296.

Squire, L. R. (1987). *Memory and brain*. New York: Oxford University Press.

Tulving, E., & Schacter, D. L. (1990). Priming and human memory systems. *Science, 247,* 301–306.

Tulving, E., Hayman, C. A. G., & Macdonald, C. A. (1991). Long-lasting perceptual priming and semantic learning in amnesia: A case study. *Journal of Experimental Psychology: Learning, Memory and Cognition, 17,* 595–617.

Venstrom, D., & Amoore, J. E. (1968). Olfactory threshold in relation to age, sex, or smoking. *Journal of Food Science, 33,* 264–265.

Warrington, E. K., & Weiskrantz, L. (1974). The effect of prior learning on subsequent retention in amnesic patients. *Neuropsychologia, 12,* 419–428.

Weldon, M. S. (1991). Mechanisms underlying priming on perceptual tests. *Journal of Experimental Psychology: Learning, Memory, and Cognition, 17,* 526–541.

= 6 =

Imagery for Odors

Robert G. Crowder
Yale University

Frank R. Schab
Opinion Research Corporation

Mental imagery is in principle memory, but memory characterized by coding that is faithful to the original experience, providing some of the same structural information present in perception (e.g., Bower, 1970) rather than more abstract representations. In Hebb's (1968) interpretation of this idea, which we can trace at least to Hume (1969), imagery represents some of the very same cell assemblies that are consequences of perception, but aroused from the top down, conceptually, rather than from the bottom up, sensorily. In his own classic example, the *phantom-limb phenomenon* results from activity in the same neural units that previously received input from the limb in question, but, of course, subsequent to amputation of that limb. Thus, an amputee may suffer itching *in* a leg that is no longer there!

Such experiences as well as both behavioral (Finke & Shepard, 1986) and neuropsychological (Farah, 1988; Kosslyn, 1987) evidence notwithstanding, the claim that imagery engages some of the same neural mechanisms or representations that underlie perception has not gone unchallenged (see Pylyshyn, 1973, 1984). Criticisms and alternative interpretations of mental imagery invoke the use of tacit knowledge of the way objects behave in the real world to simulate the use of percept-like representations with more abstract representations (Pylyshyn, 1981). Critics also cite demonstrations that visual experience is not necessary for visual imagery because, for example, congenitally blind persons exhibit essentially normal performance on some visual imagery tasks (Kerr, 1983), and methodological weaknesses exist in experimental paradigms used to study imagery (Intons-Peterson, 1983). The theory that ultimately proves correct will be capable of accounting for the large and diverse body of results, including large individual differences both within and across different types of imagery tasks (Finke & Kosslyn, 1980; Kosslyn, 1988; Kosslyn, Brunn, Cave, & Wallach, 1984) and data from sensory modalities other than vision. In audition, for example, we seem to have a case where spectral aspects of timbre are represented in a way that affords imagery processing, but not dynamic aspects of timbre (Pitt & Crowder, 1992).

Our objective here is to evaluate existing evidence and also to present some new evidence regarding the ability to image odors. Our question, simply put, is this: "Can percept-like memory representations of odors be activated in the absence of appropriate stimulation of the olfactory receptors?"

Those of us who have ever ordered a meal in a restaurant are confident that imagery plays a role in our choices. And those of us who realize that flavor experience includes a predominant role for smell, know that this imagery must be largely olfactory, along with possible visual, gustatory, idiosyncratic, and fiscal contributions. Other experiences, perhaps more specifically olfactory, apparently have led some to take for granted the existence of olfactory imagery (e.g., Howard, 1983). But experience is not evidence. It is where the need for psychological analysis steps in; it poses the question of whether and how olfactory imagery may be brought into the laboratory, uncontaminated by those external contributions which are so inevitable in everyday experience. That is the mandate of this chapter. Although many of us are confident about our ability to image odors (Brower, 1947; Lindauer, 1969), our introspections on this may ultimately prove fallacious, just as average people's confidence in their ability to identify objects by smell alone has been shown to be unrealistically high (see de Wijk, Schab, & Cain, chapter 3, this volume).

One reason for the scarcity of experimental data on odor imagery is the difficulty of designing sensitive and appropriate laboratory techniques for studying the phenomenon. Looking to the literature on visual imagery turns out to be of little help, because some of the standard paradigms for studying visual imagery make little or no sense when translated to the olfactory domain. For example, the *processing* of an olfactory image, in the tradition of Shepard and Metzler's (1971) demonstration of mental rotation, seems at this point to be an elusive goal, as does an olfactory adaptation of the *scanning* of images in the manner of Kosslyn (1980) and his associates. Size scaling (Bundesen & Larson, 1975; Sekular & Nash, 1972) appears to offer no approach, either. Olfactory responses are notoriously sluggish, so we do not naturally think of reaction-time methods like that of Posner, Boies, Eichelman and Taylor (1969) from the start, although slow processing does not in principle disqualify response timing as an index. In fact, several experiments reported elsewhere in this volume (Schab & Crowder, chapter 5, this volume) as well as outside of this forum (Schab, de Wijk, & Cain, 1991) show that orderly response-time data can be obtained in experiments involving olfactory stimuli.

Of the remaining demonstrations of visual imagery, one subclass depends on observing the consequences of instructing subjects to generate visual images of concepts *in their heads* and observing subsequent recall success. On occasion (e.g., Bugelski, Kidd, & Segman, 1968) imagery instructions have been validated from striking levels of performance achieved thereby. Knowing what little we do about expected memory for odors themselves, however, this strategy resembles groping in the dark. Other experiments have capitalized on the phenomenon of selective interference to validate imagery (Bower, 1972; Brooks, 1968). These studies, in vision, examine the amount of interference between an imagery-based task and the actual processing of new visual input. We report an olfactory analog of such an experiment in this chapter.

Lyman and McDaniel (1990, Experiment 2) have offered an experimental design with promise for bringing olfactory imagery under laboratory control, using techniques closely related to work on visual-pictorial imagery. The names of common, household odorants were presented for learning, under either of two instructions, to separate groups: One group was asked to form a visual image of the object associated with that odor (e.g., lemon). An independent group was asked to form an olfactory image (" . . .to see how well people can imagine the scent of the referent of these names," p. 660). Half the people in each group were tested by recognition of pictures of the named objects and half were tested by a standard odor-recognition procedure. Thus, the design was a 2 × 2 within-subjects crossing of encoding instructions (imagine what the named object looks like vs. imagine what the object smells like) and recognition code (pictures vs. odors).

Analysis of resulting d' scores shows (a) people recognized pictures better than odors, overall, and (b) no reliable main effect of encoding instructions. The interesting result is an interaction showing that (c) encoding with visual imagery was superior in picture recognition and (d) encoding with odor imagery was superior in odor recognition. The most straightforward interpretation of this crossover interaction is in terms of transfer-appropriate processing at encoding (Morris, Bransford, & Franks, 1977): When the recognition test will be with pictures, pictorial-imagery processing leads to best performance, and when testing will be by odors, processing of olfactory imagery leads to best performance. As Lyman and McDaniel (1990) appreciate, this interpretation assumes that images share processing characteristics of the genuine stimuli within a modality, which Hebb (1968) also assumed.

But we cannot relax, confident that the case for olfactory imagery has been made once and for all by the Lyman and McDaniel (1990) study, because other interpretations are possible. A wealth of converging evidence suggests that instructions for pictorial imagery and testing by pictures do engage a common processing mode that entails the visual system. It is flirting with circularity, however, to say the same of odor imagery. Clearly, any code that is shared between odor-imagery instructions and recognition testing with odors could be the vehicle for good recognition. To take a ludicrous example, if people in the odor-imagery encoding condition pondered the financial expense, of each substance named, and if they thought also about the expense when tested by odors but not when tested by pictures, the obtained interaction still would have occurred. The same is true of a more serious alternative: thinking about semantic properties of the substance named. A true skeptic of odor imagery could argue with relative ease that when instructed to image an object's odor—and when later presented with the odor for testing—people will think about the object's properties and other associations (because odor imagery is supposedly impossible). The act of thinking about the same properties on learning and testing accordingly enhances recognition memory for the odor, rather than the act of generating some percept-like image at the time of learning.[1]

The same ambiguity attaches to other studies on odor imagery as well, for example when similar multidimensional scaling solutions are found for actual and *imagined* odors (Carrasco & Ridout, 1992; Lyman, 1989), and when actual and *imagined* odors, interpolated between the learning and testing of target odors, yield similar patterns of interference. In general, without controlling for semantic factors, qualitatively similar results for odors perceived and *imagined* are not necessarily evidence for the existence of odor imagery. The similarity may be mediated by semantic factors.

One research program specifically aimed at the study of olfactory imagery comes from the psychophysical tradition (Algom, 1992; Algom & Cain, 1991). In these experiments, the target dimension is not the

---

[1]As we argue in chapter 1, semantic mediation is a confounding variable in the entire published literature on odor recognition memory.

quality of odor experiences (identity of the substances), but rather their intensities as revealed by numerical magnitude judgments. In perceptual control conditions (Algom & Cain, 1991, Experiment 1), subjects estimated magnitudes of five different intensities of suprathreshold amyl acetate (banana quality). The resulting psychophysical scales were then compared with those obtained in a memory condition, in which an initial session was used to teach other subjects symbolic codes (i.e., colors) corresponding to each of the five same intensities. Later, in a different session, these colors were presented alone, and subjects in the second group were asked to perform magnitude estimation of the corresponding odor intensities from memory. Similar psychophysical functions were obtained in the perceptual and memorial conditions, even to the point that the mean exponents describing these functions were not reliably different. This preliminary result is not inconsistent with the view that the remembered odors in the memory condition were faithful images of earlier sensory experiences.

However, the results do not demand that particular interpretation. For example, subjects in the memory group could have made surreptitious numerical magnitude estimates during their training session (although not told to do so) and then remembered these numerical estimates later, in the scaling session. Magnitude judgments for odor mixtures give a pattern of data that is less ambiguous. In these experiments (Algom & Cain, 1991, Experiments 2, 3, and 4), leaf alcohol was mixed with amyl acetate to produce nine mixtures (either none, weak concentrations, or strong concentrations of the two odorants). In the perceptual condition, subjects rated the intensities of these nine combinations. The resulting estimates showed a pattern of *compression* in which the intensity of Odorant A made little difference in magnitude estimates of the mixture, provided Odorant B was at a high concentration, and vice versa. (See Algom, 1992, for other multidimensional cases in which compression is not the rule.) It was as if the strong concentrations of one odorant masked what would otherwise have been noticeable variations in intensity of the other odorant.

In the memory conditions, subjects learned symbols for the different unmixed concentrations of Odorants A and B in solo, but never directly experienced any odor mixtures. The target estimates were gathered in a later session where subjects were instructed to rate the intensities of combinations of odors associated with two simultaneously presented symbols they previously learned. For example, a combination of two color chips might represent a weak version of Odorant A combined with a strong version of B.

The telling result was that these memory conditions produced virtually identical compressed functions to those obtained for the perceptual conditions. Even though subjects would have no reason to guess that masking is the rule in odor mixture, their magnitude estimates for odor mixtures that they had never smelled showed this masking. Algom (1992) discusses how this seems to represent some sort of *implicit knowledge* of olfactory principles. For our interest in imagery, the similarity of the perceptual and memory conditions suggests support for the Hebbian (1949) principle that perception and memory (imagery) share neural machinery to some degree (see Farah, 1988).

In our own research we have used three experimental designs. The first was based on the technique of selective interference, wherein the strategy is to determine what codes are involved in a memory task by means of finding what type of processing or coding interferes with what type of information (Bower, 1972; Brooks, 1968). We gave 47 students (mean age was 24.9 years) from local Detroit) colleges a series of 15 odorants to learn in preparation for a later recognition test. The substances were common household products from the battery used by Rabin and Cain (1984) and were presented in porcelain jars for inspection. On testing, 10 min afterward, the subjects were given a randomized order of these odors from the learning set, mixed in with the same number of new distractors, and made simple old-new judgments for each.

The main variable was the type of interfering event experienced during the 10-min retention interval. Subjects were assigned to one of the four conditions listed in Table 6.1.

The critical condition was, of course, the odor imagery condition. As compared to the control condition, interference from the odor imagery condition resembling that of the odor condition indicates that people do indeed form olfactory images resembling the real thing. The visual

TABLE 6.1
Experimental Conditions of Experiment 1

Condition	Subjects	Retention Interval Activity
Control	8 women 4 men	Subjects did nothing and were exc used for the duration of the interval
Odor	7 women 4 men	Subjects learned a second set of 15 odors, presumably for a later test
Odor imagery	8 women 4 men	Subjects were read the names of a second set of 15 odors and formed olfactory images to the names
Visual imagery	7 women 5 men	Subjects were read the names of a second set of 15 odors and formed visual images to the names

imagery condition guards against the possibility that mental imagery of any kind would be as detrimental to memory as interference from odors themselves.

The main results are shown in Table 6.2. Performance measures included the proportion of hits, the proportion of false alarms, and recognition sensitivity (d'). A main effect for condition was found only on the proportion of hits, $F(3,39) = 3.92$, $p = .015$. Newman–Keuls tests show that the proportion of hits was significantly lower for the odor imagery condition than the control and odor conditions. This effect was completely unexpected. We hypothesized that performance in the odor imagery condition would fall between performance in the control and odor conditions. In fact, the obtained pattern of results for hits is more consistent with the hypothesis that odor imagery is not possible. The attempt to do the impossible during the retention interval may have placed the heaviest demand of all on subjects, leaving correspondingly fewer resources for the rehearsal of target odors. Neither false alarms nor recognition sensitivity (d') were reliably affected by the activity interpolated during the 10-min pause between presentation and testing, $F(3,39) < 1$. Our best bet, therefore, must remain that, for unselected subjects, recognition memory for odors was independent of what went on during the retention interval.

Rather than consign these data to a drawer, we included gender as a factor because we suspected that male and female subjects might show different patterns. They did, and to an extent statistically that cannot be overlooked. For d' scores the interaction between condition and sex was highly reliable, $F(3,39) = 6.51$, $p < .001$. Newman–Keuls comparisons for the males showed no differences among conditions, but for the females the two conditions with interpolated odors (odors and odor

TABLE 6.2
Summary of odor imagery Experiment 1

| Variable | Condition | | | |
	Control	Odor	Odor Imagery	Visual Imagery
P(Hits)				
Men	.87	.90	.82	.73
Women	.92	.88	.73	.89
P(FAs)				
Men	.30	.24	.15	.37
Women	.23	.35	.25	.15
d'				
Men	1.81	2.19	2.14	1.03
Women	2.42	1.82	1.34	2.59

imagery) were worse than the control and visual imagery conditions, which were not reliably different from one another. By itself, the odor condition was not reliably different from the control condition, however. The results for females are strong in dissociating the effects of visual and olfactory interference, and this dissociation goes in the direction of a similar effect for odors themselves and imagery for odors. But we have no ready interpretation for why odor imagery should have proven numerically more interfering than smelling the same 15 odors, which did not reliably interfere with memory. One possibility is that the interfering effect of smelled odors would in the long run prove to be reliably present and more disruptive than odor imagery. By this first interpretation, the odor imagery condition simply mimics the odor condition, and imagery for odors is accordingly inferred. This assumes that subjects use some kind of olfactory code for recognizing the target odors in all four conditions.

But any code that is shared among these three activities (encoding the original odors in all conditions, smelling the interpolated odors, and forming olfactory images of the interpolated odors) could have produced the females' pattern of results. This alternative code might be semantic in some sense. We know enough not to expect visual imagery to engage semantic processing (Paivio, 1971), and the formation of images might well lead to more effective semantic processing during the interpolated task than passively smelling these odors.

Both interpretations have the serious disadvantage that they leave the sex interaction unexplained. The first is further embarrassed by the lack of a reliable interference effect in the odor condition. The second is compromised by requiring the assumption of some unknown coding format that is engaged by either smelling or imaging the odors of the tested substances, but not by imaging their visual aspects. We hope to see replications and convergence from other laboratories on this finding. At least, all of us should be vigilant for sex interactions in future experiments on odor memory.

In our next endeavor to study odor imagery, we examined whether *odor imagery instructions* could enhance subsequent performance on an odor identification task, as compared with visual imagery instructions. We recruited 18 women (mean age was 23 years) from local Detroit colleges. The experiment was described as involving word ratings with no mention made of odors. Subjects were tested singly or in groups of two and first listened to a list of 50 object names presented by a tape player at a rate of 6 words per min. Subjects were instructed to imagine what each word's referent looked like (visual imagery condition) or smelled like (odor imagery condition) as each word was read. The subjects also rated the vividness of their images on a 7-point scale.

Following this task, they performed a set of simple physics problems for 5 min as a distractor, and were then presented with 20 odors corresponding to 20 of the 50 object names presented earlier (these odors never corresponded to the first five or last five words on the tape). Subjects attempted to identify the odors by name and wrote the names on paper. The odors consisted of common household objects taken from the same source as those used in the previous experiment. Odors were presented in small porcelain jars and were covered with gauze to deny subjects any visual cues to the odors' identity. Following the odor identification task, subjects were given a recognition test on the original 50 object names and 50 new object names.

The results show higher vividness ratings in the visual group (5.89, $SD = .70$) than in the odor imagery group (4.94, $SD = .66$), $F(1,16) = 8.52$, $p < .01$, but no difference between the two imagery conditions on the subsequent odor identification performance: The mean number of odors correctly identified was 7.25 ($SD = 3.73$) for the olfactory imagery group and 8.80 ($SD = 2.35$) for the visual imagery group. This difference, which points in the opposite direction than we had predicted, was not statistically significant, $t(16) < 1$. Interestingly, however, recognition memory *for the names* reliably was better in the odor imagery group ($d' = 4.1$) than in the visual imagery group ($d' = 3.46$), $t(16) = 2.22$, $p < .05$, despite the fact that performance in both conditions was almost at ceiling. This effect was due largely to a lower false alarm rate in the odor imagery than in the visual imagery group. Together, the failure of the odor imagery instructions to enhance odor identification above visual imagery instructions, and the observed advantage of those given odor imagery instructions on the recognition memory test, while not demonstrative of, are at least consistent with, the notion that when motivated to form an olfactory image, people engage some nonolfactory, possibly semantic, form of processing.

In our final experimental effort to bring odor imagery into the laboratory, we departed from the classic Perky phenomenon first studied within Tichener's laboratory. Segal and Fusella (1970) resurrected this method and applied the tools of modern perceptual analysis (largely signal detection theory) to it. The experimental question is this, translated into the olfactory modality: Are people's threshold sensitivity (d') to some target odor, say lemon, changed if they are maintaining a mental image of the odor of lemon at the same time, as opposed to detecting this same target without the accompanying imagery? In the visual modality (Segal & Fusella, 1970) this confusion between reality and a mental imagery seems to occur (and also has been found in the auditory mode by Farah & Smith, 1983), but we cannot anticipate the answer for olfaction. Our first experiment included only these two basic conditions: odor imagery and no imagery. Other controls would become important if an effect occurred, including one condition where olfactory imagery would be maintained of the wrong target (chocolate imagined while lemon was being detected) and another in which a visual image had to be maintained during olfactory detection. But in the absence of a difference between the no-imagery and (appropriate) imagery conditions, such additional controls are much less interesting.

Subjects were first given instructions in forming mental images of the target odorants, such as chocolate, lemon, orange, vinegar or other household substances (we used Durkee extracts from the grocery store for the actual substances). The detection protocol was the two-bottle, ascending method of limits protocol, in which all subjects start with dilutions too weak to detect and are asked which of two plain, opaque bottles provided for them to sniff has the substance. The other bottle, in all comparisons, has odorless water. The strength of the odorant in the correct bottle is then increased until subjects are first able to choose correctly for five tests in a row (chance probability is 1/32). This criterion defined the threshold, and then the next substance was tested. (Two subjects never reached a run of five successes prior to the strongest dilution, both with vinegar, and it was arbitrarily assumed that they would have chosen correctly if we could have tested them with still stronger concentrations than the base.) Three odors were tested with simultaneous imagery and three with no imagery instruction. In a counterbalanced arrangement, the same odors served for some subjects in the imagery condition and for other subjects in the control condition.

In principle, we could have opted to define either an identification threshold or a detection threshold in this manner. The former asks when the subject first perceives the substance as, say, lemon. The second asks, on the contrary, when the subject first identifies which bottle has *something* other than water in it, whether or not the subject can say what that something is. We adopted the latter, less complicated, detection threshold.

For every subject, six thresholds were tested—strawberry, orange, lemon, rum, peppermint, and vinegar. Nineteen dilution strengths for each of these were prepared before the experiment. Starting with a base solution that was easily discriminable to several people around the laboratory, the dilutions were systematically weakened by adding 6 cc of distilled water to the *parent* solution. (i.e., solution 6 was derived by taking 6 cc of solution 5 and adding an additional 6 cc of water, likewise 14 from 13, etc.) In informal pretests, nobody could detect solution 19 for any of the six odors.) Each numbered dilution was stored in an unmarked, clear plastic bottle that could be squeezed by the subjects to deliver the odor to their nostrils. Six identical plastic bottles were filled with distilled water only, and these were exchanged during testing so that subjects would not learn that the warmer bottle always contained the water.

For each odor the first two-bottle comparison was between the most dilute solution for that odorant versus plain water. The subjects were allowed to sniff freely between the two and choose the bottle that contained what they thought was not water, guessing if necessary. After making a response, the subject was handed the next pair, including a different bottle of water and the next-higher concentration of the target odor. This continued until the subject correctly identified the target bottle on five consecutive comparisons at the same concentration level, at which point the threshold for that subject, for that odor, was recorded.

For 15 of the 30 subjects, half the odors just listed were assigned randomly to the imagery condition and the other half to the no-imagery condition, with the restriction that the three fruit odors (lemon, orange, strawberry) could never serve in the same condition. The remaining 15 subjects were yoked to each of these with exactly the complementary assignment of the six odors to conditions. In a similar way, the order in which the six odors were tested was random with the restriction that the three odors representing one of the two conditions, for that subject, could never be tested consecutively.

At the beginning of the session, the experimenter explained what was meant by imagery for odors, in lay terms. All subjects readily assented that they personally could generate such mental images at will. The two-bottle ascending method-of-limits technique was then explained. Testing of imagery and no-imagery odors was in all respects identical except that, before testing of the former three substances, subjects were asked to form and maintain a mental image of that particular odor during the sniffing of test bottles. They were allowed unlimited time to form such an image, and the testing did not proceed until the subject indicated that a satisfactory image had been achieved. For odors in the no-imagery condition, the two-choice tests began immediately, with no prior announcement of what the target odor was going to be for the ascending series.

In this experiment the higher numbered bottles denote the weaker solutions, and so our threshold numbers are actually measures of acuity. Criterion considerations do not enter the picture, given our forced-choice method. Across all subjects and conditions the sensitivities for the six odors ranged from 12.9 (vinegar) to 15.9 (strawberry), indicating that we were successful in producing graded series of dilutions in the optimal range.

The presence of imagery had no effect on odor detection. Mean acuity was 13.91 (SD = 2.7) in the imagery condition and 14.24 (SD = 1.9) in the no-imagery condition. This negligible difference actually favored the wrong condition. Fifteen of the 30 subjects had greater sensitivity with imagery than without imagery, 14 showed the opposite effect, and 1 was tied. We describe this as a single experiment, as it is, but any even number of subjects can be tested with this counterbalancing scheme. We began with approximately a dozen subjects then essentially replicated the study, when no differences were evident in the first part, in order to add weight to what looked like it was turning out to be a null result. These two replications of an identical experimental design obviously produced identical results.

We also thought at one point that a control experiment would be necessary, in the case of negative results. In the control experiment the design would be exactly the same in all ways as in the experiment just reported, except the odor-imagery condition would be replaced by a condition with a faint but detectable background odor, matching the target odor for that series. But on reflection, that control experiment seemed too predictable to be useful: By simple application of Weber's Law, detection of a target against a somewhat salient background of that same target stimulus must necessarily be more difficult than against a background of plain air. The sensitivity of the measurement procedure we used is sufficiently well established (Cain & Gent, 1991) that it should not be called into question either. Unfortunately, this experiment was conducted in parallel with our first experiment described earlier, so we had no idea that gender was a controlling factor in the other study. Therefore, we have no record of whom, among our 30 subjects, were males and females. Still, this cannot compromise our negative result, for if one sex showed an imagery effect and the other not, then the difference would be in the expected direction, but perhaps of marginal reliability. To produce our finding of no difference, one gender would have had to show a facilitating effect of imagery and the other an inhibitory effect, with respect to sensitivity. Instead, the distribution of difference scores, across subjects, was reasonably normal (and centered at about zero).

So this detection experiment led us to a tentative conclusion quite different from the one we originally expected, that people cannot really generate and maintain a true olfactory image, their intuitions to the contrary notwithstanding. A stable memory representation of some kind must exist within the olfactory system—otherwise we could not identify the flavor of banana reliably—but this representation seems not to be open to top-down control, at least based on the findings of this experiment. Instead, our intuitions regarding odor imagery may well be based on the activation of semantic associations rather than percept-like representations.

For the question of olfactory imagery as a whole, reviewed in this chapter, the very least we can say is that the case has not yet been made with an authoritative demonstration. In the experiments reported here, as well as in an experiment in which an odor, but not the image of that same odor, cued recall of words unrelated to the odor (Schab, 1990, Experiment 2), no evidence whatever of imagery emerged. In some of the studies we reviewed here, the olfactory-imagery interpretation was always open to plausible alternatives. As an experimental question this debate is quite young, and so we would be foolish to make a categorical claim that people cannot imagine the olfactory quality of smells. However, the burden of evidence falls increasingly now on those who claim this activity is possible.

We might repeat that this negative conclusion is against the background of our own prior conviction that imagery for odors was indeed plausible. So, to whatever extend experimenter bias was a factor (which we doubt), it operated against the conclusions we reached.

REFERENCES

Algom, D. (1992). Memory psychophysics: An examination of its cognitive and perceptual prospects. In D. Algom (Ed.), *Psychophysical approaches to cognition*. Amsterdam: North Holland.

Algom, D., & Cain, W. S. (1991). Remembered odors and mental mixtures: Tapping reservoirs of olfactory knowledge. *Journal of Experimental Psychology: Human Perception and Performance, 17,* 1104–1119.

Bower, G. H. (1970). Analysis of a mnemonic device. *American Scientist, 58,* 496–510.

Bower, G. H. (1972). Mental imagery and associative learning. In L. W. Gregg (Ed.), *Cognition in learning and memory* (pp. 51–88). New York: Wiley.

Brooks, L. R. (1968). Spatial and verbal components of the act of recall. *Canadian Journal of Psychology, 22,* 349–368.

Brower, D. (1947). The experimental study of imagery: II. The relative predominance of various imagery modalities. *Journal of General Psychology, 37,* 199–200.

Bugelski, B. R., Kidd, E., & Segman, J. (1968). Image as a mediator in one-trial paired-associate learning. *Journal of Experimental Psychology, 76,* 69–73.

Bundesen, C., & Larson, A. (1975). Visual transformation of size. *Journal of Experimental Psychology: Human Perception and Performance, 1,* 214–220.

Cain, W. S., & Gent, J. F. (1991). Olfactory sensitivity: Reliability, generality, and association with aging. *Journal of Experimental Psychology: Human Perception and Performance, 17,* 382–391.

Carrasco, M., & Ridout, J. B. (1992, June). *Olfactory perception and olfactory memory: A multidimensional analysis.* Paper presented at the fourth annual conference of the American Psychological Society, San Diego, CA.

Farah, M. J. (1988). Is visual imagery really visual? Overlooked evidence from neuropsychology. *Psychological Review, 95,* 307–317.

Farah, M. J., & Smith, A. F. (1983). Perceptual interference and facilitation with auditory imagery. *Perception and Psychophysics, 33,* 475–478.

Finke, R. A., & Kosslyn, S. M. (1980). Mental imagery acuity in the peripheral visual field. *Journal of Experimental Psychology: Human Perception and Performance, 6,* 126–139.

Finke, R. A., & Shepard, R. N. (1986). Visual functions of visual imagery. In K. R. Boff, L. Kaufman, & J. P. Thomas (Eds.), *Handbook of perception and human performance* (pp. 37–55). New York: Wiley.

Hebb, D. O. (1949). *Organization of behavior.* New York: Wiley.

Hebb, D. O. (1968). Concerning imagery. *Psychological Review, 75,* 466–477.

Howard, D. V. (1983). *Cognitive psychology.* New York: MacMillan.

Hume, D. (1969). *A treatise in human nature.* Baltimore: Pelican.

Intons-Peterson, M. J. (1983). Imagery paradigms: How vulnerable are they to experimenter's expectations? *Journal of Experimental Psychology: Human Perception and Performance, 9,* 394–412.

Kerr, N. H. (1983). The role of vision in visual imagery experiments: Evidence from the congenitally blind. *Journal of Experimental Psychology: General, 112,* 265–277.

Kosslyn, S. M. (1980). *Image and mind.* Cambridge, MA: Harvard University Press.

Kosslyn, S. M. (1987). Seeing and imaging in the cerebral hemispheres: A computational approach. *Psychological Review, 94,* 148–175.

Kosslyn, S. M. (1988). Imagery in learning. In M. S. Gazzaniga (Ed.), *Perspectives in memory research* (pp. 245–273). Cambridge, MA: MIT Press.

Kosslyn, S. M., Brunn, J. L., Cave, K. R., & Wallach, R. W. (1984). Individual differences in imagery ability: A computational analysis. *Cognition, 18,* 195–244.

Lindauer, M. S. (1969). Imagery and sensory modality. *Perceptual and Motor Skills, 29,* 203–215.

Lyman, B. J. (1989, April). *Multidimensional scaling of perceived and imagined odors.* Paper presented at AChemS XI, Sarasota, FL.

Lyman, B. J., & McDaniel, M. A. (1990). Memory for odors and odor names: Modalities of elaboration and imagery. *Journal of Experimental Psychology: Learning, Memory, and Cognition, 16,* 656–664.

Morris, C. D., Bransford, J. D., & Franks, J. J. (1977). Levels of processing versus transfer appropriate processing. *Journal of Verbal Learning and Verbal Behavior, 16,* 519–533.

Paivio, A. (1971). *Imagery and verbal processes.* Hillsdale, NJ: Lawrence Erlbaum Associates.

Pitt, M. A., & Crowder, R. G. (1992). The role of spectral and dynamic cues in imagery for musical timbre. *Journal of Experimental Psychology: Human Perception and Performance, 18,* 728–738.

Posner, M. I., Boies, S. J., Eichelman, W. H., & Taylor, R. L. (1969). Retention of visual and name codes of single letters. *Journal of Experimental Psychology: Monographs, 79* (1, Pt. 2).

Pylyshyn, Z. W. (1973). What the mind's eye tells the mind's brain: A critique of mental imagery. *Psychological Bulletin, 80,* 1–24.

Pylyshyn, Z. W. (1981). The imagery debate: Analogue media versus tacit knowledge. *Psychological Review, 88,* 16–45.

Pylyshyn, Z. W. (1984). *Computation and cognition.* Cambridge, MA: MIT Press.

Rabin, M. D., & Cain, W. S. (1984). Odor recognition: Familiarity, identifiability, and encoding consistency. *Journal of Experimental Psychology: Learning, Memory, and Cognition, 10,* 316–325.

Schab, F. R. (1990). Odors and the remembrance of things past. *Journal of Experimental Psychology: Learning, Memory, and Cognition, 16,* 648–655.

Schab, F. R., de Wijk, R. A., & Cain, W. S. (1991, April). *Odor memory over the course of 100 seconds*. Paper presented at the 13th annual meeting of AChemS, Sarasota, FL.

Segal, S. J., & Fusella, V. (1970). Influence of imagined pictures and sounds on detection of visual and auditory signals. *Journal of Experimental Psychology, 83,* 458–464.

Sekular, R., & Nash, D. (1972). Speed of size scaling in human vision. *Psychonomic Science, 27,* 93–94.

Shepard, R. N., & Metzler, J. (1971). Mental rotation of three-dimensional objects. *Science, 171,* 701–703.

= 7 =

Age-Associated Differences in Memory for Odors

Claire Murphy
San Diego State University

The olfactory system shows age-related impairment at every level studied to date: thresholds increase, suprathreshold intensity decreases, and the ability to identify odors decreases (Chalke & Dewhurst, 1957; Doty, Shaman, Applebaum, et al., 1984, Fordyce, 1961; Joyner, 1963; Kimbrell & Furtchgott, 1963; Minz, 1968; Murphy, 1983; Murphy & Cain, 1986; Murphy, Nunez, Withee, & Jalowayski, 1985; Schiffman, Moss, & Erickson, 1976; Stevens, Bartoshuk, & Cain, 1984; Stevens & Cain, 1986, 1987; Stevens, Plantinga, & Cain, 1982; Strauss, 1970; Venstrom & Amoore, 1968; and see Murphy, 1986, 1989 for reviews). Whereas increases in threshold and decreases in suprathreshold intensity presumably reflect strictly sensory impairment, loss of the ability to identify odors has both sensory and cognitive aspects. A person with lower olfactory sensitivity will perceive an odor as weaker and may consequently find it harder to identify or to remember.

ODOR IDENTIFICATION

Schiffman's (1979) report that food identification was impaired in the elderly hinted at the importance of studying odor identification in the elderly. The young college students in her study were far better than the elderly at identifying blended foods placed in the mouth.

Murphy (1982, 1985) replicated this effect and then demonstrated that without olfaction the young fell to the same level of identification as the elderly, suggesting that olfactory or odor identification deficits underlie the effect. With practice and feedback both age groups could improve their performance, but the elderly never achieved the levels of identification reached by the young subjects. Murphy and Cain (1986) explored odor identification over the life span and reported progressive loss in the ability to identify a battery of 80 common odors. Present correct was a declining linear function of age (see Fig. 7.1).

Doty, Shaman, and Dann (1984) using the University of Pennsylvania Smell Identification Test (UPSIT), a scrath-and-sniff test of odor that employs microencapsulated odorants and a four-alternative, forced-choice, response mode, showed major deficits in odor identification in the elderly. The number of subjects in the upper age group was limited, but the results are startling. More than 50% of the elderly showed major impairment in the odor identification task. As with most studies of odor identification, males showed greater impairment than did females.

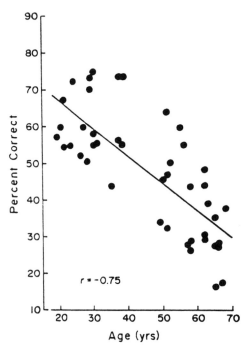

FIG.7.1.   Odor identification ability for a battery of 80 common odors, plotted as a function of the age of the subject.

The National Geographic Smell Survey, conducted on a selected sample (readers of the National Geographic Magazine who chose to return the survey), bore out the earlier general findings: Aging brings with it a significant drop in the ability to identify odors (Wysocki & Gilberg, 1989). In the National Geographic Survey, fewer people in their 60s, 70s, and 80s could detect the odor samples and, of those, fewer could identify them. Males had more difficulty than did females in both tasks.

ODOR RECOGNITION MEMORY

Within the realm of memory, larger effects of age have been argued for recall, which requires a person to conjure up information, than for recognition, which requires a person to identify information already presented from a larger set that includes distractor information (Botwinick & Storandt, 1974; Craik, 1977; Erber, 1974; Harwood & Naylor, 1969; Rabinowitz, Craik, & Ackerman, 1982; Schonfield & Robertson, 1966). The young outperform the elderly at recall of verbal information (e.g., paired associates, paragraphs, and shopping lists) as well as of visual information (e.g., memory for designs, visual-spatial stimuli, and name–face associations; Flicker, Ferris, Crook, Bartus, & Reisberg, 1986). Robust age-related impairment in recognition memory has been clearly demonstrated only at long retention intervals (Harwood & Naylor, 1969).

The degree to which the elderly and the young initiate encoding strategies and the types of strategies they employ may explain some of the difference in the degree of age-related impairment seen in recall and recognition memory studies. When required to remember verbal or visual stimuli, the young show more self-initiated and a greater variety of encoding strategies. The young also employ more elaborate strategies, whereas the elderly rely on the less complicated, less effortful, and less effective strategy of rehearsal (Craik & McDowd, 1987).

Theoretically, recall involves encoding, storage, and retrieval processes, whereas recognition primarily requires encoding and storage. Experiments using stimuli appealing to modalities other than olfaction suggest that aging impairs both encoding and retrieval, but hits hardest at retrieval (Craik, 1977). This fact may account for the larger differences in recall than in recognition (Craik & McDowd, 1987). It has been postulated that the elderly possess fewer resources to expend in the memory task and will show larger age-related decrements in more demanding tasks. Indeed, age differences in cognitive tasks increase with task complexity and with the inferred number of steps involved in performing the task (Salthouse & Lichty, 1985). Nevertheless, some age-related decrements in recognition memory do occur. The challenge involved in equating difficulty of recall and recognition tasks suggests that experiments showing a great degree of superiority of recognition over recall in the elderly should be viewed with caution. In difficult recognition memory tasks, the young outperform the elderly (Erber, 1974; Harwood & Naylor, 1969).

If odor recognition memory resembles memory for stimuli in modalities already studied in the elderly, we might expect little age-related impairment in odor recognition memory. Any deficit in recognition memory could occur only in initial encoding. That is, the elderly could remember fewer odors immediately after exposure, but could forget them at the same rate as the young. Retention interval appears to be an important factor in recognition memory in the elderly.

We conducted a series of four experiments to begin the exploration of recognition memory for odors in the elderly. Complete details of these experiments can be found in Murphy, Cain, Gilmore, and Skinner (1991).

In all of these experiments, young, university students and elderly persons involved in a university-based education and enrichment program served as subjects. All reported excellent health and no hospitalizations within the previous year. All had normal cognitive function; scores on the Raven Progressive Matrices (Raven, 1960) for the elderly subjects were above the 90th percentile for age. Odorants were 76 common household items, such as baby powder, strawberry syrup, leather, popcorn, and cigarette butts. Faces were 50 black-and-white oval bust pictures of U.S. presidents and vice presidents. Symbols were 50 engineering and electrical designs drawn from templates.

Recognition Memory With Short Delay

In this experiment on odor recognition memory in the normal elderly, we addressed what we considered to be fundamental questions. We explored whether the elderly show impaired odor recognition memory relative to the young, whether retention interval plays a role in differential memory performance, and whether odor sensitivity plays a role in differential memory performance.

We employed a standard recognition memory paradigm. Each subject participated in a four-part session on a single day. In Part 1 they were exposed to odors, faces, and symbols. Subjects were not required to name the odors, nor were they told that they would later be asked to remember them. In Part 2, immediately after the first, they performed a recognition memory task, indicating whether stimuli had been pre-

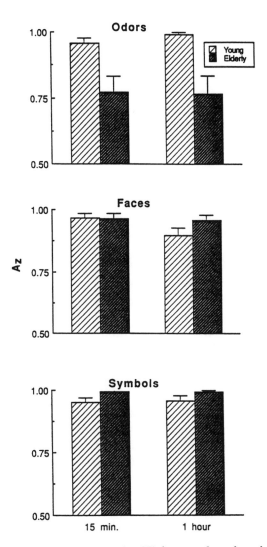

FIG.7.2. Recognition memory scores (+ SE) for everyday odors, faces of presidents and vice presidents, and engineering symbols 15 min and 1 hour after inspection in young and elderly subjects. Chance performance equals 0.5.

sented in the first part or not. In Part 3, an hour later, they performed the recognition memory task again. Threshold for butanol was determined in Part 4.

A_z, the index of memory performance, was calculated from hits, false alarms, correct rejections, and misses (Swets, 1986; Swets & Pickett, 1982). Both young and elderly subjects performed well on the faces and symbols (Fig. 7.2). The young also performed very well on odors, which suggests that the three types of stimuli had comparable inherent difficulty. The elderly, however, performed only midway between chance and perfect performance in odor recognition.

Odor threshold was significantly affected by age. The young subjects were 14 times more sensitive than the elderly. Threshold and age accounted for 44% of the variance in recognition memory performance. The individual contributions of age and threshold were 15% and 10%, respectively.

Thus, the first experiment establishes that there is no difference in recognition memory for graphic stimuli between elderly and young, the elderly have significantly poorer performance for recognition memory for odors, and poorer olfactory sensitivity in the elderly underlies some proportion of the decline in memory performance.

Recognition Memory With Long Delay

In the second experiment, we tested recognition memory at 6 months in order to determine whether the elderly might show differences in recognition memory for odors or graphic stimuli over intervals much longer than those used in the first experiment. We investigated the relationship between familiarity and recognition memory performance and explored the relationship of identification ability and recognition memory.

Ability to identify a stimulus undoubtedly reflects semantic processing. Familiarity ratings may also reflect semantic information. At the very least, familiarity constitutes recognition memory for the occurrence of the stimulus in a person's past. Familiarity undoubtedly reflects knowledge of the identity of a stimulus, thus familiarity and identity can be redundant measures. Familiarity can also reflect vaguer meanings, such as whether a stimulus brings to mind a place or circumstance.

In the first of four sessions, subjects were exposed to odors, faces, and symbols, rated their familiarity and were then given a recognition memory task. In the second session, 2 to 3 weeks later, subjects performed recognition memory testing and odor threshold testing. In the third session, 6 months later, subjects were again given the recognition memory test. Finally, in the fourth session, after all recognition memory testing was completed, the odors were presented for identification.

The elderly's recognition memory for faces and symbols exceeded their memory for odors. As retention interval increased to 6 months, the difference between the memory elderly's for odors and their memory for graphic stimuli also increased. After 2 weeks, the elderly's recognition memory for odors dropped to the chance level. For the young, odor memory resembled memory for faces and symbols (see Fig. 7.3).

Familiarity was related to memory performance for both odors and faces. In order to explore the association, we distributed the familiarity ratings for odors, faces, and symbols, separately, into quintiles (i.e., lowest fifth, next lowest fifth, etc.) for use as a stratifying variable in an ANOVA of number of hits on target stimuli. We used the quintiles to normalize for the lower average ratings that the elderly gave to odors. Hence, although an elderly person may have rated only a few items high enough to fall within the highest quintile, for example, that person's hit

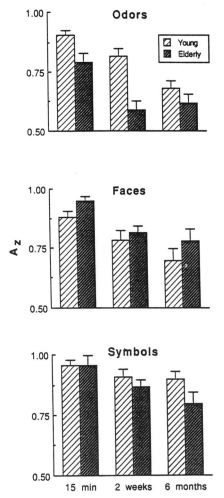

FIG. 7.3.   Memory performance (+ SE) for odors, faces, and symbols at intervals of 15 min, 2 weeks, and 6 months in young and elderly subjects.

rate on those items became the point of comparison for the hit rate on a larger number of items that were rated as having high familiarity by others. If the difference in memory between young and elderly stemmed entirely from differences in the distribution of their familiarity ratings, then there should be no significant effect of age on familiarity ratings. As shown in Fig. 7.4, familiarity did prove to be important to odor recognition memory. The lower average familiarity ratings of the elderly did, to a degree, predict their poorer performance in odor memory.

Memory performance was also correlated with identification, both for odors and faces. Regardless of age, a person who could identify many

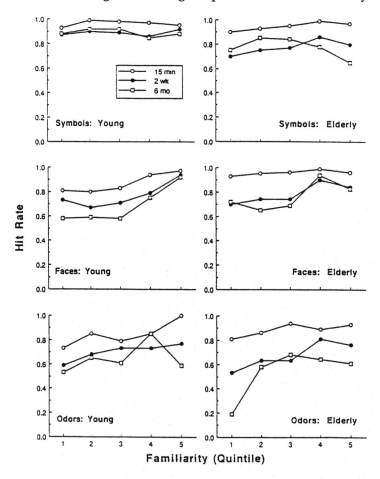

FIG. 7.4. Memory performance versus familiarity ratings for symbols, faces, and odors, respectively, distributed into quintiles for young and elderly subjects. Quintile 1 contains the lowest 20% of the familiarity ratings that the young and elderly gave to each type of stimulus; quintile 2 contains the next higher 20% of the ratings; and so on.

odors would tend to recognize many, and a person who could identify fewer odors would recognize fewer. The correlation between odor identification and odor memory performance suggests that subjects self-initiated semantic encoding.

Short-Term Recognition Memory

In a third experiment, we investigated the important question of whether the elderly are deficient in short-term odor recognition memory. We also explored further the effect of familiarity. In the second experiment, the elderly tended to remember odors that they found highly familiar just about as well as the young could. However, they showed a tendency toward poorer performance for unfamiliar odors. In this experiment, we used previous data on familiarity to select three groups of odors that clustered at different positions on the familiarity continuum. If the elderly have particular difficulty with unfamiliar odors, we would expect to see it in this set of stimuli.

The 30 odorants rated most familiar in Experiment 2 became members of a high-familiarity set, and the 30 rated least familiar became members of what we termed a medium-familiarity set. Twenty-five pure chemicals without well-known, real-world referents became members of a low-familiarity set. Visual stimuli were sets of 30 faces and 30 engineering symbols, as used before, and 30 ameboid forms presumed to be unfamiliar. Subjects were presented with only one stimulus at a time, and 26 seconds after presentation were presented with the same or another stimulus from the same modality and asked whether it was old or new. No interpolated task occurred between inspection and recognition.

The short-term, visual-recognition memory task proved easy for both young and elderly; however, the short-term odor-recognition memory task was more difficult for the elderly than for the young (Fig. 7.5). In addition, the elderly showed the poorest performance for odors of low familiarity.

Short-Term Recognition Memory With Verbal Distraction

The fourth experiment explored whether verbal processing plays a role in short-term memory by interpolating a task of backward counting during the interval when subjects would otherwise be free to engage in semantic encoding strategies.

The procedure was similar to that employed in the third experiment, except that during the 26-sec retention interval, half the young and half the elderly performed a distractor task, counting backward by threes

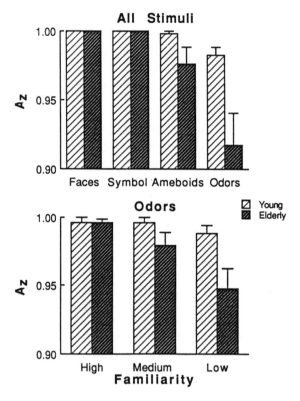

FIG. 7.5. Performance for odors separately at three levels of familiarity (upper panel). Short-term memory performance (+ SE) for visual stimuli and odors in young and elderly subjects (lower panel).

from a raⁱ domly chosen three-digit number, and half performed no distractor task. A session consisted of 20 trials, 10 for odors and 10 for ameboid drawings.

Recognition memory performance of the elderly fell significantly below that of the young for both odors and ameboids (Fig. 7.6). The interpolated task of backward counting impaired memory performance in both modalities and both age groups. Engen, Kuisma, and Eimas (1973) report that backward counting disrupted odor memory, although the small number of subjects left the reliability of the effect unclear. Walk and Johns (1984) interpreted their own work with young subjects to mean that an interpolated task will disrupt odor memory only if the task employs odor distractors. The present investigation clearly demonstrates that disruption of odor memory does not require an odor distractor. If the disruption of odor memory by distraction implies semantic encoding of odors in memory, then the implication exists for

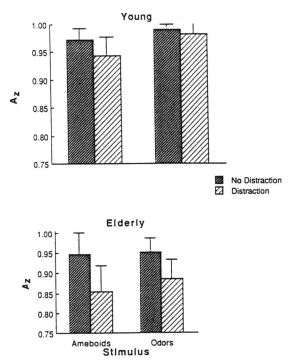

FIG. 7.6.   Short-term memory performance (+ SE) for odors and ameboid forms in young and elderly with and without distraction (counting backward).

the ameboids, too, since the effect occurred regardless of modality. However, although ameboids may seem difficult to label as a whole, subjects do tend to verbalize distinctive features of the ameboids.

The young subjects performed very well in the recognition memory task, consonant with other studies, forgot odors, faces, and symbols slowly over time (Bahrick, Bahrick, & Wittlinger, 1975; Engen, 1987; Gehring, Toglia, & Kimble, 1976). The elderly showed rapid forgetting only for the odors. As the retention interval increased, differences between the young and the elderly grew larger, with the elderly falling to chance performance at 2 weeks. Young subjects performed above chance even at 6 months.

Decreased olfactory sensitivity undoubtedly influenced the recognition memory performance of our elderly subjects. Threshold varied significantly with memory performance when memory was tested at 15 min and 1 hour. To the elderly the odor probably seemed less intense, which may account in part for why the elderly gave lower estimates of familiarity in the second experiment.

Because the ability to identify an odor with its veridical label is powerful evidence that the label is available for semantic encoding of odors, the results of these experiments strongly suggest a role for semantic factors in recognition memory for odors. The significant correlations between odor identification and memory indicated that subjects, particularly elderly subjects, who had available to them a greater number of correct verbal labels for odors scored higher on recognition memory for odors than subjects who had fewer verbal labels available to them.

The influence of familiarity on odor- and face-recognition memory reflects recognition that a stimulus has occurred in a person's past, but it may reflect much more, including identity. Conceivably, familiarity could also influence recognition memory via distinctiveness. In a series, high-frequency words will prove harder to recognize later than low-frequency words that stand out as different. In a series of odors or faces of presidents and vice presidents, where subjects can identify fewer than half the stimuli, knowing the identity of a stimulus may make it more memorable simply because it is different. It seems unlikely, however, that the major influence of odor familiarity would not be semantic.

The present experiments on elderly persons strongly support semantic processing of odor memories. Other studies of young persons also support semantic encoding. Walk and Johns (1984) argued for both perceptual and semantic encoding of odors. They found that presentation of a perceptually similar distracting odor in the interval between presentation and test disrupted odor memory more than did presentation of a name semantically unrelated to that of the target. Walk and Johns interpreted the result as evidence for perceptual encoding. However, their distractor task—generation of associations to the distracting stimulus—largely entailed semantic processing. These associations and their semantic content, rather than the odor itself, may have disrupted the odor memory. Since these associations were generated to a similar distracting odor, they would be expected to disrupt not only a perceptual code, but also a semantic code. Walk and Johns actually noted that their subjects used verbal mediation to help them remember the target odorants. Similarly, it is possible that the subjects in Lyman and McDaniel's (1986) study may have employed semantic processing to improve odor memory since the instructions for elaborative processing may have increased the quantity and quality of semantic processing.

None of these investigations represents a direct test of perceptual encoding of odors, so it is impossible at this point to assert the degree to which encoding of odors is perceptual and the degree to which it is semantic. The difficulty in preventing subjects from generating semantic codes for odors and their natural tendency to do so have, thus far, prevented an effective test of perceptual encoding of odors. Differences in the degree to which individual subjects are able to image visual stimuli have prompted research on high- and low-imagery subjects, where high and low imagery was defined in modalities other than olfaction. It is entirely possible that people differ in their ability to image odors. If this is true, then the degree to which perceptual and semantic encoding contribute to odor memory may logically be partly dependent on this ability.

ODOR RECALL

Studies of odor memory in elderly and young subject, previously described in detail, have suggested that odor recognition memory is significantly impaired relative to visual memory, in old age (Murphy, Cain, Gilmore, & Skinner, 1991). Differences in olfactory threshold sensitivity accounted for a proportion of the variance in odor memory. Additional variance was accounted for by differential semantic encoding. Odor recall has not been characterized in the elderly.

Short- and long-delay recall for odors are highly demanding cognitive tasks because they, besides encoding, storage, and retrieval, also require correct identification. In general, aging appears to have a greater impact on recall than on recognition (Botwinick & Storandt, 1974; Craik, 1977; Erber, 1974; Harwood & Naylor, 1969; Rabinowitz, Craik, & Ackerman, 1982; Schonfield & Robertson, 1966). We therefore hypothesized that normal aging would have adverse effects on odor-recall performance.

Preliminary results from work in progress in our laboratory suggest the presence of large age-related effects on short- and long-delay recall for odors (Acosta, Morgan, Nordin, & Murphy, 1994). Complete details regarding these experiments will be found in Nordin and Murphy (manuscript in preparation). Nordin and Murphy addressed the question of age-related loss in odor recall performance in a study comparing recall for odors and verbally presented words, the latter modality for comparison. This is being accomplished by giving young adults and healthy elderly adults (screened for dementia) the California Verbal Learning Test (CVLT; Delis, Kramer, Kaplan, & Ober, 1983) as well as an analogous test that applies odors. More specifically, the CVLT provides information on functions such as short- and long-delay recall, serial recall strategies, position recall strategies (primacy and recency effects), learning effects over trials, and recognition and response bias. Moreover, for the odor test, free identification is also assessed to determine what role identification versus memory plays in recall performance.

The odorants used are among the most identifiable (from a battery of 80 odors) for healthy elderly subjects and matched in familiarity with the words used in the CVLT, enabling a direct comparison between tests. Preliminary studies with 16 young and 16 elderly persons suggest poorer short- and long-delay recall ability, and long-delay recognition memory in elderly than in young for both odors and verbally presented words. Interestingly, the difference in short-delay recall ability, learning over trials, and recognition memory between groups appears to be larger for odors than for verbally presented words. The poor identification ability of the elderly appears to account for a large proportion of the poor recall performance. In these preliminary studies, the age-related effect size was largest for odor recall (eta square = 0.63), followed by odor identification (0.59) and odor-recognition memory (0.54). We plan to expand this study of odor memory in the normal elderly by testing for intrusions and perseverations with an interpolated task. Intrusion errors are characteristic of Alzheimer's patients' performance on the CVLT and perseverations tend to be higher in patients with Huntington's disease. Thus, the two measures contribute to the profiles of cortical and subcortical impairment. The findings from these studies may prove to be valuable for the development of a standardized odor memory test, which may be a useful tool in aging and in clinical populations.

ALZHEIMER'S DISEASE

Alzheimer's disease is a degenerative, dementing illness characterized by memory loss, decline in cognitive function, and significant neuropathology (Katzman, 1986). To date, the disease is only diagnosed on autopsy, since biopsy is difficult to justify in a disease with no cure. It has been suggested that Alzheimer's disease represents a type of accelerated aging process. Thus, studying patients with Probable Alzheimer's disease has the potential to shed light on the effects of age in general.

There are several recent reports that the entorhinal cortex, prepyriform cortex and anterior olfactory nucleus (all areas involved in processing of olfactory information) are particularly hard hit by the neuropathological changes characteristic of Alzheimer's disease: cell loss, neuritic plaques, neurofibrillary tangles, and granulovacuolar degeneration (Averback, 1983; Esiri & Wilcock, 1984; Reyes et al., 1985; Simpson & Yates, 1984). It has been clear for some time that the amygdala and hippocampus, areas of the brain involved in memory which are also important for olfactory information processing, are particular targets of neuropathology in Alzheimer's disease (Ball et al., 1985; Kemper, 1983).

The concentration of these neuropathological alterations in olfactory areas suggests that impairment in olfaction or in olfactory-mediated tasks might be expected in patient's with Alzheimer's disease. The fact that these areas project directly into the amygdala-hippocampal complex suggests that odor memory may be particularly vulnerable in Alzheimer's disease.

Available information suggests impairment in odor identification in patients with the clinical diagnosis of Probable Alzheimer's disease. Waldton (1974) described a marked functional impairment of odor identification in a group of 66 female senile dementia patients. It is not clear what percentage of this group would meet the National Institute of Neurological and Communicative Disorders and Stroke (NINCDS) and Alzheimer's Disease and Related Disorders Association (ADRDA) criteria for senile dementia of the Alzheimer's type. The patients exhibited progressive decline in the ability to identify six odorants, relative to elderly controls. Age-matched controls are important in these studies since deficits in the ability to identify odors have also been demonstrated in the normal elderly person, as described earlier.

Impaired olfactory identification in 11 subjects with Alzheimer's Type Dementia was also reported in Serby, Corwin, Novatt, Conrad, and Rotrosen (1985). Similarly, deficits in identification of a battery of five odors were reported in 8 of 18 Alzheimer's patients and 1 of 26 aged controls by Peabody and Tinklenberg (1984). Warner, Peabody, Flattery, and Tinklenberg (1986) then examined 17 Alzheimer's patients in the early stages of the disease (*DSM-III* diagnosis) and 17 age-matched controls and reported impaired performance on a standardized, multiple-choice test of odor identification (the UPSIT). Doty, Reyes, and Gregor (1987) reported both a decline in the ability to identify odors on the UPSIT and an increase in olfactory threshold in a group of Alzheimer's patients. Koss, Weiffenbach, Haxby, and Friedland (1988) replicated the identification deficit on the UPSIT, but found a *nonsignificant* threshold loss in the 10 mildly demented possible or probable Alzheimer's patients whom they studied. Impairment in odor identification, odor recognition, and olfactory thresholds in a group of 18 Alzheimer's patients was reported by Knupfer and Spiegel (1986).

This literature convincingly demonstrates a deficit in odor identification in Alzheimer's disease. Sensory function is necessary but not sufficient for this task. Odor identification is a task that requires considerable memory (Murphy, 1985; Murphy & Cain, 1986). To perform well, a subject must sniff an odorant, detect its odor, recall its name, and attempt to match the name with offered alternatives, recalling just what the alternatives smell like. Normal elderly people show increasing difficulty with this type of task.

Although deficits in identification and discrimination of odors are well established, odor memory in Alzheimer's disease has received only scant attention to date, in spite of the fact that dementia is central to the disease. Memory impairment is one of the hallmarks of Alzheimer's disease and occurs early in the disease process. Degree of dementia in Alzheimer's disease correlates with the number of plaques and neurofibrillary tangles in important central neural structures, particularly the hippocampus. Odor memory in the Alzheimer's patient is particularly intriguing because olfactory pathways are known to project to areas involved in memory function which are heavily hit by the neuropathological changes of Alzheimer's disease. The entorhinal cortex feeds directly into the hippocampal-amygdala complex, areas known to be involved in memory function and areas of the brain showing the highest concentration of plaques and tangles in Alzheimer's disease. Understanding odor memory in Alzheimer's disease seems particularly relevant for characterization of the functional impairment in the disease and may play a role in diagnosis.

In our initial study, we investigated episodic memory for odors and visual stimuli in a small group of patients who met the NINCDS ADRDA criteria and were thus diagnosed as having Possible or Probable Alzheimer's disease by two different neurologists from the Alzheimer's Disease Research Center at the University of California at San Diego Medical Center. Their scores on the Blessed Dementia Scale indicated mild to moderate dementia (Blessed, Tomlinson, & Roth, 1968). Olfactory thresholds were determined on all subjects using a two-alternative, forced-choice ascending series with butanol described earlier. Thresholds were significantly higher for patients than for age-matched controls, $p < .05$.

Recognition memory was explored for the same set of common odors, faces of presidents and vice presidents and electronic symbols described earlier (Murphy et al., 1991). Ten of each were first presented in mixed order for inspection and rating of familiarity. Subjects were not informed that they would subsequently be required to remember stimuli, and they were not given feedback about their performance on the task. After the familiarity session, patients were presented with 30 stimuli: 10 odors, 10 faces, and 10 symbols. Five of each were selected from those presented in the first session, along with an equal number of distracters, for recognition 10 min later.

The Alzheimer's patients' performance was compared to that of the elderly and young subjects tested in the same task (with twice as many trials) described earlier (Murphy et al., 1991). The average age of elderly patients and controls was 72 years. The Alzheimer's patients showed impairment in odor memory which significantly exceeded the impairments of the normal elderly controls. In fact, recognition memory for odors fell to chance performance in this group of patients (Murphy, Lasker, & Salmon, 1987).

Further study of Alzheimer's patients in this task considered the pattern of responses to explore the nature of the memory loss. Twenty patients with mild to moderate dementia were tested in the same paradigm. Patients were completely unable to distinguish between odor targets and distracters. They produced more false alarms to odors than did the controls. Both memory for odors and memory for symbols showed impairment, but odor memory fared worst (Seery & Murphy, 1989). These data suggested the possibility that patients with Alzheimer's disease may have a tendency toward intrusion errors in odor recognition memory. This hypothesis merits serious testing.

Moberg and his colleagues (1987) also reported that Alzheimer's patients show deficits in recognition memory for odor.

Further exploration of the fine structure of odor memory loss in the Alzheimer's patients has the potential to shed light on the disease process as well as to provide a better understanding of the neuropathological changes which underly the loss. Our ongoing work with olfactory threshold in Alzheimer's disease has shown a significant increase in threshold in Alzheimer's patients, that is correlated with the degree of dementia (Murphy, Gilmore, Seery, Salmon, & Lasker, 1990).

AGING AND AUTOBIOGRAPHICAL MEMORY

The study discussed in this section investigates the relationship between pleasantness of odor cues and the memories they elicit in elderly and young persons (Reed & Murphy, 1991). This study was part of a larger project investigating the effects of current mood and aging on qualitative dimensions of autobiographical memories (Reed, 1990).

Little research exists on the subject of autobiographical memory for odors. What does exist raises extremely interesting questions. Rubin, Groth, and Goldsmith (1984) compared autobiographical memory for odors and for words and pictures in college students. They found that the memories evoked by odors were more often ones not thought or spoken about before. In addition, in one experiment they tended to be more pleasant or to evoke more emotion, although in a second experiment this effect only approached significance. One more recent study (Schab, 1990) documents the ability of odors to stimulate memories, but argues that pleasantness of the odor cue had no effect.

A number of studies have demonstrated that a subject's mood at the time of memory encoding is one of the associated aspects of a particular memory. Based on Bower's (1981) associative network theory of mood and memory, many studies have provided evidence for the phenomena of mood congruent memory (i.e., memories are better retrieved when their affective valence matches the mood at the time of attempted retrieval), and mood state dependence (i.e., memories are better retrieved when mood at the time of attempted retrieval matches the mood at the time of encoding).

It has been reported that similarity of incidental or background stimuli facilitate memory retrieval (Riccio, Richardson, & Ebner, 1984). Odors present during memory encoding can be one of the many associated aspects of a particular memory. Anecdotal clinical information supports this hypothesis. For example, posttraumatic stress patients have been known to reexperience traumatic events precipitated by related smells (Kline & Rausch, 1985), and cancer patients in chemotherapy have identified olfactory cues of anticipatory nausea and vomiting (Dobkin, Zeichner, & Dickson-Parnell, 1985).

Because of anatomical and physiological connections in the brain between olfactory pathways and parts of the limbic system, odors may be particularly susceptible to the conditioning of affective experience. According to Kirk-Smith and Booth (1987), "Human responses to odour are acquired in complex settings, by association with emotionally significant effects. Odours thus help to carry the meaning of their sources, evoking recognition and affect" (p. 159). They further state that the effects of odors may be determined by a variety of contextual cues, including the perceiver's state of mind. Indeed, we have all had affectively laden childhood memories elicited by certain smells, such as grandmother's cookies or mother's perfume, suggesting that the association of affect and smell in memory storage does not require trauma or intense affect.

Surprisingly, there has been little systematic inquiry into this phenomenon. The present study by Reed and Murphy (1991) examines subjects' pleasantness and importance ratings of autobiographical memories that were elicited by both a pleasant and an unpleasant odor, cinnamon and mothballs. Hedonic ratings of odors had been determined previously.

Sixty-six individuals from three age groups (young adults, middle-aged adults, and the elderly) participated. All were recruited through advertisements at San Diego State University and identified themselves as undergraduate or graduate students, faculty, staff, or participants in adult education courses.

After completing tasks necessary for the larger project, subjects were presented with the odorants in amber glass jars and instructed to smell them, one at a time. Subjects were instructed to press a button stopping the timer on a reaction time apparatus when they had recalled a specific memory associated with the odor. After briefly describing the memory, they were asked to rate it on a 7-point Likert scale for four dimensions: pleasantness-then (at the time the event initially happened), pleasantness-now (as they are remembering it), importance-then (at the time of the event), and importance-now. The pleasant odor (cinnamon) was presented first, then the unpleasant odor (mothballs).

Reaction time was significantly longer in the elderly, regardless of the odorant presented. Pleasantness-then, pleasantness-now, and importance-then all varied significantly with odor pleasantness, regardless of the subjects' age. For all subjects, the more pleasant odor triggered memories that were rated higher for pleasantness-then, pleasantness-now, and importance-then than did the unpleasant odor. Neither odor nor age group or their interaction had an effect on the importance-now rating.

Several subjects were unable to retrieve specific memories to the odor cues. Although these data were not recorded or analyzed separately, qualitative impressions are noteworthy. Some of these subjects did report that the smells evoked a generalized feeling but not a specific memory. One subject burst into tears immediately after smelling the cinnamon and, only after a moment, was able to report a nostalgic memory about a favorite, but now deceased, grandmother. Another subject was able only to report bits and pieces of a vague but affect-laden memory, then stated "It almost feels like I made it up." These attempts at retrieval resulted in intangible memory associations, but clear affect.

Little empirical research has been conducted on memories elicited by odor cues, with the implicit assumption that the hedonic value of the odor has no effect on the type of memory elicited. Results of this study suggest otherwise. Although only one pleasant and one unpleasant odor were employed, the results imply that further exploration of the nature of the relationship between olfactory cues and memories is warranted.

ACKNOWLEDGMENT

Supported by NIH grants AG 08203 and AG 04085 from the National Institute on Aging. I gratefully acknowledge the collaboration of William S. Cain, Magdalena M. Gilmore, Steven Nordin, and Michelle J. Reed on the studies described in this chapter.

REFERENCES

Acosta, L., Morgan, C. D., Nordin, S., & Murphy, C. (1994). Odor memory and learning in healthy elderly versus young adults: Recall, recognition memory and identification. *Chemical Senses, 19*(5), 433.

Averback, P. (1983). Two new lesions in Alzheimer's disease. *Lancet, 19,* 1203.

Bahrick, H. P., Bahrick, P. O., & Wittlinger, R. P. (1975). Fifty years of memory for names and faces: A cross sectional approach. *Journal of Experimental Psychology: General, 104,* 54–75.

Ball, M. J., Fishman, M., Hachinski, V., Blume, W., Fox, A., Kral, V. A., Kirshen, A. J., Fox, H., & Merskey, H. (1985). A new definition of Alzheimer's disease: A hippocampal dementia. *Lancet, 1,* 14–16.

Blessed, G., Tomlinson, B. E., & Roth, M. (1968). The association between quantitative measures of dementia and of senile change in cerebral grey matter of elderly subjects. *British Journal of Psychaitry, 114,* 797–811.

Botwinick, J., & Storandt, M. (1974). *Memory, related functions and age.* Springfield, IL: Charles C. Thomas.

Bower, G. H. (1981). Mood and memory. *American Psychologist, 36,* 129–148.

Chalke, H. D., & Dewhurst, J. R. (1957). Accidental coal-gas poisoning. *British Medical Journal, 2,* 915–917.

Craik, F. I. M. (1977). Age differences in human memory. In J. E. Birren & K. W. Schaie (Eds.), *Handbook of the psychology of aging* (pp. 384–420). New York: Van Nostrand Reinhold.

Craik, F. I. M. & McDowd, J. M. (1987). Age differences in recall and recognition. *Journal of Experimental Psychology: Learning, Memory, and Cognition, 13,* 474–479.

Delis, D., Kramer, J. H., Kaplan, E., & Ober, B. A. (1983). California Verbal Learning Test. *The Psychological Corp.*

Dobkin, P., Zeichner, A., & Dickson-Parnell, B. E. (1985). Concomitants of anticipatory nausea emesis in cancer patients in chemotherapy. *Psychology Reports, 56*(2), 671–676.

Doty, R. L., Reyes, P., & Gregor, T. (1987). Olfactory dysfunction in Alzheimer's disease. *Brain Research Bulletin, 18,* 597–600.

Doty, R. L., Shaman, P., Applebaum, S. L., Giberson, R., Siksorski, L., & Rosenberg, L. (1984). Smell identification ability: Changes with age. *Science, 226,* 1441–1443.

Doty, R. L., Shaman, P., & Dann, M. (1984). Development of the University of Pennsylvania Smell Identification Test: A standardized microencapsulated test of olfactory function. *Physiology and Behavior, 32,* 489–502.

Engen, T. (1987). Remembering odors and their names. *American Scientist, 75,* 497–503.

Engen, T., Kuisma, J. E., & Eimas, P. D. (1973). Short-term memory of odors. *Journal of Experimental Psychology, 99,* 222–225.

Erber, J. (1974). Age differences in recognition memory. *Journal of Gerontology, 29,* 177–181.

Esiri, M., & Wilcock, G. (1984). The olfactory bulbs in Alzheimer's disease. *Journal of Neurology, Neurosurgery Psychiatry, 47,* 56–60.

Flicker, C., Ferris, S. H., Crook, T., Bartus, R. T., & Reisberg, B. (1986). Cognitive decline in advanced age: Future directions for the psychometric differentiation of normal and pathological age changes in cognitive function. *Developmental Neuropsychology, 2,* 309–322.

Fordyce, I. D. (1961). Olfaction tests. *British Journal of Industrial Medicine, 18,* 213–215.

Gehring, R. E., Toglia, M. P., & Kimble, G. A. (1976). Recognition memory for words and pictures of short and long retention intervals. *Memory and Cognition, 4,* 256–260.

Harwood, E., & Naylor, G. F. K. (1969). Recall and recognition in elderly and young subjects. *Australian Journal of Psychology, 21,* 251–257.

Joyner, R. E. (1963). Olfactory acuity in an industrial population. *Journal of Occupational Medicine, 5,* 37–42.

Katzman, R. (1986). Alzheimer's disease. *The New England Journal of Medicine, 314,* 964–973.

Kemper, T. L. (1983). Organization of the neuropathology of the amygdala in Alzheimer's disease. In R. Katzman (Ed.), *Banbury report 15: Biological aspects of Alzheimer's Disease* (pp. 31–36). New York: Cold Spring Harbor Laboratory.

Kimbrell, G. M., & Furtchgott, E. (1963). The effect of aging on olfactory threshold. *Journal of Gerontology, 18,* 364–365.

Kirk-Smith, M. P., & Booth, D. A. (1987). Chemoreception in human behaviour: Experimental analysis of the social effect of fragrances. *Chemical Senses, 12*(1), 159–166.

Kline, N. A., & Rausch, J. L. (1985). Olfactory precipitants of flashbacks in post-traumatic stress disorders: Case reports. *Journal of Clinical Psychiatry, 46*(9), 383–384.

Knupfer, L., & Spiegel, R. (1986). Differences in olfactory test performance between normal aged, Alzheimer and vascular type dementia individuals. *International Journal of Geriatric Psychiatry, 1,* 3–14.

Koss, E., Weiffenbach, J., Haxby, J., & Friedland, R. (1988). Olfactory detection and identification performance are dissociated in early Alzheimer's disease. *Neurology, 38,* 1228–1232.

Lyman, B. J., & McDaniel, M. A. (1986). Effects of encoding strategy on long-term memory for odours. *Quarterly Journal of Experimental Psychology, 38A,* 753–765.

Minz, A. I. (1968). Condition of the nervous system in old men. *Zeitschrift Altersforschung, 21,* 271–277.

Moberg, P. J., Pearlson, G. D., Speedie, L. J., Lipsey, J. R., Strauss, M. E., & Folstein, S. E. (1987). Olfactory recognition: Differential impairments in early and late Huntington's and Alzheimer's diseases. *Journal of Clinical and Experimental Neuropsychology, 9,* 650–664.

Murphy, C. (1982). Effects of exposure and context on hedonics of olfactory-taste mixtures. In J. T. Kuznicki, R. A. Johnson, & A. F. Rutkiewic (Eds.), *Selected sensory methods: Problems and approaches to measuring hedonics,* ASTM STP 773. Philadelphia: American Society for Testing and Materials.

Murphy, C. (1983). Age-related effects on the threshold, psychophysical function, and pleasantness of menthol. *Journal of Gerontology, 38,* 217–222.

Murphy, C. (1985). Cognitive and chemosensory influences on age-related changes in the ability to identify blended foods. *Journal of Gerontology, 40,* 47–52.

Murphy, C. (1986). Taste and smell in the elderly. In H. L. Meiselman & R. S. Rivlin (Eds.), *Clinical measurement of taste and smell* (pp. 343–371). New York: Macmillan.

Murphy, C. (1989). Aging and chemosensory perception of and preference for nutritionally significant stimuli. *Annals of the New York Academy of Sciences, 561,* 251–266.

Murphy, C., & Cain, W. S. (1986). Odor identification: The blind are better. *Physiology and Behavior, 37,* 177–180.

Murphy, C., Cain, W. S., Gilmore, M. M., & Skinner, R. B. (1991). Sensory and semantic factors in recognition memory for odors and graphic stimuli: Elderly versus young persons. *American Journal of Psychology, 104,* 161–192.

Murphy, C., Gilmore, M. M., Seery, C. S., Salmon, D. P., & Lasker, B. P. (1990). Olfactory thresholds are associated with degree of dementia in Alzheimer's disease. *Neurobiology of Aging, 11,* 465–469.

Murphy, C., Lasker, B. R., & Salmon, D. P. (1987). Olfactory dysfunction and odor memory in Alzheimer's disease, Huntington's disease and normal aging. *Society for Neuroscience Abstracts, 13,* 151.

Murphy, C., Nunez, K., Withee, J., & Jalowayski, A. A. (1985). The effects of age, nasal airway resistance and nasal cytology on olfactory threshold for butanol. *Chemical Senses, 10,* 418.

Peabody, C. A., & Tinklenberg, J. R. (1984). Olfactory deficits and primary degenerative dementia. *American Journal of Psychiatry, 142,* 524–525.

Rabinowitz, J. C., Craik, F. I., & Ackerman, B. P. (1982). A processing resource account of age differences in recall. *Canadian Journal of Psychology, 36,* 325–344.

Raven, J. (1960). *Guide to standard progressive matrices.* London: H. K. Lewis.

Reed, M. J. (1990). *The influence of mood and age on the affective qualities of autobiographical memories.* Unpublished doctoral dissertation, University of Houston.

Reed, M. J., & Murphy, C. (1991, August). *Influence of aging on the affective qualities of autobiographical memories.* Paper presented at the American Psychological Association Meeting, Los Angeles.

Reyes, P. F., Golden, G. T., Fariello, R. G., Fagel, L., & Zalewska, M. (1985). Olfactory pathways in Alzheimer's disease (AD): Neuropathological studies. *Neuroscience Abstracts, 11,* 168.

Riccio, D. C., Richardson, R., & Ebner, D. L. (1984). Memory retrieval deficits based upon altered contextual cues: A paradox. *Psychological Bulletin, 96(1),* 152–165.

Rubin, G. R., Groth, R. E., & Goldsmith, D. J. (1984). Olfactory cuing of autobiographical memory. *American Journal of Psychology, 97(4),* 493–507.

Salthouse, T. A., & Lichty, W. (1985). Tests of the neural noise hypothesis of age-related cognitive change. *Journal of Gerontology, 40,* 443–450.

Schab, F. R. (1990). Odors and the remembrance of things past. *Journal of Experimental Psychology: Learning, Memory, and Cognition, 16(4),* 648–655.

Schiffman, S. S. (1979). Changes in taste and smell with age: Psychophysical aspects. In J. M. Ordy & K. R. Brizzee (Eds.), *Sensory systems and communication in the elderly.* New York: Raven Press.

Schiffman, S. S., Moss, J., & Erickson, R. P. (1976). Thresholds of food odors in the elderly. *Experimental Aging Research, 2,* 389–398.

Schonfield, D., & Robertson, B. A. (1966). Memory storage and aging. *Canadian Journal of Psychology, 20,* 228–236.

Seery, C. S., & Murphy, C. (1989). Characteristics of odor memory in Alzheimer's disease. *Society for Neuroscience Abstracts, 15,* 862.

Serby, M., Corwin, J., Novatt, A., Conrad, P., & Rotrosen, J. (1985). Olfaction in dementia. *Journal of Neurology, Neurosurgery and Psychiatry, 48(8),* 848–849.

Simpson, J., & Yates, C. M. (1984). Olfactory tubercle choline acetyltransferase activity in Alzheimer-type dementia: Down's syndrome and Huntington's disease. *Journal of Neurology, Neurosurgery and Psychiatry, 47,* 1138–1139.

Stevens, J. C., Bartoshuk, L. M., & Cain, W. S. (1984). Chemical senses and aging: Taste vs. smell. *Chemical Senses, 9,* 167–179.

Stevens, J. C., & Cain, W. S. (1986). Smelling via the mouth: Effects of aging. *Perception and Psychophysics, 40,* 321–323.

Stevens, J. C., & Cain, W. S. (1987). Old-age deficits in the sense of smell as gauged by thresholds, magnitude matching, and odor identification. *Psychology and Aging, 2,* 36–42.

Stevens, J. C., Plantinga, A., & Cain, W. S. (1982). Reduction of odor and nasal pungency associated with aging. *Neurobiology of Aging, 3,* 125–132.

Strauss, E. L. (1970). A study on olfactory acuity. *Annals of Otology, Rhinology, and Laryngology, 79,* 95–104.

Swets, J. A. (1986). Form of empirical ROCs in discrimination and diagnostic tasks: Implications for theory and measurement of performance. *Psychological Bulletin, 99,* 181–198.

Swets, J. A., & Pickett, R. M. (1982). *Evaluation of Diagnostic Systems.* New York: Academic Press.

Venstrom, D., & Amoore, J. E. (1968). Olfactory threshold in relation to age, sex, or smoking. *Journal of Food Science, 33,* 264–265.

Waldton, S. (1974). Clinical observations of impaired cranial nerve function in senile dementia. *Acta Psychiatry Scandinavia, 50,* 539–547.

Walk, H. A., & Johns, E. E. (1984). Interference and facilitation in short-term memory for odors. *Perception and Psychophysics, 36,* 508–514.

Warner, M. D., Peabody, C. A., Flattery, J. J., & Tinklenberg, J. R. (1986). Olfactory deficits and Alzheimer's disease. *Biological Psychiatry, 21,* 116–118.

Wysocki, C. J., & Gilbert, A. N. (1989). National Geographic Smell Survey: Effects of age are heterogenous. *Annals of The New York Academy of Sciences, 510,* 12–28.

= 8 =

Odor Memory in Nonhumans

Stephen F. Davis
Emporia State University

H. Wayne Ludvigson
Texas Christian University

There are more odors in heaven and earth, Horatio, than you can find listed in any standard work on the subject or in all the advertising and caralogues of the perfumery trade. The woods are full of odors, especially in dewy mornings of spring and in the moist twilight after sundown. The woods are also full of wild creatures with noses automatically tuned to catch odor meanings and ready to flee, or chase, or mate, or fight to the death as one or another may appraise the significance for him of the communication. The great major themes of life and death and love burden the airborne odor molecules, criss crossing and tangling with one another as well as with many minor themes all in apparent anarchy until each sender's plea, or threat, or pleasant welcome finds an appropriate receptor, when order is restored, much as the confused babble of a telephone exchange becomes rational as calls are properly plugged in.

—Bedichek (1960, pp. 131-132)

The importance of airborne chemicals in the control of the behavior of many animals has long been known and at least minimally documented. Recently, however, there has been an upsurge of research on olfaction, accompanied by a heightened conviction that olfaction plays a pervasive role of great significance for the behavior and physiological processes of many, if not most, animals.

133

Olfaction in nonhuman animals—which, following the convenient although misleading convention of psychologists, we refer to as animals—takes on special significance when it is realized that animals themselves produce or emit some of the most important odors in their environment, a fact that partially justifies labeling their role as communicative. Conspecific- and self-generated odors, then, are the stimuli for much of odor memory here discussed. Indeed, they may be considered the symbols of animal chemical communication.[1] Considering the presumed importance of chemical communication for many animals, it may be worthwhile to keep in mind that memories may differ for animal-emitted odors, as compared with other odors. Similarly, although an animal emission may affect a conspecific, that is no assurance that a memory is involved at all.

The extent to which memory may be involved in chemical communication among animals, or in their other interactions with odors, depends first on its definition. Much animal behavior has traditionally been considered to be the result of stimulus–response (S–R) bonds, although this is much less believed today, depending on the animal considered. Further, it has often been suggested that memory is not involved in S–R bonds. Although this latter contention is illogical (Baker & Mercier, 1989), many contemporary psychologists would none-the-less claim that the nature of an S–R memory differs significantly from memories that may properly be said to *represent* objects or events—these latter being termed cognitions. For the present purposes, we consider memory of either variety, assuming the distinction has some merit, but we are sensitive to the variety that appears easily to be called representational. Indeed, in concentrating on studies of learned associations involving odors, we are dealing with cognitive representations—at least according to current views of many experts in the field of animal learning.

Considering representational memory, a certain ambiguity in speaking of odor memory remains and bears upon the translation of findings from research on animals to the domain of humans, and vice versa. When referring to odor memory in humans, one might first mean memory of the odor, as against a memory of something that is aroused by the odor. Furthermore, much is made of the distinction between recognition and recall memory in humans. For humans, it is said that not only is the ability to recognize odors as good as is the ability to recognize colors, but that permanence of recognition memories is "a special attribute of olfaction"; in contrast, recall memory for odors, as compared with sights or sounds, is limited, at best (Engen, 1987, p. 497).

---

[1]Grounds for treating chemical emissions as symbols are not a subject of the present chapter, although the analysis below may be relevant.

Whatever else might be made of this recognition–recall distinction, to say that a stimulus cannot be recalled seems tantamount to saying that a representation of the stimulus cannot be retrieved from memory, to use the term central to current cognitive psychology. Thus, absence of odor recall would suggest either the absence of representations of odors in memory or a problem with the retrieval process. On the other hand, recognition of odors implies, at minimum, a clear ability of the odor stimulus to elicit reactions and perhaps representations of (nonodorous) stimuli or events associated with the odor.

With these translations in mind, the work on animal odor memory may not appear so different from that on human odor memory. Virtually nothing can be said about recall memory for odors in animals, because the proper experiments appear not to have been undertaken. Recall of odor might be demonstrated if it could be shown that a nonodorous stimulus previously associated with an odor can arouse a reaction subsequently associated with the odor. Since it would also have to be shown that the reaction is not mediated by a representation of the nonodorous stimulus present when the odor became associated with the reaction, the demonstration poses an interesting problem in experimental design and inference. However, much more can be said about recognition memory. It is to this task that we now turn.

PHEROMONES AND MEMORY

Much of chemical communication among animals is thought to involve pheromones, chemicals that are excreted by an animal and have some rather specific or stereotyped effect on a conspecific. The effect could be on behavior, and be rather immediate, or on hormonal or other internal physiological processes, taking some time to run its course. Usually omitted from the definition of a pheromone, but virtually always implied, is the assumption that the release of the pheromone is triggered by quite specific conditions, ranging from internal physiological changes to external stimulation of a particular kind, or a combination of these.

The chemicals affecting behavior are often categorized according to the nature of their effect: those affecting internal physiological processes are called *priming pheromones*, whereas those affecting behavioral reactions are termed *releasing* or *signaling pheromones* (Wilson, 1963). These effects are said to serve physiological regulatory and communication functions, respectively (Gleason & Reynierse, 1969).

For the priming effects, there may be little reason to invoke memory at all. For the direct behavioral effects that appear unlearned (i.e., dependent only on those kinds of sensory experiences normally inevitable for all members of a species), the neural structures that mediate the effects must often represent, in some sense, objects and events in the animal's environment. As remarkable as these unlearned memories must be in some instances, space constraints prevent our discussion of them here. Instead we limit ourselves to behavioral effects that depend on idiosyncratic experiences, ones that may be said to involve acquiring and retaining information about, or a reaction to, an odorous chemical.

In this context we refer to acquired meaning of odors, where "meaning" refers either to representations of objects or events associated with the odor in question or to other hypothetical processes/reactions of the organism, such as emotional responses. Furthermore, we concentrate on laboratory investigations of mammals, particularly rats and particularly those studies in which the animals themselves seem to provide the odor stimulus — and even then the review is far from exhaustive.

To a large extent, research on odor memory in nonhumans has not progressed to the point where one can say a great deal about the nature or function of the memories themselves. Much of the work has been concerned with more basic tasks, such as determining whether, and the conditions under which, odors function as conditioned or discriminative stimuli for learned reactions. Indeed, the questions of primary interest often revolve around the nature of the odorous stimuli, including their functional properties, although there are often implied collateral questions regarding resulting memories. For example, we ourselves have been particularly concerned with odors that animals themselves emit, the specific conditions resulting in the emissions of these odors, and whether these odors are qualitatively distinctive. These questions, however, are basic to an understanding of the memories and functions of these odors, that is, what these odors mean to the receiving animal and what effects they have.

EARLY INVESTIGATIONS

Rather than researching odor memory, per se, early studies attempted to delineate the role(s) of odor in the acquisition of new behaviors. One of the first thorough investigations was by Liggett (1928), who reported the use of four methods with rat subjects: localization, anosmia, odor-present versus odor-absent discrimination, and discrimination between two simultaneously presented odors. Although the first two methods yielded positive results regarding the importance of odor cues, the latter two methods did not. Interestingly, Liggett also failed to obtain good odor-based discriminations when human subjects were tested under comparable conditions. As subsequent researchers (e.g.,

Brown & Ghiselli, 1938; Honzik, 1936; Swann, 1933) were successful in establishing odor-based discriminations, the Liggett data appear to have been compromised by the unusual nature of the odors and tasks that were used.

A determination of the role of brain processes in olfactory learning also was on the research agenda of these early investigators. Destruction of the olfactory bulbs consistently resulted in the abolition of a previously established odor discrimination (Lashley & Sperry, 1943; Swann, 1933) and/or the inability to form such a discrimination (Swann, 1934). Lesions in other parts of the brain met with mixed results. For example, Swann (1935) found that up to 85% destruction of the cerebral cortex failed to interfere with olfactory discrimination in rats. This finding led to an investigation of subcortical mechanisms (Brown & Ghiselli, 1938). Sieck (1972) reported that bilateral ablation of the olfactory bulbs interfered with the acquisition of passive avoidance; however, this intervention improved active avoidance performance. The results were interpreted in terms of alterations to the limbic system that resulted in overreactivity to external stimuli.

The role of the olfactory sense in guiding more complex maze learning also has been investigated. Based on the finding showing superior learning by rats that were provided an artificial odor trail marking the correct path in a maze, Lindley (1930) and Honzik (1936) reported more comprehensive studies employing anosmic rats as subjects (also see Demand, 1940). Honzik's research is instructive. Using the multiple-unit, elevated maze apparatus, he reported that the learning of anosmic rats was inferior to that of normals. Further tests indicated that vision appeared to be the most important cue in this task. However, olfaction became the dominant cue when blind rats were tested.

These early studies clearly indicate that odors can be used effectively by rats as discriminative stimuli in a variety of learning tasks. More recently, several investigators have been more directly concerned with odor memory. For example, Barnett (1963) reported a study by Neuhaus in which rats were trained to associate food with the odor of butyric acid. Subsequently, when the rats were presented with two odors, they consistently chose the butyric acid that had been paired with food.

Using a similar strategy, Thorpe (1939) reported that *Drosophila melanogaster* raised on a peppermint-scented food source retained a memory of that odor and showed greater acceptance of this odor when they were tested later as imagoes. In order to rule out the possibility of simple habituation, Hershberger and Smith (1967) raised insects in the same manner as did Thorpe. However, additional insects were exposed to the peppermint odor alone for 24 hours prior to testing. The results indicate that insects raised on a peppermint-scented food medium subsequently chose the peppermint odor in significantly greater numbers than did either insects raised on a nonscented food medium and those insects that had been exposed to the peppermint odor alone after it had been paired with food (i.e., an extinction condition). These data establish the existence of an acquired odor memory in Drosophila. Additionally, it is clear that this learning is susceptible to extinction just as other forms of learning are. It also has been reported that rat mothers emit an odor that serves as an attractant for pups (Coopersmith & Leon, 1984). As these odors are directly influenced by the animal's diet (i.e., there is no common maternal odor), this behavior would reflect the development of an odor memory by the pups.

Although this body of literature supports the acquisition of odor memories by nonhumans, several additional considerations are worthy of mention. Although the role(s) of odors as cues and discriminative stimuli has received some research attention, precious few data dealing primarily with odor memory have been reported. This situation appears to have been caused, in part, by the lack of sensitive, relevant behaviors to measure such effects. Finally, although the existence of odor memory has been established in rats, data from a significant number of other species have yet to be made available.

ODOR MEMORY AS MEASURED
BY CONDITIONED AVERSIONS

The associability of odors and odor memory also have been investigated via the conditioned taste-aversion paradigm. To produce a conditioned taste aversion, typically, the presentation of a novel taste is followed by a toxicosis-including agent such as lithium chloride (LiCl). This procedure routinely results in the development of a strong aversion to the novel taste (e.g., Garcia & Koelling, 1966, 1967; Grote & Brown, 1971; Nachman, 1970). That oflaction may play a role in taste-aversion conditioning was demonstrated by Elkins, Fraser, and Hobbs (1977), who found that bilateral removal of the olfactory bulbs resulted in weaker aversions.

If an odor, not a novel taste, is conditioned, the outcome may be quite different, however. Some investigators (e.g., Palmerino, Rusiniak, & Garcia, 1980) reported that only a weak aversion, if any at all, is developed to the odor. Additionally, these investigators reported that the strength of the potential aversion rapidly decreasesd as the interval between the conditioned stimulus (CS) and unconditioned stimulus (US) increases. For example, a delay of 15 min was sufficient to significantly attenuate an odor aversion, whereas delays of 30 min or greater completely eliminated it.

On the other hand, conditioning of an odor aversion has frequently been successful (Batsell & Ludvigson, 1989; Domjan, 1973; Lorden, Kenfield, & Braun, 1970; Panhuber, 1982; Taukulis, 1974). In this context, a series of studies reported by Rudy and Cheatle (1977, 1979) illustrates how the lack of appropriate behavioral measures and programmatic research may be successfully addressed. Rudy and Cheatle (1977) conditioned an odor aversion to the scent of lemon extract in 2-day-old rat pups by placing them in an environment of lemon-scented wood shavings and then administering LiCl. The dependent variable was the amount of time the subject spent in proximity to the lemon odor or a second scent (see Cornwell-Jones, 1976). The conditioned pups spent significantly less time in the presence of the aversive odor than did a variety of control groups. It is noteworthy that although conditioning took place when the pups were 2 days old, testing was not conducted until the pups were 8 days old. Clearly, the memory of the aversively conditioned odor persisted during the 6-day interval.

Additional studies (Rudy & Cheatle, 1979) indicate that these acquired aversions were subject to the normal extinction process, and that neonatal pups ranging in age from 2 to 14 days acquired odor aversions in a comparable manner. These investigators also demonstrated that 2-day-old pups were unable to tolerate any delay in the presentation of the US, whereas 8-day-old pups displayed strong odor conditioning with CS–US intervals up to 90 min. Moreover, it also was shown that preexposure to the CS interfered with the acquisition of the conditioned odor aversion for 8-day-old but not 2-day-old pups. Based on these results it was suggested that odor-memory mechanisms are fully functional in the 8-day-old pups, but not in the 2-day-old pups.

Finally, these authors demonstrated that once an odor aversion had been acquired by 7-day-old pups it was amenable to higher order conditioning procedures. More specifically, 24 hours following a single pairing of the lemon scent with LiCl, animals were exposed to an orange scent and then immediately reexposed to the lemon scent. In a subsequent test, pups conditioned in this manner spent significantly less time near the orange scent than did nonconditioned, control pups.

Kucharski and Hall (1988) also reported successful odor-aversion conditioning in 6-day-old rat pups. They further demonstrated that bilateral access to olfactory memories develops postnatally. Such preliminary developmental data suggest a potentially fruitful avenue for additional research.

This pattern of well-established odor aversions and odor memories in neonatal rat pups stands at odds with the contradictory data reported for adult animals. However, the conditionability of odors for adult animals may be dramatically altered. If the olfactory stimulus is presented in compound with a novel taste and followed by toxicosis, then the resultant odor aversion may be significantly enhanced or potentiated relative to that of animals conditioned just to the odor. Although this taste-mediated odor potentiation effect is not consonant with the more typical finding of overshadowing (e.g., Pavlov, 1927; Revusky, 1971) that occurs when weak and strong stimuli form a compound CS, it has been replicated sufficiently often (e.g., Palmerino, Rusiniak, & Garcia, 1980; Rusiniak, Hankins, Garcia, & Brett, 1979; Rusiniak, Palmerino, & Garcia, 1982) to establish it as a genuine phenomenon, even if we do not yet know all the factors critical for its appearance.

One factor apparently critical for the appearance of potentiation is familiarity of the environment, according to a recent report by Striegel and Batsell (1990). These investigators found that potentiation failed to appear if either the training or test environment was unfamiliar. Another critical factor appears to be the duration of exposure of the odor-taste compound CS (Westbrook, Homewood, Horn, & Clarke, 1983). Short (2 min) exposures result in overshadowing, whereas long (15 min) exposures produce potentiation. Along similar lines, Holder and Garcia (1987) reported that the odor and taste stimuli must be presented simultaneously for the odor potentiation effect to be shown. Additionally, they reported that (a) odor intensity was positively related to the strength of potentiation, (b) odor did not serve to potentiate the taste aversion, and (c) that, even at maximum intensity, an odor aversion was impossible to establish without presenting a taste along with it.

Additional aspects of the basic odor-conditioning paradigm have been investigated. Suggesting that the novel taste serves to strengthen an odor-illness association, Lett (1984) reported that extinction of the taste aversion following odor-taste conditioning did not attenuate the odor potentiation. This effect was shown following either one or two conditioning episodes. Demonstrating that odor may be successfully paired with a different type of internal US, Russell et al. (1984) reported the successful conditioning of odor as a CS for histamine release. The US in this situation was a challenge to the immune system. The potential gains in understanding of the immune reaction by including consideration of such an associative process are obvious.

While the role of natural animal odors often appears to be that of a US, Williams (1987, 1989; Williams & Scott, 1989), in the development of his stress-coping-fear-defense (SCFD) theory, devised an ingenious method for the aversive conditioning and subsequent testing of such cues. For example, Williams and Scott (Experiment 1) demonstrated that one defeat, which involved several bites, by an alpha male rat was sufficient to establish the odor of the alpha male as an aversive CS for the defeated animal. This CS function was subsequently demonstrated in the defensive burying situation where it was shown that the presence of the alpha male odors resulted in an increase in freezing behavior and a decrease in burying in the defeated animals.[2] The presence of alpha odors during the defensive burying testing of nondefeated animals failed to significantly increase the duration of freezing behavior. It was also shown (Williams & Scott, 1989, Experiment 3) that natural cat odor could be conditioned and subsequently assume a similar CS role. More specifically, groups of rats that had experienced five or more electric footshocks in the presence of cat odor displayed significantly more freezing behavior in a subsequent defensive burying test with cat odor present than did animals conditioned with cat odor but tested in the absence of cat odor. In that more freezing was shown by animals receiving five pairings of electric shock and cat odor than animals receiving five pairings of electric shock and citronella odor, it may be that the rat is selectively prepared to make the former association. However, for such natural odors to assume this CS role, they apparently must be paired with the receipt of a painful stimulus several times. (Williams and Scott, 1989, Experiment 3, reported that one pairing of cat odor and shock failed to produce a discernible effect.) Likewise, Williams and Scott (1989, Experiment 2) demonstrated that simple exposure to cat odor prior to defensive burying testing failed to influence the display of freezing behavior in the subsequent burying test.

Finally, the ethoexperimental approach to the study of aversive conditioning of conspecific odors adopted by Williams and his colleagues offers promise for the general study of odor memory. The creation of a seminatural laboratory environment will afford the investigator a wider range of highly probable response alternatives from which to choose. Clearly, the measurement of freezing behavior has proven most effective in the program of research reported by Williams and Scott (1989).

EXPERIENCE-CONTROLLED ANIMAL EMISSIONS

My attention was first called to odors of mood by a rattlesnake hunter, Mr. John A. Peterson, a building contractor of Austin, Texas. He smells out his prey, as the savages of Queensland are said to do. Moreover this man

---

[2]It is not completely clear from the report that *odors of defeat* (i.e., odors from the defeated rat or rats) were not also present along with alpha rat odors.

assures me that he can tell the mood of the rattler, whether stretched out dozing in the sun or coiled for combat, angry and menacing. Resting quietly the creature smells, he says, like a green watermelon just cut open; in the other case, like a wet dog. There is much in snake lore to confirm this observation. . . . Other authorities do not confine the odor communications to rattlesnakes, but include many if not all macrosmatic species. "Mood," the dictionaries say means temper of mind, humor, especially the sum of those mental dispositions which give the dominant emotional character of the moment—specifically, joyful, somber, ecstatic, lustful, dominating, pugnacious, etc. The theory is that each mood has a distinctive flavor. The more discriminating the nose, the more information may be communicated odorwise from smelled to smeller. In short, each basic body odor changes flavor with the creature's mood. (Bedichek, 1960, p. 131)

Odors Engendered by Appetitive Reinforcers

An extensive literature has been generated in recent years concerned with the apparent ability of rats to respond to significant environmental events by emitting distinctive odors—odors that can influence the behavior of conspecifics. The significant events studied have often been common reinforcing or punishing operations, such as presentation of food or other rewarding objects and withholding of food that the rats are anticipating. Similarly electric shock or other kinds of stressors have been employed.

Much of the work employing reward and nonreward can be traced to the observations of McHose and Ludvigson (1966), who found that rats apparently emit distinctively different odors as a consequence of receiving rewards of different value in a straight runway apparatus. The rewards differed in terms of amount and/or delay of reward for most rats (experimental rats) in a squad. Since these differing rewards were signaled by discriminative stimuli present when the rats left the runway start box, the differential odorous emissions were evidently elicited by the discriminative stimuli as well as the rewards themselves, although only with later work did that inference gain certainty (see Ludvigson, Mathis, & Choquette, 1985).

Evidence that the experimental rats indeed emitted differential odors came from the behavior of the control rats that responded differentially in a runway depending on the relative goodness of the rewards that preceding experimental rats had received in that runway. Because the control rats themselves always received the same reward, regardless of the reward received by preceding experimental rats, their behavior seemed to represent a reaction to odors left by experimental rats—a reaction that was either unlearned or learned outside the context of the experiment. That is, any meaning the odors had for the control rats must not have been specific to the experimental context. It is significant perhaps, as discussed later, that this reaction was rather weak.

This initial observation was followed by a host of others concerned first with simply establishing the reality of such reward odors and nonreward odors. In many studies the question of whether both, or only one, of these odors existed could not be addressed. Only later were data garnered that implicated both emissions.

The experimental paradigm for many subsequent studies (e.g., Pitt, Davis, & Brown, 1973; Seago, Ludvigson, & Remley, 1970) also employed the straight runway and was initiated by Ludvigson and colleagues (Ludvigson, 1969; Ludvigson & Sytsma, 1967; see also Amsel, Hug, & Surridge, 1969; Howard & McHose, 1974; Morrison & Ludvigson, 1970). The basic procedure involved arranging reward contingencies such that any odors emitted by a preceding rat in reaction to particular rewards received (or not received) could serve as discriminative stimuli for subsequent experimental subjects. For control subjects, any such odors were arranged to be nondiscriminative or virtually so. The often observed result was that the experimental rats did indeed respond differentially depending on the treatment given to preceding animals. Specifically, on trials on which preceding rats had received food and the rat in question was itself about to receive food, it ran fast. In contrast when preceding rats expected food but did not receive it, and this outcome predicted absence of food for the rat in question, it ran slowly. The results of the Ludvigson and Sytsma (1967) study are shown in Fig. 8.1. Interestingly, appropriate double-alternation patterning developed in Group P (odors maximally discriminative), and such responding failed to develop in Group NP (odors minimally discriminative).

Several details are worth noting. First, these differential reactions occurred only in the goalwise portion of the runway, where differential odors should have accrued. This is part of the basis for the inference of the odors. Second, the experimental arrangement assured that any distinctive odors emitted could easily become associated with goal events, that is, that learned reactions or meaning could accrue to the odors in the experimental context. Third, these learned reactions were very strong, suggesting that odors, at least conspecific-generated ones, can command powerful memories of associated events significant to the life of these animals. Fourth, similar results have been obtained when nonlaboratory wood rats served as subjects (Davis, Gustavson, & Petty-Zirnstein, 1985).

Following the seminal studies (e.g., Ludvigson & Sytsma, 1967; McHose & Ludvigson, 1966) in this line of research, some have

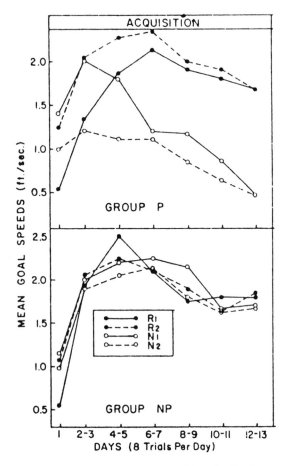

FIG. 8.1. Mean goal speeds during acquisition. Note the development of rational patterning, fast on reward (R) trials and slow on nonreward (N) trials, by Group P, which had odor cues maximally discriminative. Such patterning was now shown by Group NP, in which odor cues were minimally discriminative (Ludvigson & Sytsma, 1967).

confirmed that these odor emissions may elicit unlearned reactions. However, these reactions appear fairly weak and short lived. For example, odor from nonreward appears mildly aversive on first encounter, but rather quickly becomes neutral if it signals nothing untoward (Collerain, 1978; Collerain & Ludvigson, 1972, 1977; Ludvigson, McNeese, & Collerain, 1979). If it is made to signal reward, instead of nonreward, its natural significance, it can readily come to elicit approach, rather than aversively motivated avoidance (Eslinger & Ludvigson, 1980). Thus, odor of nonreward must have only weak unlearned meaning for the rat, and it can easily acquire a meaning quite opposite to what it would naturally be associated with. Learned memories seem crucial for establishing the link between odor emission and action in this case.

Other lines of research have revealed findings similar or related to those already mentioned. For example, French investigators have found evidence that rats emit distinctive odors when frustrated,[3] rewarded, or isolated from other rats (e.g., Cattarelli, Vernet-Maury, & Chanel, 1974, 1977), and that these odors elicit characteristic patterns of emotional reactions in the rat along dimensions that they termed reassuring and fear arousing. From recordings of mitral cell responses, Voorhees and Remley (1981) found that individual cells respond differently to reward and nonreward odors, suggesting that the odors themselves are qualitatively different.

These studies, as well as others (e.g., Davis, Weaver, Janzen, & Travis-Neideffer, 1984; Davis, Whiteside, Bramlett, & Peterson, 1981) suggest that at least some of the emissions produced under different stimulating conditions are qualitatively distinctive, although such an inference is difficult from behavioral data only. Direct chemical analysis would obviously be of great help and, no doubt, highly illuminating. This question of the distinctiveness of chemical emissions arising from different environmental events comes to the fore in a number of studies, seeking to investigate the motivational specificity of conspecific odors of reward and nonreward. Before turning to the data bearing on motivational specificity, it will be instructive to consider recent research dealing with subject-generated odors that have influenced the selection of specific diets. The results of these studies bear an interesting relationship to the motivational specificity results, as will be discussed.

Odorous Emissions in Diet Selection and Foraging

A series of experiments (Galef, 1983; Galef & Wigmore, 1983) indicated that a recently fed rat (a demonstrator) may transfer information regarding a food it has consumed to a second (observer) rat. Typically after an observer has been in contact with a demonstrator that has recently eaten a novel food, the observer prefers that food to another novel food. According to Galef (1987), observer rats can use both olfactory and gustatory cues from the demonstrator, including diet-engendered odors emitted from the demonstrator's digestive tract (Galef & Stein, 1985) and odors and tastes from food particles clinging to the

---

[3]Their operation of frustration may sometimes involve fear or conflict: Cues previously associated with electric shock are presented that deter the animal from obtaining reward, thus frustrating it (E. Vernet-Maury, personal communication, July 13, 1976).

pelage of the demonstrator. These conclusions, and others, regarding this interesting and presumably functionally significant phenomenon, are based on findings such as the following: (a) interactions as short as 2 min are sufficient for the successful exchange of information, (b) contact with the mouth of the demonstrator is a predictor of the diet preference of the observer, (c) demonstrators that have been stomach-loaded, thus eliminating direct food and gustatory cues, remain a reliable source of information, and (d) a rat demonstrator, as opposed to a surrogate object, is essential to provide the appropriate context for transmission of dietary information. Furthermore, Galef and Kennett (1985) reported that cues emitted by demonstrators were effective for up to 4 hours after ingestion of the diet. In a related experiment, Richard, Grover, and Davis (1987) indicated that appropriate diet selection by observer animals persisted throughout the course of a 24-hour test session in a simulated free-foraging situation.

It is presumed that these studies reveal a mechanism by which rats select food in natural foraging situations. Indeed, some of the studies provide rather direct evidence for this supposition (Galef & Wigmore, 1983; Richard et al., 1987). Given that supposition, it would be expected that memory of the diet-associated cue would last some hours. Indeed, it appears that there can be at least an 8-day hiatus between contact with the demonstrator and the preference test (Galef, 1987): Memory of the specific diet cues along with some sort of memory mediating preference for the foods generating these cues (e.g., a memory of the demonstrator) must persist at least that long.

Motivationally Specific Emissions

Several studies, using donor rats that receive one reinforcer and test rats that receive another reinforcer, lead to the conclusion that the odor generated by a rat upon receipt of a reinforcer is at least somewhat specific to or characteristic of the particular reinforcer received and/or the rat's particular motivational state (Davis et al., 1974; Davis, Prytula, Noble, & Mollenhour, 1976; Travis, Ludvigson, & Eslinger, 1988). In these studies, a donor under a given motivational state, for example hunger, was placed into the start box of a runway, either reinforced (with, in this case, food) or not reinforced, and then removed. Given this treatment, the donor would presumably leave a discriminable odor whose properties depend on the treatment just received. A test rat (thirsty, in this case) was then placed into the start box and allowed to traverse the runway to receive either its reinforcer (water, in this case) or nothing. The critical finding was that when the donor's reinforcer/ motivation was different from its own, the test rat displayed no evidence of correctly anticipating the occurrence and nonoccurrence of its own impending reinforcer as it left the start box. In contrast, strong evidence of differential anticipation readily occurred when the rats' reinforcers/motivations were the same. Representative data are presented in Fig. 8.2.

Two intriguing conclusions can be drawn: (a) the rat's odor emissions on reinforced and/or nonreinforced trials are not the same when food and hunger, as against water and thirst, are motivating the animal (i.e., the odor generated appears to be at least partially specific to the motivational state and/or reward received), and (b) somehow the donor's odor emission is not as effective a discriminative stimulus when the reinforcers/motivations are different as when they are the same (i.e., its control of the receiving rat's behavior appears to be at least partially specific). The reader may note that it is fortunate indeed that the latter effect occurs, or the former might never have been detected.

These results pose interesting questions. While the donors seem able to provide highly specific information about experiences they have had, much as the demonstrators can in the diet-selection studies, the question of just how that occurs remains to be answered. In fact, it even remains to be determined whether it is the emission on rewarded trials, as opposed to nonrewarded trials, that is specific, or whether both are specific. It seems more plausible to suppose that different rewards are differently marked, rather than different types of nonreward (no food, no water, etc.), but this is yet to be determined. If that should prove to be the case, the motivational specificity and the diet-selection results might involve at least some of the same mechanisms.

At this point the reader might wonder whether the reinforcer-related odors in these studies simply are remnants of the reinforcer itself left by the donor, rather than odors that are genuinely generated or emitted by the donor. Pertinent to this question, remnants could not have been operating in some studies (McHose & Ludvigson, 1966; Voorhees & Remley, 1981), and others have effectively ruled out such reinforcer-related cues as necessary for the effects. Instead of giving the donors reward versus nonreward, some researchers have given them reward versus delayed reward without much change in behavioral effect on the test rats (Davis, Weaver, Janzen, & Travis-Neideffer, 1984; Ludvigson, 1970; Travis-Neideffer, 1981). The same reward is given on all trials— only delayed on half—thus, this procedure evidently assures that any remnants of reward would be available on all trials and thus nondifferential. One is led to the inference, therefore, that the animals themselves emit or discharge some odor tht effectively differentiates the reinforcers (or the nonreinforced experiences).

One is tempted to explain the conclusion that the control of behavior

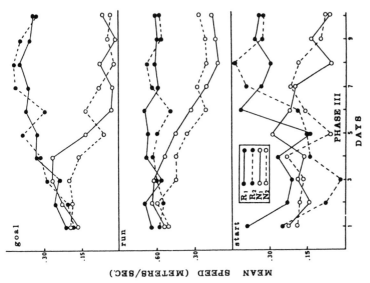

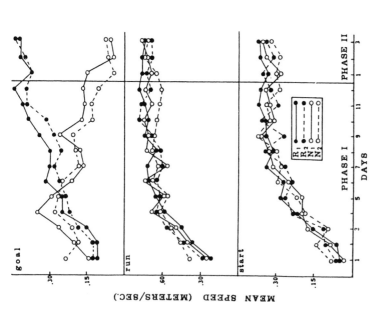

FIG. 8.2. A study of the motivational specificity of the signal value of odor cues. During Phases I and II (left panel), startbox-placed odor-donor rats were water deprived, whereas runway-trained rats were food deprived. Runway-trained animals developed rational patterning only in the goal measure during Phase I (RRNNRRNN trial sequence) and Phase II (NNRRNNRR trial sequence). Patterning during these phases was apparently based only on odors exuded by preceding runway-trained animals, with donor odors serving no discriminative function. Prior to Phase III the deprivation state of the runway-trained animals was shifted to coincide with that of the odor donors. The result was that the runway animals established patterned responding in the start and run measures (right panel), suggesting that the donor odor cues were utilized only in Phase III when motivational conditions for donors and runway animals were the same (Davis, Prytula, Noble, & Mollenhour, 1976).

148

exerted by an odor emission is specific to the motivation/reward generating the emission in terms of a constraint on learning, a popular conception in recent years. However, it may have little to do with any ability or even propsensity to form an association. The failure of motivationally incongruent or irrelevant donor emissions to control discriminative behavior could result if a test rat tends not to retain a memory of such an emission as it traverses the runway and encounters its reinforcer. Of course, when donor and test rats receive the same reinforcer and differential behavior is evident, the memory is evidently retained. Therefore, the test rat would have to retain, or fail to retain, the memory of the odor depending on some property of it—its meaning, so to speak. Alternatively, a learning-constraint account suggests that the test rat retains a memory of the donor's odor, but only associates it with the occurrence of its reinforcer if the meaning is appropriate to, or congruent with, that of its reinforcer.

For these motivational specificity results, the former hypothesis is favored because the irrelevant odors can become signals of impending reinforcement when they are deposited in the goal box instead of the start box, albeit not as readily or as effectively as is the case for relevant odors (cf. Travis-Neideffer, 1981). Presumably the greater propinquity of the odor and reinforcer when the odor is in the goal box would aid the association, but would not alter any tendency to associate only appropriate signals or any constraint against associating irrelevant ones. That is, although recent years have brought much talk of biological constraints on learning, there may be no such constraint operating here. The data appear more likely to be the result of a propensity to disregard or fail to retain memories of stimuli that do not signal what the animal is anticipating.

Considering these data on motivationally specific animal-generated odors, one wonders whether the food-related odor cues used in diet selection are in fact animal generated in much the same way. Similarly, one wonders whether the motivational specificity effects and the diet selection phenomena are really different manifestations of the same processes. In both cases, there are odor cues from and/or associated with a conspecific and a particular reinforcer that then influence the behavior of a test rat in approaching and consuming reinforcers. In the diet selection studies, the memory of these cues guides the rat to the food that resulted in the diet odor cues, perhaps because the cues signify that the food is safe. In the motivational specificity studies, the odor cues associated with a particular reinforcer also influence the subsequent approach to the goal by functioning as discriminative stimuli, so long as they are relevant or so long as they signify an available reinforcer. When they do not signify a relevant available reinforcer, they exert less influence, perhaps because they are ignored or not retained in working memory long enough to become discriminative stimuli.[4]

Odors Engendered by Aversive Reinforcers

Not only is there abundant evidence that encounters with positive reinforcers can cause rats to emit distinctive odors that can be used as discriminative signals by other rats, there is evidence that stress causes one or more distinctive emissions as well. Electric shock has been implicated for some years as a stimulus for a stress odor (Valenta & Rigby, 1968). This odor can interfere with the acquisition of one-way shock avoidance (Dua & Dobson, 1974), an effect that Fanselow (1985) suggested may be a result of its ability to produce analgesia in rats.

Batsell, Ludvigson, and Kunko (1990) found that rats emitted an odor when confronted with a signal (a taste) of impending illness brought about by LiCl. The rats readily distinguished this aversion odor from odors emitted as a consequence of receiving water reward or nonreward, although it cannot be said with certainty that aversion odor differs qualitatively from nonreward odor because of the impossibility of ruling out discrimination on the basis of odor concentration. Clearly, such odor emissions might guide foraging and food selection by rats in a natural environment.

The mechanism underlying the operation of this aversion odor is not yet understood. Although Batsell et al. (1990) found that the odor depressed speed of approach to it on the first trial on which it was encountered in a runway appratus—suggesting an innate or unconditioned avoidance of it, it is still possible that the ability of the aversion odor to command avoidance depends on prior associative learning. That is, there was opportunity in this study for the odor to have been associated with illness during the aversive conditioning that established the taste as a signal of illness. Since there were four conditioning trials, rats might have emitted an odor in anticipation of illness beginning on Trial 2; this emission would then have been present when the animal was rendered ill by LiCl and could thus have acquired its aversiveness. That is, the odor may have influenced avoidance via a memory of illness. Support for just this interpretation has been presented by Batsell (1989). He found that if the air around the rat was exhausted during the

---

[4]They would seem ignored or not retained only if they have not previously been relevant in the situation. If they have recently been successful in predicting a reward schedule, then they continue to function even if no longer relevant (cf. Travis, Ludvigson, & Eslinger, 1988).

conditioning phase, the aversion odor failed to suppress approach speeds in subsequent runway tests.

This rather remarkable observation is reminiscent of an early work concerned with the ability of odor from nonreward to suppress approach to a goal box containing it. In a little-noted but important work, Pratt (1971) found that most of the classic latent extinction effect in a runway apparatus results from a reaction to odors inadvertently left by preceding subjects. She also found that part of the ability of nonreward odor to suppress approach speed to it is acquired, although part seems unlearned also. That is, if during latent extinction placements, the rat can smell its own odor, it evidently associates the odor with the frustrating experience produced by the unrewarded placement. This substantially increases the potency of the odor in slowing subsequent approach to it.

MEANING AND FUNCTION OF ODOR FOR ANIMALS

Human observers of animal behavior tend to characterize it as stereotyped, rigid, and unlearned in comparison with that of human behavior. Applying this bias to odor memory in animals, we would expect to find much evidence of unlearned reactions to odors, including odors emitted by animals themselves. As noted earlier, this is not always observed in the more complex animals, and there is evidence that even animal-emitted odors must sometimes acquire their power to control behavior. Indeed, in the rat, and probably other complex mammals, this may be the rule. One wonders whether the function of odor for the rat is, therefore, not greatly different from its function for humans.

Engen (1987) argued, with respect to humans, that the "salient aspect of the sense of smell is the persistence of memories of episodes associated with odor . . ." and not memories of associated names of odors or other verbal responses (p. 503). Odor perception "is not organized lexically by nouns but around the similarity of objects causing odors and especially the contexts in which odors usually occur. A corollary is that they tend to be described in terms of personal references rather than by more general names like those proposed by traditional classification systems" (p. 502). The main function of smell in humans, then, "is not to recall odors for cognitive reasons but to respond to odors actually encountered" (p. 503).

There are several suggestions here that may be applied to animals. First, Engen's (1987) views suggest that the memories or meanings elicited by odors depend to a large extent on individual past experiences the receiving animal has had with the odors. This itself is a somewhat

surprising suggestion about animals, considering the data on stereotyped reactions to pheromones in animals. Coupled with the fact that
many of the most important odors are animal generated, it is even more
surprising, because it implies that the chemical symbols used in the
chemical communication of higher animals may have little unlearned
meaning, but may readily acquire meaning. Interestingly, the use of a
set of such symbols with arbitrary meaning is not unlike our language
use.

Do complex animals emit chemical emissions that (a) are discrimin-
ably distinctive to themselves and conspecifics, (b) elicit only weak
reactions, primarily orientational-attentional reactions, in consepcifics
prior to experience of these compounds in association with significant
stimuli, but (c) can readily acquire associations with significant experienced stimuli and thereby influence the emitter and/or the conspecific's
behavior? Do macrosmatic animals have a repertoire of such emissions,
and is it extensive enough to significantly affect adaptation? These are
some of the questions suggested by the present research. But there are
others, also. For the chemical emissions to be effective in communication there must be shared rules regarding their use; that is, they must (a)
be emitted only under rather specific stimulating conditions, and (b)
possess meanings that are shared by conspecifics using the symbols, or
otherwise elicit responses appropriate to the stimulating conditions.

It seems to be assumed tacitly that animals that employ systems of
chemical communication must have stereotyped reactions to the emissions, or there would be no predictable reaction to them, and the
emissions could serve no function in adaptation. However, if the few
suggestive data we have are correct, there do not seem to be highly
stereotyped reactions to at least some of these chemicals. This suggests
that much of the stereotypy may reside with the compounds emitted
upon encountering given stimulating conditions, not with the reaction
to the compounds. For this source of innate mechanism in rats, there is
considerable evidence. Indeed, were it not for this mechanism, we
might know precious little about these experience-dependent emissions
in rats, since our techniques often assume similar, if not identical,
emissions to a given stimulus across animals.

Considering the whole question from an evolutionary perspective,
one would guess that evolution toward a human-like set of symbols that
is both stimulus arbitrary and response arbitrary would progress
through stages beginning with symbols that are both stimulus stereotyped and response stereotyped. In the service of greater flexibility,
then, one or the other of the stereotyped reactions might be eliminated
or diminished in importance. However, if the breakdown in stereotypy
occurred in the nature of the emissions elicited by a stimulus, there

would surely be a serious problem of communication: Stereotyped reactions would then occur to the wrong stimuli, and the whole process of communication would lose its adaptive advantage.

In contrast, a weakening of rigid, stereotyped reactions to the emissions might have advantages. A given stimulus situation might require different responses for maximal adaptation for different competing colonies of animals with overlapping, nonequivalent habitats. For example, a given food patch might be relatively rich for one colony but lean for another. A chemical signal of this patch emitted by a member of one colony would then elicit a maladaptive response from a member of the other colony if the response to the signal were highly rigid. Conceivably different colonies of animals encountering this patch could react differently to the patch and thereby increase their foraging success, assuming their respective environments remained stable for some time. Experience with such patches could then provide the appropriate meanings for any compounds previously emitted in the vicinity of the patches by conspecifics. Here the shared rules necessary for communication would be generated by (a) an unlearned tendency to emit a given emission under given conditions, and (b) a stable environment that provided similar learning for all members of a group.

It is more difficult to envisage how the shared rules could be established were particular stimuli not to elicit particular emissions. That is, if members of a colony began emitting different compounds to the same stimuli (lean patches that they had just consumed, for example), an individual conspecific would have to forage regularly with only one (or a few) particular conspecifics to realize any gain from the emissions of the foraging partners since, in general, the differing emissions would not mean anything to them. To realize a gain from the idiosyncratic emissions of many conspecifics, they would have to learn a great many associations, which would probably be adaptive only under special or extreme circumstances. Thus it is not clear why a breakdown in stimulus stereotypy should occur.

It thus seems more likely that the flexibility would appear in the reaction to the emission. If this analysis is correct, the rat may be approaching the half-way point toward a flexible symbol system. It appears to have a set of symbols that can acquire arbitrary meanings, but the symbols themselves are not arbitrary. In light of this particular example, it is all the more remarkable that at least humans among animals have evolved flexibility at both ends of the causal chain involving symbols.

Returning to the conceptions of Engen (1987) discussed earlier, there is a suggestion that one suspects might not hold for macrosmatic animals. Engen and others argued that humans readily recognize odors but do not recall images of them. One interpretation of this proposition is that an odorous stimulus will readily elicit processes that can control particular responses, but that a stimulus will not elicit a representation of an odor that can then control responding. Put this way, it may be at variance with the common wisdom enunciated by Bedichek (1960) at the beginning of this chapter. Granted that Bedichek mainly argues that odors command representational processes, not that representations of odors are commanded by stimuli, still, if odors are as important for animals as they seem to be, one might expect that representations of particular odors would be available for controlling behavior. For example, much of recognition (i.e., discriminability) of another animal is often based on the animal's odor. The odor is a clear, often predominant, signal of the identity of the sender: Change it, and the behavior of the receiver to the sender may change dramatically. If the receiver has a representation of the sender at all, could it be that it is based on nonodorous sensory experience—such as visual appearance—even when such sensations seem unused in the identification of the sender by the receiver? Of course, where olfaction is such a dominant sense, there may be no representation of the sender involved; that is, cognitive processes may be absent. Olfaction is among our most primitive senses. Perhaps only an ability to make simple associations not involving representations evolved for use by olfaction in primitive systems, with this exclusivity remaining today. If so, this would be an interesting addition to the distinction between the cognitive and the noncognitive. In any case, the needed empirical work seems possible, and the answer should be forthcoming.

REFERENCES

Amsel, A., Hug, J. J., & Surridge, C. T. (1969). Subject-to-subject trial sequence, odor trails, and patterning at 24-h ITI. *Psychonomic Science, 15,* 119–120.

Baker, A. G., & Mercier, P. (1989). Attention, retrospective processing, and cognitive representations. In S. B. Klein & R. R. Mowrer (Eds.), *Contemporary learning theories: Pavlovian conditioning and the status of traditional learning theory* (pp. 85–113). Hillsdale, NJ: Lawrence Erlbaum Associates.

Barnett, S. A. (1963). *The rat: A study in behaviour.* Chicago: Aldine.

Batsell, W. R., Jr. (1989). *Stimulus properties of conditioned taste aversion odor.* Unpublished doctoral dissertation, Texas Christian University, Fort Worth.

Batsell, W. R., Jr., & Ludvigson, H. W. (1989). Aversive conditioning of naturally produced reward and nonreward odors in rats. *Animal Learning and Behavior, 17,* 256–260.

Batsell, W. R., Jr., Ludvigson, H. W., & Kunko, P. M. (1990). Odor from rats tasting a signal of illness. *Journal of Experimental Psychology: Animal Behavior Processes, 16,* 193–199.

Bedichek, R. (1960). *The sense of smell.* Garden City, NY: Doubleday.

Brown, C. W., & Ghiselli, E. E. (1938). Subcortical mechanisms in learning. IV. Olfactory discrimination. *Journal of Comparative Psychology, 26,* 109–120.

Cattarelli, M., Vernet-Maury, E., & Chanel, J. (1974). Influences de différentes odeurs biologiques sur le comportement émotif du rat placé dans un "espace vide d'information" *Comptes Rendus de l'Académie des Sciences de Paris, 278*, 2653–2656. (Série D)

Cattarelli, M., Vernet-Maury, E., & Chanel, J. (1977). Modulation de l'activité du bulbe olfactif en fonction de la signification des odeurs chez le rat *Physiology and Behavior, 19*, 381–387.

Collerain, I. (1978). Frustration odor of rats receiving small numbers of prior rewarded running trials. *Journal of Experimental Psychology: Animal Behavior Processes, 4*, 120–130.

Collerain, I., & Ludvigson, H. W. (1972). Aversion of conspecific odor of frustrative nonreward in rats. *Psychonomic Science, 27*, 54–56.

Collerain, I., & Ludvigson, H. W. (1977). Hurdle-jump responding in the rat as a function of conspecific odor of reward and nonreward. *Animal Learning and Behavior, 5*, 177–183.

Coopersmith, R., & Leon, M. (1984). Enhanced neural response to familiar olfactory cues. *Science, 225*, 849–851.

Cornwell-Jones, C. (1976). Selective exposure alters social and plant odor preferences of immature hamsters. *Behavioral Biology, 17*, 131–137.

Davis, S. F., Gustavson, K. K., & Petty-Zirnstein, M. K. (1985). Extending the generality of the odor hypothesis: Double-alternation responding in the woodrat (Neotoma floridana osagensis). *Animal Learning and Behavior, 13*, 137–142.

Davis, S. F., Prytula, R. E., Harper, W. E., Tucker, H. K., Lewis, C., & Flood, L. (1974). Double-alternation runway performance as a function of inter- and intra-reinforcement odor cues. *Psychological Reports, 35*, 787–793.

Davis, S. F., Prytula, R. E., Noble, J. J., & Mollenhour, M. N. (1976). Motivational specificity of the signal value of odor cues. *Animal Learning and Behavior, 4*, 407–410.

Davis, S. F., Weaver, M. S., Janzen, W. C., & Travis-Neideffer, M. N. (1984). Utilization of odor cues as a function of reward-magnitude contrast and delay of reinforcement. *The Journal of General Psychology, 112*, 173–183.

Davis, S. F., Whiteside, D. A., Bramlett, J. A., & Peterson, S. H. (1981). Odor production and utilization under conditions of nonreward and small reward. *Learning and Motivation, 12*, 364–382.

Demand, J. W. (1940). The effects of olfactory cues on the maze learning of white rats. *Transactions of the Kansas Academy of Science, 43*, 337–338.

Domjan, M. (1973). Role of ingestion in odor-toxicosis learning in the rat. *Journal of Comparative and Physiological Psychology, 84*, 507–521.

Dua, J. K., & Dobson, M. J. (!974). Role of olfactory cues in acquisition and extinction of avoidance. *Journal of Experimental Psychology, 103*, 461–465.

Elkins, R. L., Fraser, J., & Hobbs, S. H. (1977). Differential olfactory bulb contributions to bait shyness and place avoidance learning. *Physiology and Behavior, 19*, 787–793.

Engen, T. (1987). Remembering odors and their names. *American Scientist, 75*, 497–503.

Eslinger, P. J., & Ludvigson, H. W. (1980). Are there constraints on learned responses to odors from rewarded and nonrewarded rats? *Animal Learning and Behavior, 8*, 452–456.

Fanselow, M. S. (1985). Odors released by stressed rats produce opioid analgesia in unstressed rats. *Behavioral Neuroscience, 99*, 589–592.

Galef, B. G., Jr. (1983). Utilization by Norway rats (R. norvegicus) of multiple messages concerning distant foods. *Journal of Comparative Psychology, 97*, 364–371.

Galef, B. G., Jr. (1987). Social influences on the identification of toxic foods by Norway rats. *Animal Learning and Behavior, 15*, 327–332.

Galef, B. G., Jr., & Kennett, D. J. (1985). Delays after eating: Effect on transmission of diet preferences and aversions. *Animal Learning and Behavior, 13*, 39–43.

Galef, B. G., Jr., & Stein, M. (1985). Demonstrator influence on observer diet preference: Analysis of critical social interactions and olfactory signals. *Animal Learning and Behavior, 13*, 31–38.

Galef, B. G., Jr., & Wigmore, S. W. (1983). Transfer of information concerning distant foods: A laboratory investigation of the 'information centre' hypothesis. *Animal Behaviour, 31*, 748–758.

Garcia, J., & Koelling, R. A. (1966). Relation of cue to consequence in avoidance learning. *Psychonomic Science, 4*, 123–124.

Garcia, J., & Koelling, R. A. (1967). A comparison of aversions induced by X-rays, toxins, and drugs in the rat. *Radiation Research Supplement, 7*, 439–450.

Gleason, K. K., & Reynierse, J. H. (1969). The behavioral significance of pheromones in vertebrates. *Psychological Bulletin, 71*, 58–73.

Grote, F. W., & Brown, R. T. (1971). Conditioned taste aversions: Two-stimulus tests are more sensitive than one-stimulus tests. *Behavioral Research Methods and Instrumentation, 3*, 311–312.

Hershberger, W. A., & Smith, M. P. (1967). Conditioning in Drosophila melanogaster. *Animal Behaviour, 15*, 259–262.

Holder, M. D., & Garcia, J. (1987). Role of temporal order and odor intensity in taste-potentiated odor aversions. *Behavioral Neuroscience, 101*, 158–163.

Honzik, C. H. (!936). The sensory basis of maze learning in rats. *Comparative Psychology Monographs, 13*, 113.

Howard, G. S., & McHose, J. H. (1974). The effects of sodium amobarbital on odor based responding in rats. *Bulletin of the Psychonomic Society, 3*, 185–186.

Kucharski, D., & Hall, W. G. (1988). Developmental change in the access to olfactory memories. *Behavioral Neuroscience, 102*, 340–348.

Lashley, K. W., & Sperry, R. W. (1943). Olfactory discrimination after destruction of the anterior thalamic nuclei. *American Journal of Physiology, 139*, 446–450.

Lett, B. T. (1984). Extinction of taste aversion does not eliminate taste potentiation of odor aversion in rats or color aversion in pigeons. *Animal Learning and Behavior, 12*, 414–420.

Liggett, J. R. (1928). An experimental study of the olfactory sensitivity of the white rat. *Genetic Psychology Monographs, 3*, 1.

Lindley, S. B. (1930). The maze-learning ability of anosmic and blind anosmic rats. *Journal of Genetic Psychology, 37*, 245–267.

Lorden, J. F., Kenfield, M., & Braun, J. J. (1970). Response suppression to odors paired with toxicosis. *Learning and Motivation, 1*, 391–400.

Ludvigson, H. W. (1969). Runway behavior of the rat as a function of intersubject reward contingencies and constancy of daily reward schedule. *Psychonomic Science, 15*, 41–43.

Ludvigson, H. W. (1970, November). *Odor effects from delayed reward in rats.* Paper presented at the meeting of the Psychonomic Society, San Antonio, TX.

Ludvigson, H. W., Mathis, D. A., & Choquette, K. A. (1985). Different odors in rats from large and small rewards. *Animal Learning and Behavior, 13*, 315–320.

Ludvigson, H. W., McNeese, R. R., & Collerain, I. (1979). Long-term reaction of the rat to conspecific (frustration) odor. *Animal Learning and Behavior, 7*, 251–258.

Ludvigson, H. W., & Sytsma, D. (1967). The sweet smell of success: Apparent double alternation in the rat. *Psychonomic Science, 9*, 283–284.

McHose, J. H., & Ludvigson, H. W. (1966). Differential conditioning with nondifferential reinforcement. *Psychonomic Science, 6*, 485–486.

Morrison, R. R., & Ludvigson, H. W. (1970). Discrimination by rats of conspecific odors of reward and nonreward. *Science, 267*, 904–905.

Nachman, M. (1970). Learned taste and temperature aversions due to lithium chloride sickness after temporal delays. *Journal of Comparative and Physiological Psychology, 73*, 22–30.

Palmerino, C. C., Rusiniak, K. W., & Garcia, J. (1980). Flavor-illness associations: The peculiar roles of odor and taste in memory for poison. *Science, 208*, 753–755.

Panhuber, H. (1982). Effect of odor quality and intensity on conditioned odor aversion learning in the rat. *Physiology and Behavior, 28,* 149–154.

Pavlov, I. P. (1927). *Conditioned reflexes* (G. V. Anrep trans.). London: Oxford University Press.

Pitt, S., Davis, S. F., & Brown, B. R. (1973). Apparent double alteration in the rat: A failure to replicate. *Bulletin of the Psychonomic Society, 2,* 359–361.

Pratt, L. K. (1971). Odor effects in latent extinction. *Dissertation Abstracts International, 31,* 6300B.

Revusky, S. (1971). The role of interference in association over a delay. In W. K. Honig & P. R. James (Eds.), *Animal memory* (pp. 155–213). New York: Academic Press.

Richard, M. M., Grover, C. A., & Davis, S. F. (1987). Galef's transfer-of-information effect occurs in a free-foraging situation. *The Psychological Record, 37,* 79–87.

Rudy, J. W., & Cheatle, M. D. (1977). Odor-aversion learning by neonatal rats. *Science, 198,* 845–846.

Rudy, J. W., & Cheatle, M. D. (1979). Ontogeny of associative learning: Acquisition of odor aversions by neonatal rats. In N. E. Spear & B. A. Campbell (Eds.), *Ontogeny of learning and memory* (pp. 157–188). Hillsdale, NJ: Lawrence Erlbaum Associates.

Rusiniak, K. W., Hankins, W. G., Garcia, J., & Brett, L. P. (1979). Flavor-illness aversions: Potentiation of odor by taste in rats. *Behavioral and Neural Biology, 25,* 1–17.

Rusiniak, K. W., Palmerino, C. C., & Garcia, J. (1982). Potentiation of odor by taste in rats: Tests of some nonassociative factors. *Journal of Comparative and Physiological Psychology, 96,* 775–780.

Russell, M., Dark, K. A., Cummins, R. W., Ellman, G., Callaway, E., & Peeke, H. V. (1984). Learned histamine release. *Science, 225,* 733–734.

Seago, J. D., Ludvigson, H. W., & Remley, N. R. (1970). Effects of anosmia on apparent double alternation in the rat. *Journal of Comparative and Physiological Psychology, 71,* 435–442.

Sieck, M. H. (1972). The role of the olfactory system in avoidance learning and activity. *Physiology and Behavior, 8,* 705–710.

Striegel, D., & Batsell, W. R., Jr. (1990, April). *The role of environmental familiarity in taste-mediated potentiation.* Paper presented at the meeting of the Southwestern Psychological Association, Dallas, TX.

Swann, H. G. (1933). The function of the brain in olfaction. I. Olfactory discrimination and an apparatus for its test. *Journal of Comparative Psychology, 15,* 229–241.

Swann, H. G. (1934). The function of the brain in olfaction. II. The results of destruction of olfactory and other nervous structures on the discrimination of odors. *Journal of Comparative Neurology, 59,* 175–201.

Swann, H. G. (1935). The function of the brain in olfaction. *American Journal of Physiology, 111,* 257–262.

Taukulis, H. (1974). Odor aversions produced over long CS-US delays. *Behavioral Biology, 10,* 505–510.

Thorpe, W. H. (1939). Further studies on pre-imaginal olfactory conditioning in insects. *Proceedings of the Royal Society, 127,* 424–433.

Travis, M. N., Ludvigson, H. W., & Eslinger, P. J. (1988). A reexamination of the effects of motivational state on utilization of conspecific odors in the rat. *Animal Learning and Behavior, 16,* 318–322.

Travis-Neideffer, M. N. (1981). Overshadowing/generalization vs. preexperimental bias in utilization of motivation-specific odors in rats. *Dissertation Abstracts International, 42,* 07B, 3019.

Valenta, J. G., & Rigby, M. K. (1968). Discrimination of the odor of stressed rats. *Science, 161,* 599–601.

Voorhees, J. W., & Remley, N. R. (1981). Mitral cell responses to the odors of reward and nonreward. *Physiological Psychology, 9,* 164–170.

Westbrook, R. F., Homewood, J., Horn, K., & Clarke, J. C. (1983). Flavour-odour compound conditioning: Odour-potentiation and flavour-attenuation. *Quarterly Journal of Experimental Psychology, 35,* 13–33.

Williams, J. L. (1987). Influence of conspecific stress odors and shock controllability on conditioned defensive burying. *Animal Learning and Behavior, 15,* 333–341.

Williams, J. L. (1989). Ethoexperimental analysis of stress, contextual odors, and defensive behaviors. In R. J. Blanchard, P. F. Brain, D. C. Blanchard, & S. Parmigiani (Eds.), *Ethoexperimental approaches to the study of behavior* (pp. 214–228). Dordrecht, The Netherlands: Martinus Nijhoff.

Williams, J. L., & Scott, D. K. (!989). Influence of conspecific and predatory stressors and their associated odors on defensive burying and freezing responses. *Animal Learning and Behavior, 17,* 383–393.

Wilson, E. O. (1963). Pheromones. *Scientific American, 208,* 100–114.

$=9=$

Commentary and Envoi

Rachel S. Herz
Eric Eich
University of British Columbia

The purpose of this chapter is threefold: to assess and discuss the current state of memory for odors as disclosed by the writings in this volume, to note important general considerations for odor memory research, and to point to new experimental and theoretical directions that odor memory research might profitably pursue.

The principal mandate of this book has been to integrate the study of memory for odors with current theory and methodology in cognitive psychology. The first six chapters of this book are particularly centered on this goal. This is a laudable endeavour as it will ultimately make important contributions to basic science in olfaction and cognitive research. By applying the methods of cognitive psychology to the study of odor memory, a coherent theoretical and methodological basis for olfactory experimentation can be developed that will ultimately improve our understanding of this relatively under-researched sense. Moreover, odor memory research conducted under this rubric will provide a foundation for a comprehensive cognitive theory that is able to account for memory mediated beyond the visual and verbal realms.

Taken together, chapters 1-6 describe memory for odors as based on semantic processing (as being part of the same memory system as memory for visual and verbal material) of a nature thta does not respond to priming and for which imagery does not seem possible. The data presented are consistent with the conclusions drawn, and the experiments are well conceived and executed following traditional verbal-learning paradigms. Nonetheless, with reference to the literature discussed in chapters 7 and 8, we would like to present some alternative views to two of the foregoing topics, (a) the role of semantic processing in memory for odors, and (b) whether odor memory is different from memory mediated by other sensory modalities, particularly visual/verbal memory. Given that the study of odor memory is in a preparadigmatic stage, it is imiportant to consider as many alternatives to current conclusions now in order to broaden the scope of how odor memory research develops in the future.

THE SEMANTIC CODE IN MEMORY FOR ODORS

The issue of whether and how semantic processing is involved in odor memory has been in contention for a number of years. The data presented in this volume favor the position that semantic processing is heavily involved in odor memory. Particularly noteworthy were the experiments described by Schab and Crowder (chapter 2, this volume), de Wijk, Schab, and Cain (chapter 3, this volume), and Murphy (chapter 6, this volume). Among the important findings are that (a) familiarity and identifiability increase performance for odor recognition in short-term memory (STM) (de Wijk, Schab, & Cain, 1994, Experiment 2; Murphy, chapter 6, this volume) as well as in long-term memory (LTM) (Murphy, chapter 6, this volume; Rabin & Cain, 1984), (b) familiar and correctly identified odors are better remembered than unfamiliar and incorrectly identified odors (Lyman & McDaniel, 1986; Rabin & Cain, 1984) in young as well as elderly subjects (Murphy, chapter 6, this volume), (c) the availability of an odor name, unless clearly inappropriate, can drive the perceptual experience of an odor (Cain, de Wijk, Lulejian, Schiet, & See, 1992), and most critically, (d) a nonperceptual, verbal distractor task (backwards counting) can disrupt STM memory for odors, suggesting that semantic processing disrupts olfactory encoding (Murphy, chapter 6, this volume).

This evidence provides a worthy case for semantic processing in odor memory. However, two points need to be considered in more detail. First, odor identification, by definition, requires the retrieval of a verbal label in response to the perception of an odor. It is, therefore, obvious that if one can name (or identify) an odor, then it has been encoded semantically. Now, it is interesting to note that, in practice, odor identification is typically poor. Free odor identification for sets of even very familiar odors is rarely above 50% (Cain, 1979). There is undoubtedly some effect of semantic processing in memory for odors, but a perceptual code must make a considerable contribution as well. Second, the fact that a backward-counting task disrupted odor memory does not in itself demonstrate the effect of semantic encoding for odors. Although Murphy concluded that her results "strongly suggest a role for semantic factors in recognition memory for odors" (chapter 6, this volume), it is far more likely that this finding represents a resource allocation problem in working memory (Baddeley & Hitch, 1974). The capacity of working memory is a limited resource system. Encoding odors either perceptually or semantically may compete for the same pool of mental resources in STM as backward counting, thus decreasing the potential to encode whatever is to be learned. Counting backward requires a great deal of attention, and the more attention that is required to perform any distractor task the worse memory will be (Talland, 1967). This was witnessed by the fact that in Murphy's experiments the distractor task interfered with recognition memory for all of the stimulus types tested, including unfamiliar amoeboid shapes. Thus, whether or not subjects attempted to semantically encode hard-to-verbalize stimuli (odors and amoeboid shapes), verbal interference was not specific to disrupting semantic processing. Abstract visual and olfactory perceptual codes were certainly disrupted as well.

Apart from these issues, there is diverse evidence to suggest that olfactory processing is weakly connected to semantic representation. For example, although English dictionaries contain several hundred entries applicable to odor quality (Moskowitz & Gerbers, 1974), our language lacks abstract verbal categories for odors (Lawless & Cain, 1975). Cain (1980) coined the term *preverbal identification* to refer to the way we respond to odors when we cannot name them. Without being able to generate the verbal label, we can still state how familiar it is and behave appropriately to it. The frequently experienced tip-of-the-nose phenomenon is a case in point. In this situation a person can state how familiar the odor is, tell what is its likely source, and name similar odors, but cannot name the odor itself (Lawless & Engen, 1977). However, what makes the tip-of-the-nose state very different from the tip-of-the-tongue state (Brown & McNeill, 1966) is that, in the former, one has no lexical information about the odor name such as first letter, general word configuration, or the number of syllables. Recent experimental evidence regarding the relation between odor naming and odor-evoked memories has also shown that subjects do not have to be able to produce any semantic associations to an odor (either idiosyncratic or veridical) in order for that odor to elicit a full-blown episodic memory (Herz & Cupchik, 1992). Additionally, physiological evidence suggests that olfactory perception is a right hemisphere dominant function (Abraham

& Mathai, 1983; Jones-Gotman & Zatorre, 1993; Zucco & Tressoldi, 1988). As the right hemisphere is considered to chiefly mediate non-verbal functioning, this is further support for the conclusion that odor processing is primarily nonverbal.

Based on these observations, it does not seem likely that a semantic code could drive odor memory. How then are the results of the odor recognition memory experiments discussed earlier explained? We propose that when semantic information for odors is available—such as when familiar, nameable odors are tested (Murphy, chapter 6, this volume), or when an odor name is provided (Schab & Crowder, chapter 2, this volume)—then odor processing is in fact semantic. As humans are primarily verbal/visual animals there is an inherent tendency to semantically encode experience that is verbally accessible. Once verbal information is available for an odor, rather than complementing perceptual processing, processing switches from an olfactory to a semantic code and then remains at that level. Thus, when given a verbal label, visual imagery and odor imagery produce the same effects (Crowder & Schab, chapter 5, this volume), and when provided with an odor name, the odor-plus-name and name-alone priming conditions are no different (Schab & Crowder, chapter 4, this volume). This is because in both cases processing was entirely semantic for odors and non-odor cues. One of us has also conducted experiments where subjects were to associate either odors, odors plus their names, or only the names of odors with visual stimuli (Herz, 1992). Names were given with the instruction to "imagine the smell of _____ ." The results reveal the same pattern of performance for the odor-plus-name and name-only groups. However, the odor-only group yielded different results. It was concluded that once semantic information for an odor was available (as in the odor-plus-name condition), processing proceeded at a semantic level—only when no verbal information was available could odors be processed perceptually. Thus, we propose that when processing switches from an olfactory to a semantic code (as when an odor name is available), it is no longer olfactory information that is being processed, rather it is truly verbal information that is encoded. This explains why the results of experiments like those described in this volume make it seem as though memory for odors operates under the same mechanisms as memory for words. It is because memory for odors is the same as memory for words when odors have been encoded semantically in the first place!

Neurological studies (see Murphy, chapter 7, this volume for a review) also provide evidence for a dissociation between the semantic and perceptual processing of odors. Comparing visual, tactile, auditory, and olfactory modalities, Goodglass, Barton, and Kaplan (1968) found that patients with aphasia were poor at odor naming, but that their olfactory perception was unimpaired. Moreover, even though aphasia impaired naming across sensory modalities, performance on olfactory items was worse than for items in other modalities. Thus, it appears that (a) semantic and perceptual processing of odors are independent, and (b) the link between language and perception is weaker in olfaction than in other sensory modalities.

In summary, we agree with Schab and Crowder (chapter 2, this volume) that establishing the nature of the code underlying odor recognition memory is necessary for the future development of odor memory research in general. The personalized nature of much odor naming (e.g., "Aunt Sue's summer cabin in Wisconsin," see Schab & Crowder, chapter 2, this volume) suggests that odors are not stored in semantic-associative networks but rather in personal meaning-associative networks—that is, in terms of their meaning and meaningfulness to us (Engen, 1987). In spite of the fact that there is typically no formalized structure for verbally learning about odors, we do learn about odors through experience and categorize them in terms of their similarity to the objects that cause them and in relation to the context in which they are likely to occur. The manner of organization of this coding system affects odor memory (Engen, 1982, 1987), and, although words are part of odor memory, it is not limited to a semantic code.

Murphy pointed out in chapter 6 that there is as yet no direct evidence for a purely perceptual olfactory code. We propose the following experiment for future researchers as a test for such a code. A recognition memory experiment for odors could be conducted following verbal learning procedures similar to those discussed in previous chapters. This experiment would, however, depart from previous practice by using only unfamiliar odors as stimuli and Korsakoff patients as participants. Korsakoff patients show impaired semantic processing (Butters & Cermak, 1980), yet their memory for odors does not appear to be disrupted (Mair et al., chapter 7, this volume). Therefore, these individuals may be especially likely to demonstrate odor processing using a predominantly olfactory code. Additionally, by using unfamiliar odors processing using a predominantly olfactory code. Additionally, by using unfamiliar odors the possibility of semantic processing would be further compromised. For example, even if subjects attempted to verbalize an olfactory experience, such as "this is a strange odor," no previously established semantic referent for the odor would be available, thus making semantic encoding of this kind unreliable—particularly for Korsakoff patients.

ODOR MEMORY AS A SPECIALIZED SYSTEM

It was concluded earlier in this volume, based on data regarding odor recognition memory, that odor memory is not a specialized memory system different from memory in other modalities, nor was a multiple memory systems approach in general promoted (Schab & Crowder, chapter 2, this volume). In the spirit of current cognitive psychology we take up this position with the alternative view that odor memory is a specialized subsystem of memory and that a multiple memory systems theory is a viable framework for odor memory research. Thus, at the very least, odor memory research has now entered the ranks of prevailing cognitive practice with this debate. We do not attempt any general resolutions to this question here. However, with regard to how memory for odors is conceptualized, we believe that a specialized, multiple memory systems view is most informative.

Cognitive Factors

Memory for odors has traditionally been compared with memory for visual and verbal information in terms of the shape of the retention function and sensitivity to interference effects (see Richardson & Zucco, 1989, for a review). Earlier work showed that the retention curve for odors was virtually flat in both the short term (30 sec) and long term (1 year) (Engen, Kuisma, & Eimas, 1973; Engen & Ross, 1973; Jones, Roberts, & Holman, 1978). In other words, odors seemed impervious to forgetting. This is in sharp contrast to the traditional Ebbinghaus forgetting curve found for verbal items. Recent data, however, seem to indicate that short-term odor recognition memory may decay following a pattern similar to verbal memory (Gilmore, 1991). Nonetheless, the timelessness of long-term recognition memory for odors has been a reliable finding to date (Lawless & Engen, 1977; Rabin & Cain, 1984).

The data on LTM for odors indicates that consistent recognition performance over long retention intervals is due to the relative imperviousness of odor memory to retroactive interference (RI), despite strong proactive interference (PI) effects (Lawless & Engen, 1977). Typically, verbal memory is sensitive to the effects of both RI and PI. The explanation generally offered for the findings with odors is that they are represented in memory as unitary, distinctive events with little attribute redundancy, which leads to limited acquisition but little loss over time due to low rates of interference from similar stimuli (Engen, 1987; Engen & Ross, 1973; Lawless, 1978). In this way, odors have been described as encoded similarly to faces or abstract visual forms (Cain, 1984). This is also supported by data comparing recognition memory for odors, faces, and symbols by Murphy in this book (chapter 6).

Odor memory is further unlike verbal memory in abstract cognitive terms. An asymmetry between sensation and cognition has been shown for olfaction, which is not found in visual or auditory modalities. The smell of popcorn, for example, can evoke a corresponding memory of the odor's name, but the word popcorn, or a popcorn memory, is not capable of evoking the smell of popcorn in sensory terms (Engen, 1982, 1987). As Crowder and Schab discuss in chapter 5, true odor imagery does not seem possible. By contrast, the visual or auditory sensation of popcorn (sight or sound) and its corresponding cognitive representation (memory, name, image) can elicit the other in a more or less symmetrical way.

Neurological Evidence

Neurological evidence from Korsakoff patients, reviewed by Mair and colleagues as reported in chapter 7, supports the view that odor memory is functionally dissimilar from memory in other modalities. Korsakoff patients exhibit rapid forgetting for tactile, visual, and auditory material, but relatively good STM for odors, despite odor discrimination impairment. Additionally, like normal control subjects, recognition memory for odors does not decay as a function of retention interval, unlike memory for other stimuli. In other words, Korsakoff's syndrome disrupts the ability to discriminate between odorants but this loss is not due to an inability to detect the odorants or to a rapid decay of odor memory. It is noteworthy that a syndrome characterized by severe memory impairment for visual and verbal material spares memory for odors, despite damage to olfactory neural substrates regarding odor discrimination (e.g., the mediodorsal thalamic nucleus).

Importantly, research in rats has shown that lesions of the hippocampal complex will impair the ability to solve a simultaneous olfactory discrimination, but does not alter the ability to learn and remember successive olfactory discriminations (see Otto & Eichenbaum, 1992b for a review). Successive odor discrimination involves memory—that is, remembering what odor came before. Therefore, like Korsakoff patients, olfactory damage in rodents differentially affects odor memory and odor discrimination. These characterizations of impaired versus spared dissociations in memory are consistent with a multiple memory systems view.

It is noteworthy that there is also extensive evidence from animal research that olfactory memory is different from memory mediated by other sensory modalities in the rat (see Lynch, 1993; Otto & Eichenbaum, 1992). Unlike discrimination learning in the other senses, olfactory discrimination is learned extremely rapidly (Reid & Morris, 1992), shows an unusually fast improvement rate (Slotnik & Katz, 1974), and is sensitive to damage in the hippocampal formation (Otto & Eichenbaum, 1992a). Thus, for both the model macrosomatic animal and the model microsomatic animal of the research laboratory, there is considerable evidence that odor memory is different from memory mediated by other sensory modalities.

Multiple Memory Systems and Odor Memory

The neuroanatomical evolutionary approach of Nadel (1992) and Sherry and Schacter (1987) regarding multiple memory systems proposes that different memory systems differ in the types of information they process, and that there is an advantage to having different memory systems adapted to serve different functions. In evolutionary terms, odor memory serves a vitally adaptive function. In all infrahuman species, chemical or olfactory communication is the primary sense for conveying information pertinent to survival (e.g., recognizing kin, food, prey, and the reproductive status of conspecifics); although we rely predominantly on visual/verbal communication signals for survival, the processing of olfactory information must still retain some connection to its ancestral purpose.

That this may be true is indicated by a number of features of olfaction. However, from a cognitive perspective two characteristics of olfactory experience are particularly noteworthy. For one, the unusual potency of PI in odor learning explains how learned taste aversions (Garcia & Brett, 1977) develop and why they are so difficult to modify (Engen, 1982, 1987). Smell is a major component in the interoceptive experience of taste. There is an obvious adaptive advantage for an organism to learn in only one trial that something is poisonous and must subsequently be avoided. In keeping with this theme, Engen (1991, p. 81) stated that for humans "odor memory serves the primitive protection function of making sure that significant events involving food, people or places are not forgotten." Secondly, the inability to recall or image olfactory percepts may suggest that "only an ability to make simple associations not involving representations evolved for use by olfaction in primitive systems, with this exclusivity remaining today" (Davis & Ludvigson, chapter 8, this volume). In other words, olfaction appears to have evolved for the purpose of reinstating significant primary associations, and for signaling what is good to approach and bad to avoid without the complexity of multiple associations or internal representations.

Converging evidence from cognitive, neuroanatomical, and evolutionary perspectives shows that odors are encoded, processed, and stored differently than stimuli mediated by other sensory modalities, and that odors may also serve different functions in memory than stimulus information from other senses. Moreover, a review of the literature indicates that criteria commonly used to distinguish separate memory systems—functional dissociation, independent neural systems, and functional incompatibility (Roediger, Rajaram, & Srinivas, 1990)—are supported for odor memory. Thus, a multiple memory systems framework appears well suited to account for the data from odor memory experimentation.

IMPORTANT CONSIDERATIONS FOR ODOR MEMORY RESEARCH

Individual Differences

Throughout this volume it has been demonstrated that researchers need to be cognizant of the effects that subject sex and age can have in odor memory experimentation. It is generally found that females are more sensitive to olfactory information than are males, and this appears to transgress sensory perception and extend into the domain of cognitive processing as well. For example, Herz (1992) showed that memory performance was better for females than for males when odors were used as retrieval cues. Females have also been shown to experience more emotional odor-evoked memories than males (Herz & Cupchik, 1992; Laird, 1935). Interestingly, Crowder and Schab (chapter 5, this volume) found that attempting odor imagery caused more interference for females than for males. Although it was not clear why this was the case, it nevertheless shows that subject sex can interact with odor experience at multiple levels.

The effects of age on odor perception follow the tendency of all sensory modalities, a decline in perceptual sensitivity with increased senescence. The elderly show deficits in both olfactory perceptual sensitivity and higher order cognitive processing of olfactory stimuli. Interestingly, LTM for odors in the elderly has been shown to drop off dramatically over time (Murphy, chapter 6, this volume). Importantly, this finding challenges the generality and timelessness of the flat odor memory forgetting function that has been established in young adults. Thus, in the words of Crowder and Schab (chapter 5, this volume), "all of us should be vigilant for sex (and age) interactions in future experiments on odor memory."

Task and Test

Another important consideration for study in this field is how, like the results from state-dependent memory research (Eich, 1980), the data from odor-memory experiments appear to be sensitive to both task type and test. Widely differing results have been obtained by various researchers with regard to a number of cognitive operations in olfaction, such as the presence of a recency effect in STM, the duration of odor memory, the contribution of semantic versus perceptual codes, and the proficiency of odor identification, amongst others. Methodological variations have also been shown to modify the contribution of individual-difference factors, such as the effect of sex differences on odor-naming ability (Cain, 1982, vs. Herz & Cupchik, 1992). Using a set of 80 highly familiar odors that had been previously named by either the subject or the experimenter, Cain (1982) found that females consistently outperformed males on subsequent tests of odor identification. In contrast, Herz and Cupchik (1992) found no differences in males' and females' first-hand ability to correctly name a set of 20 odors varying in familiarity. Nor were any systematic male versus female performance differences found for particular odors as Cain had shown. It is clear that a systematic review of the literature on odor memory is needed so that the differences in procedure and test that have led to these divergent outcomes can be identified and explained.

Associative Learning

The nature of olfactory learning is an important issue for odor memory theory. Davis and Ludvigson (chapter 8, this volume) present evidence that olfactory learning in animals is largely acquired and situationally dependent rather than innate and static. In organisms ranging from fruit-flies to higher mammals, responses to odors were shown to almost all be based on associative-learning principles with conditioning and extinction operating in the usual way. Thus, memories or meanings elicited by an odor vary depending on the past experiences the receiving animal has had with the odor in question.

There is also substantial evidence that hedonic responses to odors in humans are primarily acquired through associative learning via personal experience and the conditioning and modelling of cultural norms (Engen, 1982, 1988). Engen (1988) demonstrated that at early ages of development children do not manifest any differences in preferences for odors considered to be either very pleasant or very unpleasant by adults. Children age 4 gave hedonic rating values for both amyl acetate (banana) and butyric acid (rancid butter) that were both slightly below neutral but did not differ from each other, suggesting that novel odors are viewed cautiously and are somewhat disliked. However, by age 8, children's reactions were nearly identical to adult norms.

The way we learn about odors is through the context in which they were first experienced (Engen, 1987). Thus, if the smell of rose were first encountered at a beloved's funeral it would elicit negative hedonic reactions thereafter, and conversely if the smell of skunk were first encountered while at play on a lovely summer's day, it would yield positive hedonic responses in the future. Note that forming a positive association to an odor may take longer than forming a negative association to an odor (Cain, 1984). This is because one-trial aversion learning is typically more potent than one-trial of a positive reinforcement contingency, although this may vary depending on the motivational and preparatory state of the organism in question (e.g., food deprivation, developmental stage, immediate postpartum mother–infant interaction, etc.; see Schaal & Porter, 1991, for a review).

Clearly, culture also plays an important role in the development of olfactory hedonic responses, which is commonly witnessed in cultural differences in food and spice preferences. However, culture does not have to diverge much for dramatic discrepancies in olfactory responses to be shown. Britons, for example, dislike the smell of wintergreen (methyl salicylate) (Moncreiff, 1966), whereas the same odorant was given the highest pleasantness rating out of 24 odors in a U.S. study (Cain & Johnson, 1978). Wintergreen is almost exclusively associated with mint candy in the United States. However, in the United Kingdom, wintergreen was the odorant used in an analgesic rub popular during World War II. Thus, the connotation of the same odorant across two relatively similar cultures can yield very different hedonic responses depending on the contextual and personal associations that are made to it.

In summary, evidence from both human and animal experimentation indicates that the formation of olfactory memories is based on associative learning mechanisms with far reaching extrapolations. As such, any theoretical framework developed to account for odor memory data will need to take the principles of associative learning into consideration.

Context

As mentioned earlier, context is an important factor in odor memory research; however, it is only cursorily discussed in the previous chapters of this book. Davis and Ludvigson (chapter 8, this volume) described animal data that show how the familiarity of the environment, previous experience, and motivational state (e.g., hungry vs. thirsty) all strongly affect the responses animals make to olfactory stimuli. However, this topic was not raised in the previous chapters on human olfactory learning and memory, where situational effects may be even stronger. Rozin and Fallon (1987, p. 24) stated that for odors "it is the subject's conception of the object, rather than the sensory properties of the object, that primarily determine its hedonic value." This was poignantly illustrated in Mark Twain's *The Invalid's Story*, where the protagonist, a stowaway on a freight train, imagines that the smell emanating from a casket beside him is the aroma of rotting flesh. When the imagined scenario becomes too intolerable, the protagonist flees the train car, which precipitates his untimely death, only to find out too late that it was just "a lot of innocent cheese" (Twain, 1906, p. 192). This demonstrates how an odor does not have inherent meaning by itself, but rather acquires meaning through the Gestalt of the whole stimulus complex in which it is embedded (Kirk-Smith & Booth, 1987).

Experimental evidence supports this literary characterization. When panelists rated fragrances with or without brand labels, dramatic differences in both ratings of sweetness and liking were obtained (Moskowitz, 1979). Likewise, Zellner and Kautz (1990) reported that the perceived intensity of food odors was increased when the odor extracts were presented in colored as compared to colorless liquid. Thus, context, whether in terms of cognitive information or emotional expectation, may influence olfactory perception to a possibly even greater extent than the sensory properties of the odorant per se. In persuit of this hypothesis, we are currently conducting research to investigate the extent to which environmental context can alter the effectiveness of odors as retrieval cues.

NEW DIRECTIONS

There are many tangential directions that future research in odor memory can take. For one, odor cues may provide important theoretical insights for emotional-memory research. It has recently been found that a dissociation between emotion and content in episodic memory can be demonstrated with odor retrieval cues (Herz & Cupchik, in press). In two experiments, odor-evoked memories were shown to be more emotional than memories elicited by semantic cues on a variety of dependent measures. However, odors and semantic cues did not differ in their ability to accurately remind subjects of the content of to-be-remembered items or of subjects' own previous emotional responses. The finding that the emotional quality, but not the accuracy, of memory was affected by the nature of the eliciting cue suggests that a dissociation between emotional experience and memory content occurs in episodic memory. Olfactory cues may be particularly good at demonstrating this dissociation. Future experiments using odors as cues for investigating emotional memory will profit cognitive research in this domain.

The basic theoretical tenets from odor memory research can, and have, also been extrapolated to practical and personal applications, and the possibilities are nearly limitless. We have perused a number of current olfactory manipulations and will present some of the more interesting and whimsical noncommercial implementations.

With regard to the therapeutic application of odors, we found that odors are currently implemented in some psychiatric treatments. For example, a seaside smell is used by some psychiatrists in the United Kingdom during enhanced relaxation therapy with anxious patients (King, 1988). The smell of the sea is used because it is considered to be the odor most universally capable of evoking feelings of relaxed leisure and tranquility. Pertinent to the use of this fragrance, however, is the recent report that there are regional differences in the odors which elicit pleasant nostalgic responses from different people. For instance, according to Hirsch (1992), people who grew up in the heartland of the United States find the smell of farm animals to be most pleasantly reminiscent, whereas people from the east are most transported by the scent of flowers, and people on the west coast by the smell of barbecuing. Recall, however, that regional/cultural differences have already been demonstrated between the United States and the United Kingdom, and that, furthermore, despite a general consensus for associations to various odors, individual responses will vary on the basis of idiosyncratic experience.

On a related therapeutic dimension is the current application of odors in *aromatherapy*. Aromatherapy is basically a new-age form of herbal medicine, where essential oils are used in massage and as incense in conjunction with soft lighting and tranquil music to promote feelings of well being, energy, and efficacy. The key feature of the olfactory component of aromatherapy is that the specific plants employed are considered to have particular therapeutic powers. A few examples of the reputed benefits of certain flowers are for jasmine to be an antidepressant, lavender to be an anxiolytic, rosemary to sharpen memory, and water-violet to promote tranquility and grace. The previously reviewed research on odor learning and memory, however, leads one to suspect that the positive feeling states induced by aromatherapy oils are most likely a by-product of the context in which they are administered and prior positive associations that the individual has had with the fragrances in question.

On the lighter hearted side of odor application, we were entertained by the finding that there is a U.S. organization called the "Whiffy Club"—a support group for people who like the smell of skunks. People who belong to this club may keep a vial of skunk scent handy so that they can discretely enjoy the smell of skunk at any time. The club was started by an anonymous antique dealer who placed a personal ad in *USA Today*. We were also amused to run across the term *Nose Muzak* coined by the Reuter correspondent Sebastian Moffett to refer to the Japanese corporate practice of pumping perfumes through offices to improve workers' performance. There are a multitude of other entertaining examples, and interested readers are advised to keep their noses to the newsprint for further amusement.

It is theoretically notable that all of the popular olfactory manipulations we have reviewed rely on associative learning mechanisms for their effects. Having a past association to the odor in question is required in order for it to conjure the past and/or elicit positive hedonic responses and feeling states.

CONCLUDING REMARKS

Like the study of amnesia not long ago, few studies exist on memory for odors, and what does exist is poorly integrated with current cognitive theory. This book makes an admirable effort to establish a foundation upon which a framework for odor memory research can be built to ultimately lead odor memory into the mainstay of cognitive psychology.

It appears that the biggest issue for a general cognitive theory of odor memory is to determine how memory for odors is similar to memories mediated through other modalities and how it is different. This extends to the general question of whether, as we propose, a multiple memory systems framework can best explain previous findings and provide a means for addressing future unanswered questions. At one level, almost all researchers would agree that the sensory modalities share a number of commonalities both in terms of their relation to cognitive processes and in their neurological interactions. Yet, it is also clear that there are differences between the sensory modalities, and that odor memory in particular may be different.

Future investigation into the similarities and differences of odor memory with other perceptual systems is essential, and should be examined with reference to the issues raised in the preceding chapters of this volume. Critically needed are experiments which compare basic cognitive operations in odor memory with memory in other modalities within the same experiments. This will then allow conclusions regarding the similarity and differences between memory systems to be reliably made. In tandem, experiments designed to take into account the unique characteristics of olfaction are necessary so that the special attributes of odor memory can be specifically captured. It is further clear from the foregoing chapters that a combined analysis of clinical syndromes in

humans and lesion studies in animals will greatly advance our understanding of odor memory and provide us with many answers to the
underlying principles of learning and memory. It is to all of this that this
volume sets the stage for anticipating the research of the future.

ACKNOWLEDGMENT

Preparation of this commentary was aided by grants from the (Canadian) Natural Sciences and Engineering Research Council (37335) and
the (American) National Institute of Mental Health (R01-MH48502).

REFERENCES

Abraham, A., & Mathai, K. V. (1983). The effect of right temporal lobe lesions on matching
of smells. *Neuropsychologia, 21,* 277–281.
Baddeley, A. D., & Hitch, G. (1974). Working memory. In G. H. Bower (Ed.), *The
psychology of learning and motivation* (Vol. 8, pp. 47–89). New York: Academic Press.
Brown, R. W., & McNeill, D. (1966). The "tip of the tongue" phenomenon. *Journal of Verbal
Learning and Verbal Behavior, 5,* 325–327.
Butters, N., & Cermak, L. S. (1980). *Alcoholic Korsakoff's syndrome: An information processing
approach to amnesia.* New York: Academic Press.
Cain, W. S. (1979). To know with the nose: Keys to odor identification. *Science, 203,*
467–470.
Cain, W. S. (1980). Chemosensation and cognition. In H. van der Starre (Ed.), *Olfaction and
taste* (Vol. 7, pp. 347–357). London: IRL.
Cain, W. S. (1982). Odor identification by males and females: Predictions vs. performance.
Chemical Senses, 7, 129–142.
Cain, W. S. (1984). What we remember about odors. *Perfumer and Flavorist, 17,* 17–21.
Cain, W. S., de Wijk, R. A., Lulejian, C., Schiet, F., & See, L. C. (1992). *Odor identification:
Stability, specificity, feeling of knowing, and discrimination.* Manuscript submitted for
publication.
Cain, W. S., & Johnson, F., Jr. (1978). Lability of odor pleasantness: Influence of mere
exposure. *Perception, 7,* 459–465.
de Wijk, R. A., Schab, F. R., & Cain, W. S. (1994). *Short-term recognition memory for odors
as a function of odor knowledge.* Manuscript submitted for publication.
Eich, J. E. (1980). The cue-dependent nature of state-dependent retrieval. *Memory and
Cognition, 8,* 157–173.
Engen, T. (1982). *The perception of odors.* Toronto: Academic Press.
Engen, T. (1987). Remembering odors and their names. *American Scientist, 75,* 497–503.
Engen, T. (1988). The acquisition of odor hedonics. In S. Van Toller & G. H. Dodd (Eds.),
Perfumery: The psychology and biology of fragrance. New York: Chapman & Hall.
Engen, T. (1991). *Odor sensation and memory.* New York: Praeger.
Engen, T., Kuisma, J. E., & Eimas, P. D. (1973). Short-term memory of odors. *Journal of
Experimental Psychology, 99,* 222–225.
Engen, T., & Ross, B. M. (1973). Long-term memory odours with and verbal descriptions.
Journal of Experimental Psychology, 100, 221–227.
Garcia, J., & Brett, L. P. (1977). Conditioned responses to food odor and taste in rats and

wild predators. In M. R. Kare & O. Maller (Eds.), *The chemical senses and nutrition* (pp. 277–290). New York: Academic Press.

Gilmore, M. M. (1991, April). *On the encoding of odors: Is there a visual and/or semantic component?* Paper presented at the 12th annual AChemS conference, Sarasota, FL.

Goodglass, H., Barton, M., & Kaplan, E. (1968). Sensory modality and object naming in aphasia. *Journal of Speech and Hearing Research, 11,* 488–496.

Herz, R. S. (1992). *The relationship between odor and emotional memory.* Unpublished doctoral disseration. University of Toronto, Toronto.

Herz, R. S., & Cupchik, G. C. (1992). An experimental characterization of odor-evoked memories in humans. *Chemical Senses, 17,* 519–528.

Herz, R. S., & Cupchik, G. C. (in press). The emotional distinctiveness of odor-evoked memories. *Chemical Senses.*

Hirsch, A. R. (1992). Nostalgia: A neuropsychiatric understanding. *Advances in Consumer Research, 19,* 390–395.

Jones, F. N., Roberts, K., & Holman, E. (1978). Similarity judgments and recognitin memory for common spices. *Perception and Psychophysics, 24,* 2–6.

Jones-Gotman, M., & Zatorre, R. J. (1993). Odor recognition memory in humans: Role of right temporal and orbitofrontal regions. *Brain and Cognition, 22,* 182–198.

King, J. R. (1988). Anxiety reduction using fragrances. In S. Van Toller & G. H. Dodd (Eds.), *Perfumery: The psychology and biology of fragrance* (pp. 147–165). New York: Chapman & Hall.

Kirk-Smith, M. D., & Booth, D. A. (1987). Chemoreception in human behaviour: Experimental analysis of the social effect of fragrances. *Chemical Senses, 12,* 159–166.

Laird, D. A. (1935). What can you do with your nose? *Scientific Monthly, 41,* 126–130.

Lawless, H. (1978). Recognition of common odors, pictures and simple shapes. *Perception and Psychophysics, 24,* 493–495.

Lawless, H. T., & Cain, W. S. (1975). Recognition memory for odors. *Chemical Senses and Flavour, 1,* 331–337.

Lawless, H., & Engen, T. (1977). Associations to odors: Interference, mnemonics, and verbal labelling. *Journal of Experimental Psychology, 3,* 52–59.

Lyman, B. J., & McDaniel, M. A. (1986). Effects of encoding strategy on long-term memory for odours. *The Quarterly Journal of Experimental Psychology, 38,* 753–765.

Lynch, G. (1993). A cortical system for studying cortical memory. *Trends in Neurosciences, 16,* 24–25.

Moncreiff, R. W. (1966). *Odour preferences.* New York: Wiley.

Moskowitz, H. R. (1979). Mind, body and pleasure: An analysis of factors which influence sensory hedonics. In J. H. A. Kroeze (Ed.), *Preference behaviour and chemoreception* (pp. 131–147). London: Information Retrieval Limited.

Moskowitz, H. R., & Gerbers, C. L. (1974). Dimensional salience of odors. *Annals of the New York Academy of Sciences, 237,* 1–16.

Nadel, L. (1992). Multiple memory systems: What and why. Special Issues: Memory systems. *Journal of Cognitive Neuroscience, 4,* 179–188.

Otto, T., & Eichenbaum, H. (1992a). Complementary roles of orbital prefrontal cortex and the perirhinal-entorhinal cortices in an odor-guided delayed non-matching to sample task. *Behavioral Neuroscience, 106,* 763–776.

Otto, T., & Eichenbaum, H. (1992b). Olfactory learning and memory. In M. J. Serby & K. L. Chobor (Eds.), *Science of olfaction* (pp. 213–244). New York: Springer-Verlag.

Rabin, M. D., & Cain, W. S. (1984). Odor recognition, familiarity, identifiability and encoding consistency. *Journal of Experimental Psychology: Learning, Memory and Cognition, 10,* 316–325.

Reid, I. C., & Morris, R. G. M. (1992). Smells are no surer: Rapid improvement in olfactory discriminator is not due to the acquisition of a learning set. *Proceedings of the Royal Society of London, Series B, 247,* 137–143.

Richardson, J. T. E., & Zucco, G. M. (1989). Cognition and olfaction: A review. *Psychological Bulletin, 105,* 352–360.

Roediger, H. L., Rajaram, S., & Srinivas, K. (1990). Specifying criteria for postulating memory systems. *Annals of the New York Academy of Sciences, 608,* 572–595.

Rozin, P., & Fallon, A. E. (1987). A perspective on disgust. *Psychological Bulletin, 94,* 23–41.

Schaal, B., & Porter, R. H. (1991). "Microsomatic humans" revisted: The generation and perception of chemical signals. *Advances in the Study of Behavior, 20,* 135–199.

Sherry, D. F., & Schacter, D. L. (1987). The evolution of multiple memory systems. *Psychological Review, 94,* 439–454.

Slotnik, B. M., & Katz, H. M. (1974). Olfactory learning-set formation in rats. *Science, 185,* 769–777.

Talland, G. A. (1967). Short-term memory with interpolated activity. *Journal of Verbal Learning and Verbal Behavior, 6,* 144–150.

Twain, M. (1906). The invalid's story. In *How to tell a story and other essays* (pp. 182–192). New York: Harper.

Zellner, D. A., & Kautz, M. A. (1990). Color affects perceived odor intensity. *Journal of Experimental Psychology: Human Perception and Performance, 16,* 391–397.

Zucco, G. M., & Tressoldi, P. E. (1988). Hemispheric differences in odour recognition. *Cortex, 25,* 607–615.End[et

═ Author Index ═

Page numbers in *italics* denote complete bibliographical citations.

Subject Index